Just The facts101
Textbook Key Facts

Israel Recent Economic and Political Developments Yearbook

by Cram101
Textbook NOT Included

Table of Contents

Title Page

Copyright

Foundations of Business

Management

Business law

Finance

Human resource management

Information systems

Marketing

Manufacturing

Commerce

Business ethics

Accounting

Index: Answers

Just The Facts101

Exam Prep for

Israel Recent Economic and Political Developments Yearbook

Just The Facts101 Exam Prep is your link from
the textbook and lecture to your exams.

**Just The Facts101 Exam Preps are unauthorized and comprehensive reviews
of your textbooks.**

All material provided by CTI Publications (c) 2019

Textbook publishers and textbook authors do not participate in or contribute to these reviews.

Just The Facts101 Exam Prep

Copyright © 2019 by CTI Publications. All rights reserved.

eAIN 449769

Foundations of Business

A business, also known as an enterprise, agency or a firm, is an entity involved in the provision of goods and/or services to consumers. Businesses are prevalent in capitalist economies, where most of them are privately owned and provide goods and services to customers in exchange for other goods, services, or money.

:: Human resource management ::

_____ is the corporate management term for the act of reorganizing the legal, ownership, operational, or other structures of a company for the purpose of making it more profitable, or better organized for its present needs. Other reasons for _____ include a change of ownership or ownership structure, demerger, or a response to a crisis or major change in the business such as bankruptcy, repositioning, or buyout. _____ may also be described as corporate _____, debt _____ and financial _____.

Exam Probability: **Medium**

1. *Answer choices:*

(see index for correct answer)

- a. Enterprise architecture
- b. Induction training
- c. Diversity Icebreaker
- d. Restructuring

Guidance: level 1

:: Marketing ::

_____ comes from the Latin neg and otsia referring to businessmen who, unlike the patricians, had no leisure time in their industriousness; it held the meaning of business until the 17th century when it took on the diplomatic connotation as a dialogue between two or more people or parties intended to reach a beneficial outcome over one or more issues where a conflict exists with respect to at least one of these issues. Thus, _____ is a process of combining divergent positions into a joint agreement under a decision rule of unanimity.

Exam Probability: **Medium**

2. *Answer choices:*

(see index for correct answer)

- a. Negotiation
- b. Personalized marketing
- c. Marketing mix
- d. Brandjacking

Guidance: level 1

:: Problem solving ::

In other words, _____ is a situation where a group of people meet to generate new ideas and solutions around a specific domain of interest by removing inhibitions. People are able to think more freely and they suggest as many spontaneous new ideas as possible. All the ideas are noted down and those ideas are not criticized and after _____ session the ideas are evaluated. The term was popularized by Alex Faickney Osborn in the 1953 book Applied Imagination.

Exam Probability: **Low**

3. *Answer choices:*

(see index for correct answer)

- a. Cognitive acceleration
- b. Brainstorming
- c. How to Solve It
- d. Teachable moment

Guidance: level 1

:: Globalization-related theories ::

_____ is an economic system based on the private ownership of the means of production and their operation for profit. Characteristics central to _____ include private property, capital accumulation, wage labor, voluntary exchange, a price system, and competitive markets. In a capitalist market economy, decision-making and investment are determined by every owner of wealth, property or production ability in financial and capital markets, whereas prices and the distribution of goods and services are mainly determined by competition in goods and services markets.

Exam Probability: **Medium**

4. *Answer choices:*

(see index for correct answer)

- a. Economic Development
- b. Capitalism
- c. postmodernism

Guidance: level 1

:: Management ::

A _____ describes the rationale of how an organization creates, delivers, and captures value, in economic, social, cultural or other contexts. The process of _____ construction and modification is also called _____ innovation and forms a part of business strategy.

Exam Probability: **High**

5. *Answer choices:*

(see index for correct answer)

- a. Business model
- b. Wireless informatics
- c. Sensemaking
- d. Community of practice

Guidance: level 1

:: Stock market ::

A _____, securities exchange or bourse, is a facility where stock brokers and traders can buy and sell securities, such as shares of stock and bonds and other financial instruments. _____ s may also provide for facilities the issue and redemption of such securities and instruments and capital events including the payment of income and dividends. Securities traded on a _____ include stock issued by listed companies, unit trusts, derivatives, pooled investment products and bonds. _____ s often function as "continuous auction" markets with buyers and sellers consummating transactions via open outcry at a central location such as the floor of the exchange or by using an electronic trading platform.

Exam Probability: **Low**

6. *Answer choices:*

(see index for correct answer)

- a. Shadow stock

- b. stock price
- c. Correlation trading
- d. Book building

Guidance: level 1

:: Information technology ::

_____ is the use of computers to store, retrieve, transmit, and manipulate data, or information, often in the context of a business or other enterprise. IT is considered to be a subset of information and communications technology. An _____ system is generally an information system, a communications system or, more specifically speaking, a computer system – including all hardware, software and peripheral equipment – operated by a limited group of users.

Exam Probability: **Low**

7. *Answer choices:*
(see index for correct answer)

- a. PC Supporters
- b. Information technology
- c. IT as a service
- d. ActivEcho

Guidance: level 1

:: Business law ::

A _____ is an arrangement where parties, known as partners, agree to cooperate to advance their mutual interests. The partners in a _____ may be individuals, businesses, interest-based organizations, schools, governments or combinations. Organizations may partner to increase the likelihood of each achieving their mission and to amplify their reach. A _____ may result in issuing and holding equity or may be only governed by a contract.

Exam Probability: **High**

8. *Answer choices:*
(see index for correct answer)

- a. Security interest
- b. Partnership
- c. Voidable floating charge
- d. Administration

Guidance: level 1

:: Payments ::

A _____ is the trade of value from one party to another for goods, or services, or to fulfill a legal obligation.

Exam Probability: **Medium**

9. *Answer choices:*

(see index for correct answer)

- a. Direct Payments
- b. Subsidy
- c. Tuition payments
- d. County payments

Guidance: level 1

:: Industrial design ::

In physics and mathematics, the _____ of a mathematical space is informally defined as the minimum number of coordinates needed to specify any point within it. Thus a line has a _____ of one because only one coordinate is needed to specify a point on it for example, the point at 5 on a number line. A surface such as a plane or the surface of a cylinder or sphere has a _____ of two because two coordinates are needed to specify a point on it for example, both a latitude and longitude are required to locate a point on the surface of a sphere. The inside of a cube, a cylinder or a sphere is three-_____ al because three coordinates are needed to locate a point within these spaces.

Exam Probability: **High**

10. *Answer choices:*

(see index for correct answer)

- a. Air-augmented rocket

- b. Community design
- c. Corrugated box design
- d. Dimension

Guidance: level 1

:: Reputation management ::

_____ or image of a social entity is an opinion about that entity, typically as a result of social evaluation on a set of criteria.

Exam Probability: **Low**

11. *Answer choices:*

(see index for correct answer)

- a. Reputation
- b. The Economy of Esteem
- c. Whuffie
- d. personal brand

Guidance: level 1

:: Stochastic processes ::

_____ is a system of rules that are created and enforced through social or governmental institutions to regulate behavior. It has been defined both as "the Science of Justice" and "the Art of Justice". _____ is a system that regulates and ensures that individuals or a community adhere to the will of the state. State-enforced _____ s can be made by a collective legislature or by a single legislator, resulting in statutes, by the executive through decrees and regulations, or established by judges through precedent, normally in common _____ jurisdictions. Private individuals can create legally binding contracts, including arbitration agreements that may elect to accept alternative arbitration to the normal court process. The formation of _____ s themselves may be influenced by a constitution, written or tacit, and the rights encoded therein. The _____ shapes politics, economics, history and society in various ways and serves as a mediator of relations between people.

Exam Probability: **Low**

12. *Answer choices:*

(see index for correct answer)

- a. Self-similar process
- b. Law
- c. Feller-continuous process
- d. Stochastic thinking

Guidance: level 1

:: National accounts ::

_____ is a monetary measure of the market value of all the final goods and services produced in a period of time, often annually. GDP per capita does not, however, reflect differences in the cost of living and the inflation rates of the countries; therefore using a basis of GDP per capita at purchasing power parity is arguably more useful when comparing differences in living standards between nations.

Exam Probability: **Medium**

13. *Answer choices:*

(see index for correct answer)

- a. Fixed capital
- b. Gross domestic product
- c. capital formation

Guidance: level 1

:: Business ::

_____ is the activity of making one's living or making money by producing or buying and selling products. Simply put, it is "any activity or enterprise entered into for profit. It does not mean it is a company, a corporation, partnership, or have any such formal organization, but it can range from a street peddler to General Motors."

Exam Probability: **Medium**

14. *Answer choices:*

(see index for correct answer)

- a. Business
- b. Business directory
- c. Corporate social media
- d. Signed number

Guidance: level 1

:: Export and import control ::

" _____ " means the Government Service which is responsible for the administration of _____ law and the collection of duties and taxes and which also has the responsibility for the application of other laws and regulations relating to the importation, exportation, movement or storage of goods.

Exam Probability: **Medium**

15. *Answer choices:*

(see index for correct answer)

- a. Export parity price
- b. Customs
- c. International Traffic in Arms Regulations
- d. Export Management and Compliance Program

Guidance: level 1

:: Production economics ::

_____ is the joint use of a resource or space. It is also the process of dividing and distributing. In its narrow sense, it refers to joint or alternating use of inherently finite goods, such as a common pasture or a shared residence. Still more loosely, "_____" can actually mean giving something as an outright gift: for example, to "share" one's food really means to give some of it as a gift. _____ is a basic component of human interaction, and is responsible for strengthening social ties and ensuring a person's well-being.

Exam Probability: **High**

16. *Answer choices:*

(see index for correct answer)

- a. Productivity world
- b. HMI quality
- c. Total factor productivity
- d. Cost-of-production theory of value

Guidance: level 1

:: Employment ::

The _____ is an individual's metaphorical "journey" through learning, work and other aspects of life. There are a number of ways to define _____ and the term is used in a variety of ways.

Exam Probability: **Medium**

17. *Answer choices:*

(see index for correct answer)

- a. CIETC
- b. Skilled worker
- c. Make-work job
- d. Career

Guidance: level 1

:: Stock market ::

_____ is a form of corporate equity ownership, a type of security. The terms voting share and ordinary share are also used frequently in other parts of the world; "_____" being primarily used in the United States. They are known as Equity shares or Ordinary shares in the UK and other Commonwealth realms. This type of share gives the stockholder the right to share in the profits of the company, and to vote on matters of corporate policy and the composition of the members of the board of directors.

Exam Probability: **Low**

18. *Answer choices:*

(see index for correct answer)

- a. Common stock
- b. Open outcry
- c. Stop price
- d. Bear raid

Guidance: level 1

:: ::

A _____ is an organization, usually a group of people or a company, authorized to act as a single entity and recognized as such in law. Early incorporated entities were established by charter. Most jurisdictions now allow the creation of new _____ s through registration.

Exam Probability: **Medium**

19. *Answer choices:*

(see index for correct answer)

- a. Character
- b. hierarchical
- c. hierarchical perspective
- d. levels of analysis

Guidance: level 1

:: ::

_____ or accountancy is the measurement, processing, and communication of financial information about economic entities such as businesses and corporations. The modern field was established by the Italian mathematician Luca Pacioli in 1494. _____ , which has been called the "language of business", measures the results of an organization's economic activities and conveys this information to a variety of users, including investors, creditors, management, and regulators. Practitioners of _____ are known as accountants. The terms "_____" and "financial reporting" are often used as synonyms.

Exam Probability: **Low**

20. *Answer choices:*
(see index for correct answer)

- a. functional perspective
- b. Sarbanes-Oxley act of 2002
- c. Accounting
- d. interpersonal communication

Guidance: level 1

:: Consumer theory ::

_____ is the quantity of a good that consumers are willing and able to purchase at various prices during a given period of time.

Exam Probability: **Low**

21. *Answer choices:*

(see index for correct answer)

- a. Business contract hire
- b. Revealed preference
- c. Income elasticity of demand
- d. Hicksian demand function

Guidance: level 1

:: Classification systems ::

_____ is the practice of comparing business processes and performance metrics to industry bests and best practices from other companies. Dimensions typically measured are quality, time and cost.

Exam Probability: **Low**

22. *Answer choices:*

(see index for correct answer)

- a. Biological dark matter
- b. Holdridge life zones
- c. Benchmarking
- d. International Standard Classification of Education

Guidance: level 1

:: Corporate crime ::

_____ LLP, based in Chicago, was an American holding company. Formerly one of the "Big Five" accounting firms, the firm had provided auditing, tax, and consulting services to large corporations. By 2001, it had become one of the world's largest multinational companies.

Exam Probability: **Low**

23. *Answer choices:*

(see index for correct answer)

- a. State-corporate crime
- b. Langbar International
- c. Arthur Andersen LLP v. United States
- d. Arthur Andersen

Guidance: level 1

:: Management accounting ::

In economics, _____ s, indirect costs or overheads are business expenses that are not dependent on the level of goods or services produced by the business. They tend to be time-related, such as interest or rents being paid per month, and are often referred to as overhead costs. This is in contrast to variable costs, which are volume-related and unknown at the beginning of the accounting year. For a simple example, such as a bakery, the monthly rent for the baking facilities, and the monthly payments for the security system and basic phone line are _____ s, as they do not change according to how much bread the bakery produces and sells. On the other hand, the wage costs of the bakery are variable, as the bakery will have to hire more workers if the production of bread increases. Economists reckon _____ as a entry barrier for new entrepreneurs.

Exam Probability: **Medium**

24. *Answer choices:*
(see index for correct answer)

- a. Management accounting
- b. Constraints accounting
- c. Fixed cost
- d. Variance

Guidance: level 1

:: Decision theory ::

Within economics the concept of _____ is used to model worth or value, but its usage has evolved significantly over time. The term was introduced initially as a measure of pleasure or satisfaction within the theory of utilitarianism by moral philosophers such as Jeremy Bentham and John Stuart Mill. But the term has been adapted and reapplied within neoclassical economics, which dominates modern economic theory, as a _____ function that represents a consumer's preference ordering over a choice set. As such, it is devoid of its original interpretation as a measurement of the pleasure or satisfaction obtained by the consumer from that choice.

Exam Probability: **High**

25. *Answer choices:*

(see index for correct answer)

- a. Ulysses pact
- b. Ophelimity
- c. Dynamic decision-making
- d. Utility

Guidance: level 1

:: ::

_____ is a marketing communication that employs an openly sponsored, non-personal message to promote or sell a product, service or idea. Sponsors of _____ are typically businesses wishing to promote their products or services. _____ is differentiated from public relations in that an advertiser pays for and has control over the message. It differs from personal selling in that the message is non-personal, i.e., not directed to a particular individual. _____ is communicated through various mass media, including traditional media such as newspapers, magazines, television, radio, outdoor _____ or direct mail; and new media such as search results, blogs, social media, websites or text messages. The actual presentation of the message in a medium is referred to as an advertisement, or "ad" or advert for short.

Exam Probability: **Medium**

26. *Answer choices:*

(see index for correct answer)

- a. deep-level diversity
- b. imperative
- c. information systems assessment
- d. process perspective

Guidance: level 1

:: Legal terms ::

_____, a form of alternative dispute resolution, is a way to resolve disputes outside the courts. The dispute will be decided by one or more persons, which renders the "_____ award". An _____ award is legally binding on both sides and enforceable in the courts.

Exam Probability: **High**

27. *Answer choices:*

(see index for correct answer)

- a. Arbitration
- b. Immediately adjacent
- c. Next friend
- d. Legal death

Guidance: level 1

:: Workplace ::

_____ is asystematic determination of a subject's merit, worth and significance, using criteria governed by a set of standards. It can assist an organization, program, design, project or any other intervention or initiative to assess any aim, realisable concept/proposal, or any alternative, to help in decision-making; or to ascertain the degree of achievement or value in regard to the aim and objectives and results of any such action that has been completed. The primary purpose of _____, in addition to gaining insight into prior or existing initiatives, is to enable reflection and assist in the identification of future change.

Exam Probability: **Low**

28. *Answer choices:*

(see index for correct answer)

- a. Workplace strategy
- b. Workplace wellness
- c. labour turnover
- d. Workplace deviance

Guidance: level 1

:: Economic globalization ::

_____ is an agreement in which one company hires another company to be responsible for a planned or existing activity that is or could be done internally, and sometimes involves transferring employees and assets from one firm to another.

Exam Probability: **Low**

29. *Answer choices:*

(see index for correct answer)

- a. Outsourcing
- b. reshoring

Guidance: level 1

:: Statistical terminology ::

_____ es can be learned implicitly within cultural contexts. People may develop _____ es toward or against an individual, an ethnic group, a sexual or gender identity, a nation, a religion, a social class, a political party, theoretical paradigms and ideologies within academic domains, or a species. _____ ed means one-sided, lacking a neutral viewpoint, or not having an open mind. _____ can come in many forms and is related to prejudice and intuition.

Exam Probability: **Medium**

30. *Answer choices:*
(see index for correct answer)

- a. Observable variable
- b. Level of analysis
- c. Shape parameter
- d. Bias

Guidance: level 1

:: Auditing ::

_____, as defined by accounting and auditing, is a process for assuring of an organization's objectives in operational effectiveness and efficiency, reliable financial reporting, and compliance with laws, regulations and policies. A broad concept, _____ involves everything that controls risks to an organization.

Exam Probability: **High**

31. *Answer choices:*

(see index for correct answer)

- a. Internal control
- b. Communication audit
- c. Audit risk
- d. Audit trail

Guidance: level 1

:: International trade ::

_____ involves the transfer of goods or services from one person or entity to another, often in exchange for money. A system or network that allows _____ is called a market.

Exam Probability: **High**

32. *Answer choices:*

(see index for correct answer)

- a. Export-oriented
- b. Trade
- c. The Observatory of Economic Complexity
- d. Agreement on Government Procurement

Guidance: level 1

:: Currency ::

A _____ , in the most specific sense is money in any form when in use or circulation as a medium of exchange, especially circulating banknotes and coins. A more general definition is that a _____ is a system of money in common use, especially for people in a nation. Under this definition, US dollars , pounds sterling , Australian dollars , European euros , Russian rubles and Indian Rupees are examples of currencies. These various currencies are recognized as stores of value and are traded between nations in foreign exchange markets, which determine the relative values of the different currencies. Currencies in this sense are defined by governments, and each type has limited boundaries of acceptance.

Exam Probability: **Low**

33. *Answer choices:*
(see index for correct answer)

- a. Currency
- b. Currency intervention

- c. Remonetisation
- d. Pre-decimal currency

Guidance: level 1

:: Scientific method ::

In the social sciences and life sciences, a _____ is a research method involving an up-close, in-depth, and detailed examination of a subject of study , as well as its related contextual conditions.

Exam Probability: **Low**

34. *Answer choices:*

(see index for correct answer)

- a. Causal research
- b. Case study
- c. Preference test
- d. pilot project

Guidance: level 1

:: ::

_____ refers to a business or organization attempting to acquire goods or services to accomplish its goals. Although there are several organizations that attempt to set standards in the _____ process, processes can vary greatly between organizations. Typically the word "_____" is not used interchangeably with the word "procurement", since procurement typically includes expediting, supplier quality, and transportation and logistics in addition to _____ .

Exam Probability: **High**

35. *Answer choices:*

(see index for correct answer)

- a. Sarbanes-Oxley act of 2002
- b. Purchasing
- c. empathy
- d. deep-level diversity

Guidance: level 1

:: Health promotion ::

_____ , as defined by the World _____ Organization , is "a state of complete physical, mental and social well-being and not merely the absence of disease or infirmity." This definition has been subject to controversy, as it may have limited value for implementation. _____ may be defined as the ability to adapt and manage physical, mental and social challenges throughout life.

Exam Probability: **High**

36. *Answer choices:*

(see index for correct answer)

- a. Health
- b. Integrated Management of Childhood Illness
- c. Breastfeeding promotion
- d. Myokine

Guidance: level 1

:: Production and manufacturing ::

_____ consists of organization-wide efforts to "install and make permanent climate where employees continuously improve their ability to provide on demand products and services that customers will find of particular value." "Total" emphasizes that departments in addition to production are obligated to improve their operations; "management" emphasizes that executives are obligated to actively manage quality through funding, training, staffing, and goal setting. While there is no widely agreed-upon approach, TQM efforts typically draw heavily on the previously developed tools and techniques of quality control. TQM enjoyed widespread attention during the late 1980s and early 1990s before being overshadowed by ISO 9000, Lean manufacturing, and Six Sigma.

Exam Probability: **High**

37. *Answer choices:*

(see index for correct answer)

- a. Performance supervision system
- b. Digital prototyping
- c. Cellular manufacturing
- d. Total quality management

Guidance: level 1

:: Management ::

The term _____ refers to measures designed to increase the degree of autonomy and self-determination in people and in communities in order to enable them to represent their interests in a responsible and self-determined way, acting on their own authority. It is the process of becoming stronger and more confident, especially in controlling one's life and claiming one's rights. _____ as action refers both to the process of self-_____ and to professional support of people, which enables them to overcome their sense of powerlessness and lack of influence, and to recognize and use their resources. To do work with power.

Exam Probability: **Medium**

38. *Answer choices:*

(see index for correct answer)

- a. Executive development
- b. Intopia
- c. Nonconformity
- d. Modes of leadership

Guidance: level 1

:: Real estate valuation ::

_____ or OMV is the price at which an asset would trade in a competitive auction setting. _____ is often used interchangeably with open _____, fair value or fair _____, although these terms have distinct definitions in different standards, and may or may not differ in some circumstances.

Exam Probability: **Low**

39. *Answer choices:*
(see index for correct answer)

- a. Zillow
- b. Market value
- c. Real estate appraisal
- d. Days on market

Guidance: level 1

:: Project management ::

_____ is the right to exercise power, which can be formalized by a state and exercised by way of judges, appointed executives of government, or the ecclesiastical or priestly appointed representatives of a God or other deities.

Exam Probability: **Medium**

40. *Answer choices:*

(see index for correct answer)

- a. Task management
- b. Authority
- c. Decision table
- d. Project manufacturing

Guidance: level 1

:: Actuarial science ::

_____ is the possibility of losing something of value. Values can be gained or lost when taking _____ resulting from a given action or inaction, foreseen or unforeseen . _____ can also be defined as the intentional interaction with uncertainty. Uncertainty is a potential, unpredictable, and uncontrollable outcome; _____ is a consequence of action taken in spite of uncertainty.

Exam Probability: **High**

41. *Answer choices:*

(see index for correct answer)

- a. CRESTA
- b. Anders Lindstedt
- c. Risk
- d. Mathematical statistics

Guidance: level 1

:: Data collection ::

A _____ is an utterance which typically functions as a request for information. _____ s can thus be understood as a kind of illocutionary act in the field of pragmatics or as special kinds of propositions in frameworks of formal semantics such as alternative semantics or inquisitive semantics. The information requested is expected to be provided in the form of an answer. _____ s are often conflated with interrogatives, which are the grammatical forms typically used to achieve them. Rhetorical _____ s, for example, are interrogative in form but may not be considered true _____ s as they are not expected to be answered. Conversely, non-interrogative grammatical structures may be considered _____ s as in the case of the imperative sentence "tell me your name".

Exam Probability: **Medium**

42. *Answer choices:*

(see index for correct answer)

- a. Guardian
- b. Question
- c. North Atlantic Population Project
- d. Bus monitoring

Guidance: level 1

:: Income ::

_____ is a ratio between the net profit and cost of investment resulting from an investment of some resources. A high ROI means the investment's gains favorably to its cost. As a performance measure, ROI is used to evaluate the efficiency of an investment or to compare the efficiencies of several different investments. In purely economic terms, it is one way of relating profits to capital invested. _____ is a performance measure used by businesses to identify the efficiency of an investment or number of different investments.

Exam Probability: **Low**

43. *Answer choices:*

(see index for correct answer)

- a. Return of investment
- b. IRD asset
- c. Pay grade
- d. Income Per User

Guidance: level 1

:: Regression analysis ::

A _____ often refers to a set of documented requirements to be satisfied by a material, design, product, or service. A _____ is often a type of technical standard.

Exam Probability: **Medium**

44. *Answer choices:*

(see index for correct answer)

- a. Separation
- b. Bayesian multivariate linear regression
- c. Specification
- d. Multinomial logistic regression

Guidance: level 1

:: Management ::

A _____ is a method or technique that has been generally accepted as superior to any alternatives because it produces results that are superior to those achieved by other means or because it has become a standard way of doing things, e.g., a standard way of complying with legal or ethical requirements.

Exam Probability: **Low**

45. *Answer choices:*

(see index for correct answer)

- a. Double linking
- b. Project management information system
- c. Event chain methodology
- d. PhD in management

Guidance: level 1

:: Business process ::

A _____ or business method is a collection of related, structured activities or tasks by people or equipment which in a specific sequence produce a service or product for a particular customer or customers. _____ es occur at all organizational levels and may or may not be visible to the customers. A _____ may often be visualized as a flowchart of a sequence of activities with interleaving decision points or as a process matrix of a sequence of activities with relevance rules based on data in the process. The benefits of using _____ es include improved customer satisfaction and improved agility for reacting to rapid market change. Process-oriented organizations break down the barriers of structural departments and try to avoid functional silos.

Exam Probability: **Medium**

46. *Answer choices:*

(see index for correct answer)

- a. Hi-tech export
- b. Communication-enabled business process
- c. Business process
- d. Open door policy

Guidance: level 1

:: International trade ::

_____ or globalisation is the process of interaction and integration among people, companies, and governments worldwide. As a complex and multifaceted phenomenon, _____ is considered by some as a form of capitalist expansion which entails the integration of local and national economies into a global, unregulated market economy. _____ has grown due to advances in transportation and communication technology. With the increased global interactions comes the growth of international trade, ideas, and culture. _____ is primarily an economic process of interaction and integration that's associated with social and cultural aspects. However, conflicts and diplomacy are also large parts of the history of _____ , and modern _____ .

Exam Probability: **Medium**

47. *Answer choices:*

(see index for correct answer)

- a. Portuguese India Armadas
- b. International Organisation of Employers
- c. East forum Berlin
- d. Globalization

Guidance: level 1

:: Labour relations ::

_____ is a field of study that can have different meanings depending on the context in which it is used. In an international context, it is a subfield of labor history that studies the human relations with regard to work – in its broadest sense – and how this connects to questions of social inequality. It explicitly encompasses unregulated, historical, and non-Western forms of labor. Here, _____ define "for or with whom one works and under what rules. These rules determine the type of work, type and amount of remuneration, working hours, degrees of physical and psychological strain, as well as the degree of freedom and autonomy associated with the work."

Exam Probability: **High**

48. *Answer choices:*

(see index for correct answer)

- a. Labor relations
- b. Jesse Simons
- c. Lockout
- d. Boulwarism

Guidance: level 1

:: Stock market ::

The _____ of a corporation is all of the shares into which ownership of the corporation is divided. In American English, the shares are commonly known as "_____s". A single share of the _____ represents fractional ownership of the corporation in proportion to the total number of shares. This typically entitles the _____ holder to that fraction of the company's earnings, proceeds from liquidation of assets, or voting power, often dividing these up in proportion to the amount of money each _____ holder has invested. Not all _____ is necessarily equal, as certain classes of _____ may be issued for example without voting rights, with enhanced voting rights, or with a certain priority to receive profits or liquidation proceeds before or after other classes of shareholders.

Exam Probability: **Medium**

49. *Answer choices:*

(see index for correct answer)

- a. Purple chip
- b. Market-based valuation
- c. Street name securities
- d. Stock promoter

Guidance: level 1

:: ::

A _____ is any person who contracts to acquire an asset in return for some form of consideration.

Exam Probability: **Low**

50. *Answer choices:*

(see index for correct answer)

- a. hierarchical perspective
- b. cultural
- c. co-culture
- d. open system

Guidance: level 1

:: Organizational structure ::

An _____ defines how activities such as task allocation, coordination, and supervision are directed toward the achievement of organizational aims.

Exam Probability: **High**

51. *Answer choices:*

(see index for correct answer)

- a. Automated Bureaucracy
- b. Unorganisation
- c. Organization of the New York City Police Department
- d. Organizational structure

Guidance: level 1

:: ::

An _____ is the production of goods or related services within an economy. The major source of revenue of a group or company is the indicator of its relevant _____ . When a large group has multiple sources of revenue generation, it is considered to be working in different industries. Manufacturing _____ became a key sector of production and labour in European and North American countries during the Industrial Revolution, upsetting previous mercantile and feudal economies. This came through many successive rapid advances in technology, such as the production of steel and coal.

Exam Probability: **Medium**

52. *Answer choices:*

(see index for correct answer)

- a. information systems assessment
- b. Industry
- c. Sarbanes-Oxley act of 2002
- d. functional perspective

Guidance: level 1

:: Business ethics ::

_____ is a type of harassment technique that relates to a sexual nature and the unwelcome or inappropriate promise of rewards in exchange for sexual favors. _____ includes a range of actions from mild transgressions to sexual abuse or assault. Harassment can occur in many different social settings such as the workplace, the home, school, churches, etc. Harassers or victims may be of any gender.

Exam Probability: **Medium**

53. *Answer choices:*

(see index for correct answer)

- a. Marketing ethics
- b. Sexual harassment
- c. Society for Business Ethics
- d. Repugnant market

Guidance: level 1

:: Business ::

The seller, or the provider of the goods or services, completes a sale in response to an acquisition, appropriation, requisition or a direct interaction with the buyer at the point of sale. There is a passing of title of the item, and the settlement of a price, in which agreement is reached on a price for which transfer of ownership of the item will occur. The seller, not the purchaser typically executes the sale and it may be completed prior to the obligation of payment. In the case of indirect interaction, a person who sells goods or service on behalf of the owner is known as a salesman or saleswoman or salesperson, but this often refers to someone _____ goods in a store/shop, in which case other terms are also common, including salesclerk, shop assistant, and retail clerk.

Exam Probability: **High**

54. *Answer choices:*

(see index for correct answer)

- a. Serviced office broker
- b. Corporate social media
- c. Uncorporation
- d. Business interaction networks

Guidance: level 1

:: Television commercials ::

_____ is a phenomenon whereby something new and somehow valuable is formed. The created item may be intangible or a physical object.

Exam Probability: **High**

55. *Answer choices:*

(see index for correct answer)

- a. Creativity
- b. The LeBrons
- c. Eyebrows
- d. World History. Bank Imperial

Guidance: level 1

:: Generally Accepted Accounting Principles ::

In business and accounting, _____ is an entity's income minus cost of goods sold, expenses and taxes for an accounting period. It is computed as the residual of all revenues and gains over all expenses and losses for the period, and has also been defined as the net increase in shareholders' equity that results from a company's operations. In the context of the presentation of financial statements, the IFRS Foundation defines _____ as synonymous with profit and loss. The difference between revenue and the cost of making a product or providing a service, before deducting overheads, payroll, taxation, and interest payments. This is different from operating income.

Exam Probability: **Low**

56. *Answer choices:*

(see index for correct answer)

- a. Net income
- b. Access to finance
- c. Generally Accepted Accounting Practice
- d. Goodwill

Guidance: level 1

:: Production economics ::

In microeconomics, _____ are the cost advantages that enterprises obtain due to their scale of operation, with cost per unit of output decreasing with increasing scale.

Exam Probability: **Medium**

57. *Answer choices:*

(see index for correct answer)

- a. Marginal cost of capital schedule
- b. Economies of scale
- c. HMI quality
- d. Sharing

Guidance: level 1

:: Costs ::

In microeconomic theory, the _____, or alternative cost, of making a particular choice is the value of the most valuable choice out of those that were not taken. In other words, opportunity that will require sacrifices.

Exam Probability: **Low**

58. *Answer choices:*

(see index for correct answer)

- a. Search cost
- b. Travel and subsistence
- c. Manufacturing cost
- d. Opportunity cost

Guidance: level 1

:: Strategic alliances ::

A _____ is an agreement between two or more parties to pursue a set of agreed upon objectives needed while remaining independent organizations. A _____ will usually fall short of a legal partnership entity, agency, or corporate affiliate relationship. Typically, two companies form a _____ when each possesses one or more business assets or have expertise that will help the other by enhancing their businesses. _____ s can develop in outsourcing relationships where the parties desire to achieve long-term win-win benefits and innovation based on mutually desired outcomes.

Exam Probability: **Medium**

59. *Answer choices:*

(see index for correct answer)

- a. Defensive termination
- b. Strategic alliance
- c. Bridge Alliance
- d. International joint venture

Guidance: level 1

Management

Management is the administration of an organization, whether it is a business, a not-for-profit organization, or government body. Management includes the activities of setting the strategy of an organization and coordinating the efforts of its employees (or of volunteers) to accomplish its objectives through the application of available resources, such as financial, natural, technological, and human resources.

:: Commercial item transport and distribution ::

In commerce, supply-chain management , the management of the flow of goods and services, involves the movement and storage of raw materials, of work-in-process inventory, and of finished goods from point of origin to point of consumption. Interconnected or interlinked networks, channels and node businesses combine in the provision of products and services required by end customers in a supply chain. Supply-chain management has been defined as the "design, planning, execution, control, and monitoring of supply-chain activities with the objective of creating net value, building a competitive infrastructure, leveraging worldwide logistics, synchronizing supply with demand and measuring performance globally."SCM practice draws heavily from the areas of industrial engineering, systems engineering, operations management, logistics, procurement, information technology, and marketing and strives for an integrated approach. Marketing channels play an important role in supply-chain management. Current research in supply-chain management is concerned with topics related to sustainability and risk management, among others. Some suggest that the "people dimension" of SCM, ethical issues, internal integration, transparency/visibility, and human capital/talent management are topics that have, so far, been underrepresented on the research agenda.

Exam Probability: **High**

1. *Answer choices:*

(see index for correct answer)

- a. Export Yellow Pages
- b. Australia standard pallets
- c. Freight exchange
- d. Supply chain management

Guidance: level 1

:: Supply chain management terms ::

In business and finance, _____ is a system of organizations, people, activities, information, and resources involved in moving a product or service from supplier to customer. _____ activities involve the transformation of natural resources, raw materials, and components into a finished product that is delivered to the end customer. In sophisticated _____ systems, used products may re-enter the _____ at any point where residual value is recyclable. _____ s link value chains.

Exam Probability: **High**

2. *Answer choices:*

(see index for correct answer)

- a. Widget
- b. Price look-up code
- c. Stockout
- d. Work in process

Guidance: level 1

:: Marketing ::

_____ , in marketing, manufacturing, call centres and management, is the use of flexible computer-aided manufacturing systems to produce custom output. Such systems combine the low unit costs of mass production processes with the flexibility of individual customization.

Exam Probability: **Low**

3. *Answer choices:*

(see index for correct answer)

- a. Gladvertising
- b. Contact centre
- c. Official statistics
- d. MaxDiff

Guidance: level 1

:: Marketing ::

_____ comes from the Latin neg and otsia referring to businessmen who, unlike the patricians, had no leisure time in their industriousness; it held the meaning of business until the 17th century when it took on the diplomatic connotation as a dialogue between two or more people or parties intended to reach a beneficial outcome over one or more issues where a conflict exists with respect to at least one of these issues. Thus, _____ is a process of combining divergent positions into a joint agreement under a decision rule of unanimity.

Exam Probability: **High**

4. *Answer choices:*

(see index for correct answer)

- a. Negotiation
- b. Price war
- c. Industrial marketing
- d. Product requirements document

Guidance: level 1

:: Behavior modification ::

In psychotherapy and mental health, _____ has a positive sense of empowering individuals, or a negative sense of encouraging dysfunctional behavior.

Exam Probability: **Medium**

5. *Answer choices:*

(see index for correct answer)

- a. Thought stopping
- b. Enabling

Guidance: level 1

:: Organizational behavior ::

In organizational behavior and industrial and organizational psychology, _____ is an individual's psychological attachment to the organization. The basis behind many of these studies was to find ways to improve how workers feel about their jobs so that these workers would become more committed to their organizations. _____ predicts work variables such as turnover, organizational citizenship behavior, and job performance. Some of the factors such as role stress, empowerment, job insecurity and employability, and distribution of leadership have been shown to be connected to a worker's sense of _____ .

Exam Probability: **Low**

6. *Answer choices:*

(see index for correct answer)

- a. History of contingency theories of leadership
- b. Burnout
- c. Boreout
- d. Organizational commitment

Guidance: level 1

:: Behaviorism ::

In behavioral psychology, _____ is a consequence applied that will strengthen an organism's future behavior whenever that behavior is preceded by a specific antecedent stimulus. This strengthening effect may be measured as a higher frequency of behavior, longer duration, greater magnitude, or shorter latency. There are two types of _____, known as positive _____ and negative _____; positive is where by a reward is offered on expression of the wanted behaviour and negative is taking away an undesirable element in the persons environment whenever the desired behaviour is achieved.

Exam Probability: **Low**

7. *Answer choices:*

(see index for correct answer)

- a. Programmed instruction
- b. social facilitation
- c. Reinforcement
- d. Systematic desensitization

Guidance: level 1

:: Organizational theory ::

Decentralisation is the process by which the activities of an organization, particularly those regarding planning and decision making, are distributed or delegated away from a central, authoritative location or group. Concepts of _____ have been applied to group dynamics and management science in private businesses and organizations, political science, law and public administration, economics, money and technology.

Exam Probability: **High**

8. *Answer choices:*

(see index for correct answer)

- a. The three circles model
- b. Mutual aid
- c. Decentralization
- d. Goat rodeo

Guidance: level 1

:: Office administration ::

An _____ is generally a room or other area where an organization's employees perform administrative work in order to support and realize objects and goals of the organization. The word " _____ " may also denote a position within an organization with specific duties attached to it ; the latter is in fact an earlier usage, _____ as place originally referring to the location of one's duty. When used as an adjective, the term " _____ " may refer to business-related tasks. In law, a company or organization has _____ s in any place where it has an official presence, even if that presence consists of a storage silo rather than an establishment with desk-and-chair. An _____ is also an architectural and design phenomenon: ranging from a small _____ such as a bench in the corner of a small business of extremely small size , through entire floors of buildings, up to and including massive buildings dedicated entirely to one company. In modern terms an _____ is usually the location where white-collar workers carry out their functions. As per James Stephenson, " _____ is that part of business enterprise which is devoted to the direction and co-ordination of its various activities."

Exam Probability: **Medium**

9. *Answer choices:*

(see index for correct answer)

- a. Office administration
- b. Fish! Philosophy
- c. Office
- d. Inter departmental communication

Guidance: level 1

:: Management ::

_____ is a set of activities that ensure goals are met in an effective and efficient manner. _____ can focus on the performance of an organization, a department, an employee, or the processes in place to manage particular tasks. _____ standards are generally organized and disseminated by senior leadership at an organization, and by task owners.

Exam Probability: **Low**

10. *Answer choices:*

(see index for correct answer)

- a. Systems analysis
- b. Project stakeholder

- c. Extended enterprise
- d. Performance management

Guidance: level 1

:: Game theory ::

To _____ is to make a deal between different parties where each party gives up part of their demand. In arguments, _____ is a concept of finding agreement through communication, through a mutual acceptance of terms—often involving variations from an original goal or desires.

Exam Probability: **High**

11. *Answer choices:*
(see index for correct answer)

- a. La Relance
- b. Algorithmic game theory
- c. Focal point
- d. Rationalizability

Guidance: level 1

:: ::

The _____ is an intergovernmental organization that is concerned with the regulation of international trade between nations. The WTO officially commenced on 1 January 1995 under the Marrakesh Agreement, signed by 124 nations on 15 April 1994, replacing the General Agreement on Tariffs and Trade , which commenced in 1948. It is the largest international economic organization in the world.

Exam Probability: **Medium**

12. *Answer choices:*

(see index for correct answer)

- a. process perspective
- b. World Trade Organization
- c. empathy
- d. functional perspective

Guidance: level 1

:: ::

A _____ is a leader's method of providing direction, implementing plans, and motivating people. Various authors have proposed identifying many different _____ s as exhibited by leaders in the political, business or other fields. Studies on _____ are conducted in the military field, expressing an approach that stresses a holistic view of leadership, including how a leader's physical presence determines how others perceive that leader. The factors of physical presence in this context include military bearing, physical fitness, confidence, and resilience. The leader's intellectual capacity helps to conceptualize solutions and to acquire knowledge to do the job. A leader's conceptual abilities apply agility, judgment, innovation, interpersonal tact, and domain knowledge. Domain knowledge encompasses tactical and technical knowledge as well as cultural and geopolitical awareness. Daniel Goleman in his article "Leadership that Gets Results" talks about six styles of leadership.

Exam Probability: **Low**

13. *Answer choices:*

(see index for correct answer)

- a. Leadership style
- b. interpersonal communication
- c. levels of analysis
- d. personal values

Guidance: level 1

The _____ is an agreement signed by Canada, Mexico, and the United States, creating a trilateral trade bloc in North America. The agreement came into force on January 1, 1994, and superseded the 1988 Canada–United States Free Trade Agreement between the United States and Canada. The NAFTA trade bloc is one of the largest trade blocs in the world by gross domestic product.

Exam Probability: **High**

14. *Answer choices:*

(see index for correct answer)

- a. information systems assessment
- b. North American Free Trade Agreement
- c. Character
- d. personal values

Guidance: level 1

:: Statistical terminology ::

_____ es can be learned implicitly within cultural contexts. People may develop _____ es toward or against an individual, an ethnic group, a sexual or gender identity, a nation, a religion, a social class, a political party, theoretical paradigms and ideologies within academic domains, or a species. _____ ed means one-sided, lacking a neutral viewpoint, or not having an open mind. _____ can come in many forms and is related to prejudice and intuition.

Exam Probability: **High**

15. *Answer choices:*

(see index for correct answer)

- a. Covariate
- b. Likelihood
- c. Probability of error
- d. Bias

Guidance: level 1

:: ::

_____ Corporation was an American energy, commodities, and services company based in Houston, Texas. It was founded in 1985 as a merger between Houston Natural Gas and InterNorth, both relatively small regional companies. Before its bankruptcy on December 3, 2001, _____ employed approximately 29,000 staff and was a major electricity, natural gas, communications and pulp and paper company, with claimed revenues of nearly $101 billion during 2000. Fortune named _____ "America's Most Innovative Company" for six consecutive years.

Exam Probability: **Medium**

16. *Answer choices:*

(see index for correct answer)

- a. information systems assessment
- b. functional perspective
- c. corporate values
- d. imperative

Guidance: level 1

:: ::

In communications and information processing, _____ is a system of rules to convert information—such as a letter, word, sound, image, or gesture—into another form or representation, sometimes shortened or secret, for communication through a communication channel or storage in a storage medium. An early example is the invention of language, which enabled a person, through speech, to communicate what they saw, heard, felt, or thought to others. But speech limits the range of communication to the distance a voice can carry, and limits the audience to those present when the speech is uttered. The invention of writing, which converted spoken language into visual symbols, extended the range of communication across space and time.

Exam Probability: **Low**

17. *Answer choices:*

(see index for correct answer)

- a. similarity-attraction theory
- b. Sarbanes-Oxley act of 2002
- c. process perspective
- d. hierarchical

Guidance: level 1

:: Monopoly (economics) ::

_____ is a category of property that includes intangible creations of the human intellect. _____ encompasses two types of rights: industrial property rights and copyright. It was not until the 19th century that the term "_____" began to be used, and not until the late 20th century that it became commonplace in the majority of the world.

Exam Probability: **High**

18. *Answer choices:*

(see index for correct answer)

- a. Private finance initiative
- b. Natural monopoly
- c. Intellectual property
- d. Dominance

Guidance: level 1

:: Business law ::

A _____ is a group of people who jointly supervise the activities of an organization, which can be either a for-profit business, nonprofit organization, or a government agency. Such a board's powers, duties, and responsibilities are determined by government regulations and the organization's own constitution and bylaws. These authorities may specify the number of members of the board, how they are to be chosen, and how often they are to meet.

Exam Probability: **Low**

19. *Answer choices:*

(see index for correct answer)

- a. Board of directors
- b. Lex mercatoria
- c. Advertising regulation
- d. Negotiable instrument

Guidance: level 1

:: Labor ::

The workforce or labour force is the labour pool in employment. It is generally used to describe those working for a single company or industry, but can also apply to a geographic region like a city, state, or country. Within a company, its value can be labelled as its "Workforce in Place". The workforce of a country includes both the employed and the unemployed. The labour force participation rate, LFPR , is the ratio between the labour force and the overall size of their cohort . The term generally excludes the employers or management, and can imply those involved in manual labour. It may also mean all those who are available for work.

Exam Probability: **Medium**

20. *Answer choices:*

(see index for correct answer)

- a. Lump of labour fallacy
- b. Strikebreaker
- c. Labor force
- d. Distributed workforce

Guidance: level 1

:: Project management ::

_____ and Theory Y are theories of human work motivation and management. They were created by Douglas McGregor while he was working at the MIT Sloan School of Management in the 1950s, and developed further in the 1960s. McGregor's work was rooted in motivation theory alongside the works of Abraham Maslow, who created the hierarchy of needs. The two theories proposed by McGregor describe contrasting models of workforce motivation applied by managers in human resource management, organizational behavior, organizational communication and organizational development. _____ explains the importance of heightened supervision, external rewards, and penalties, while Theory Y highlights the motivating role of job satisfaction and encourages workers to approach tasks without direct supervision. Management use of _____ and Theory Y can affect employee motivation and productivity in different ways, and managers may choose to implement strategies from both theories into their practices.

Exam Probability: **Medium**

21. *Answer choices:*

(see index for correct answer)

- a. Theory X
- b. Scope creep
- c. Effort management
- d. Identifying and Managing Project Risk

Guidance: level 1

:: Generally Accepted Accounting Principles ::

In accounting, _____ is the income that a business have from its normal business activities, usually from the sale of goods and services to customers. _____ is also referred to as sales or turnover. Some companies receive _____ from interest, royalties, or other fees. _____ may refer to business income in general, or it may refer to the amount, in a monetary unit, earned during a period of time, as in "Last year, Company X had _____ of $42 million". Profits or net income generally imply total _____ minus total expenses in a given period. In accounting, in the balance statement it is a subsection of the Equity section and _____ increases equity, it is often referred to as the "top line" due to its position on the income statement at the very top. This is to be contrasted with the "bottom line" which denotes net income.

Exam Probability: **Low**

22. *Answer choices:*

(see index for correct answer)

- a. Revenue
- b. Generally accepted accounting principles
- c. Indian Accounting Standards
- d. Cost principle

Guidance: level 1

:: Decision theory ::

Within economics the concept of _____ is used to model worth or value, but its usage has evolved significantly over time. The term was introduced initially as a measure of pleasure or satisfaction within the theory of utilitarianism by moral philosophers such as Jeremy Bentham and John Stuart Mill. But the term has been adapted and reapplied within neoclassical economics, which dominates modern economic theory, as a _____ function that represents a consumer's preference ordering over a choice set. As such, it is devoid of its original interpretation as a measurement of the pleasure or satisfaction obtained by the consumer from that choice.

Exam Probability: **Low**

23. *Answer choices:*

(see index for correct answer)

- a. Mental accounting
- b. Utility
- c. Mean-preserving spread
- d. Dominance-based rough set approach

Guidance: level 1

:: ::

_____ is the stock of habits, knowledge, social and personality attributes embodied in the ability to perform labor so as to produce economic value.

Exam Probability: **Medium**

24. *Answer choices:*

(see index for correct answer)

- a. hierarchical
- b. functional perspective
- c. similarity-attraction theory
- d. deep-level diversity

Guidance: level 1

:: Employment ::

_____ is a relationship between two parties, usually based on a contract where work is paid for, where one party, which may be a corporation, for profit, not-for-profit organization, co-operative or other entity is the employer and the other is the employee. Employees work in return for payment, which may be in the form of an hourly wage, by piecework or an annual salary, depending on the type of work an employee does or which sector she or he is working in. Employees in some fields or sectors may receive gratuities, bonus payment or stock options. In some types of _____ , employees may receive benefits in addition to payment. Benefits can include health insurance, housing, disability insurance or use of a gym. _____ is typically governed by _____ laws, regulations or legal contracts.

Exam Probability: **Low**

25. *Answer choices:*

(see index for correct answer)

- a. Liaison job
- b. Employment
- c. Personal chef
- d. Labor geography

Guidance: level 1

:: Costs ::

In economics, _____ is the total economic cost of production and is made up of variable cost, which varies according to the quantity of a good produced and includes inputs such as labour and raw materials, plus fixed cost, which is independent of the quantity of a good produced and includes inputs that cannot be varied in the short term: fixed costs such as buildings and machinery, including sunk costs if any. Since cost is measured per unit of time, it is a flow variable.

Exam Probability: **Low**

26. *Answer choices:*
(see index for correct answer)

- a. Social cost
- b. Cost competitiveness of fuel sources
- c. Implicit cost
- d. Total cost

Guidance: level 1

:: Hospitality management ::

A _____ is an establishment that provides paid lodging on a short-term basis. Facilities provided may range from a modest-quality mattress in a small room to large suites with bigger, higher-quality beds, a dresser, a refrigerator and other kitchen facilities, upholstered chairs, a flat screen television, and en-suite bathrooms. Small, lower-priced _____ s may offer only the most basic guest services and facilities. Larger, higher-priced _____ s may provide additional guest facilities such as a swimming pool, business centre , childcare, conference and event facilities, tennis or basketball courts, gymnasium, restaurants, day spa, and social function services. _____ rooms are usually numbered to allow guests to identify their room. Some boutique, high-end _____ s have custom decorated rooms. Some _____ s offer meals as part of a room and board arrangement. In the United Kingdom, a _____ is required by law to serve food and drinks to all guests within certain stated hours. In Japan, capsule _____ s provide a tiny room suitable only for sleeping and shared bathroom facilities.

Exam Probability: **High**

27. *Answer choices:*
(see index for correct answer)

- a. Les Roches Jin Jiang International Hotel Management College
- b. IHM Pusa
- c. Restaurant management
- d. Swiss Hotel Schools Association

Guidance: level 1

:: Summary statistics ::

_____ is the number of occurrences of a repeating event per unit of time. It is also referred to as temporal _____ , which emphasizes the contrast to spatial _____ and angular _____ . The period is the duration of time of one cycle in a repeating event, so the period is the reciprocal of the _____ . For example: if a newborn baby's heart beats at a _____ of 120 times a minute, its period—the time interval between beats—is half a second . _____ is an important parameter used in science and engineering to specify the rate of oscillatory and vibratory phenomena, such as mechanical vibrations, audio signals , radio waves, and light.

Exam Probability: **High**

28. *Answer choices:*

(see index for correct answer)

- a. Quartile
- b. Location parameter
- c. Frequency
- d. Mean percentage error

Guidance: level 1

:: Management accounting ::

_____ s are costs that change as the quantity of the good or service that a business produces changes. _____ s are the sum of marginal costs over all units produced. They can also be considered normal costs. Fixed costs and _____ s make up the two components of total cost. Direct costs are costs that can easily be associated with a particular cost object. However, not all _____ s are direct costs. For example, variable manufacturing overhead costs are _____ s that are indirect costs, not direct costs. _____ s are sometimes called unit-level costs as they vary with the number of units produced.

Exam Probability: **Low**

29. *Answer choices:*

(see index for correct answer)

- a. Variable cost
- b. Indirect costs
- c. Responsibility center
- d. Cost driver

Guidance: level 1

:: ::

_____ is the collection of mechanisms, processes and relations by which corporations are controlled and operated. Governance structures and principles identify the distribution of rights and responsibilities among different participants in the corporation and include the rules and procedures for making decisions in corporate affairs. _____ is necessary because of the possibility of conflicts of interests between stakeholders, primarily between shareholders and upper management or among shareholders.

Exam Probability: **High**

30. *Answer choices:*
(see index for correct answer)

- a. empathy
- b. levels of analysis
- c. hierarchical perspective
- d. Corporate governance

Guidance: level 1

:: Statistical terminology ::

_____ is the magnitude or dimensions of a thing. _____ can be measured as length, width, height, diameter, perimeter, area, volume, or mass.

Exam Probability: **High**

31. *Answer choices:*

(see index for correct answer)

- a. Iterated conditional modes
- b. Fair coin
- c. Concentration parameter
- d. Size

Guidance: level 1

:: Management ::

_____ is the practice of initiating, planning, executing, controlling, and closing the work of a team to achieve specific goals and meet specific success criteria at the specified time.

Exam Probability: **Medium**

32. *Answer choices:*

(see index for correct answer)

- a. Event chain methodology
- b. Business-oriented architecture
- c. Outrage constraint
- d. Porter five forces analysis

Guidance: level 1

:: Management ::

In the field of management, _____ involves the formulation and implementation of the major goals and initiatives taken by an organization's top management on behalf of owners, based on consideration of resources and an assessment of the internal and external environments in which the organization operates.

Exam Probability: **High**

33. *Answer choices:*
(see index for correct answer)

- a. Strategic management
- b. Narcissistic leadership
- c. Communities of innovation
- d. Evidence-based management

Guidance: level 1

:: Organizational theory ::

_____ comprises the actual output or results of an organization as measured against its intended outputs.

Exam Probability: **Medium**

34. *Answer choices:*

(see index for correct answer)

- a. Participatory management
- b. Organizational performance
- c. Organizational theory
- d. Sociogram

Guidance: level 1

:: ::

_____ is the reason for people's actions, willingness and goals. _____ is derived from the word motive in the English language which is defined as a need that requires satisfaction. These needs could also be wants or desires that are acquired through influence of culture, society, lifestyle, etc. or generally innate. _____ is one's direction to behaviour, or what causes a person to want to repeat a behaviour, a set of force that acts behind the motives. An individual's _____ may be inspired by others or events or it may come from within the individual . _____ has been considered as one of the most important reasons that inspires a person to move forward in life. _____ results from the interaction of both conscious and unconscious factors. Mastering _____ to allow sustained and deliberate practice is central to high levels of achievement e.g. in the worlds of elite sport, medicine or music.

Exam Probability: **Medium**

35. *Answer choices:*

(see index for correct answer)

- a. interpersonal communication
- b. Motivation
- c. deep-level diversity
- d. corporate values

Guidance: level 1

:: Mereology ::

_____ , in the abstract, is what belongs to or with something, whether as an attribute or as a component of said thing. In the context of this article, it is one or more components , whether physical or incorporeal, of a person's estate; or so belonging to, as in being owned by, a person or jointly a group of people or a legal entity like a corporation or even a society. Depending on the nature of the _____ , an owner of _____ has the right to consume, alter, share, redefine, rent, mortgage, pawn, sell, exchange, transfer, give away or destroy it, or to exclude others from doing these things, as well as to perhaps abandon it; whereas regardless of the nature of the _____ , the owner thereof has the right to properly use it , or at the very least exclusively keep it.

Exam Probability: **Medium**

36. *Answer choices:*

(see index for correct answer)

- a. Simple
- b. Non-wellfounded mereology
- c. Mereology
- d. Mereotopology

Guidance: level 1

:: Management accounting ::

In economics, _____ s, indirect costs or overheads are business expenses that are not dependent on the level of goods or services produced by the business. They tend to be time-related, such as interest or rents being paid per month, and are often referred to as overhead costs. This is in contrast to variable costs, which are volume-related and unknown at the beginning of the accounting year. For a simple example, such as a bakery, the monthly rent for the baking facilities, and the monthly payments for the security system and basic phone line are _____ s, as they do not change according to how much bread the bakery produces and sells. On the other hand, the wage costs of the bakery are variable, as the bakery will have to hire more workers if the production of bread increases. Economists reckon _____ as a entry barrier for new entrepreneurs.

Exam Probability: **Low**

37. *Answer choices:*
(see index for correct answer)

- a. Fixed cost
- b. activity based costing

- c. Direct material total variance
- d. Spend management

Guidance: level 1

:: Occupations ::

An _____ is a person who has a position of authority in a hierarchical organization. The term derives from the late Latin from officiarius, meaning "official".

Exam Probability: **Medium**

38. *Answer choices:*
(see index for correct answer)

- a. Ungdommens Naturvidenskabelige Forening
- b. Barrelman
- c. Statistician
- d. Shopkeeper

Guidance: level 1

:: Management occupations ::

_____ is the process of designing, launching and running a new business, which is often initially a small business. The people who create these businesses are called entrepreneurs.

Exam Probability: **High**

39. *Answer choices:*

(see index for correct answer)

- a. Exempt secretary
- b. Chief design officer
- c. Business magnate
- d. County administrator

Guidance: level 1

:: Customs duties ::

A _____ is a tax on imports or exports between sovereign states. It is a form of regulation of foreign trade and a policy that taxes foreign products to encourage or safeguard domestic industry. _____ s are the simplest and oldest instrument of trade policy. Traditionally, states have used them as a source of income. Now, they are among the most widely used instruments of protection, along with import and export quotas.

Exam Probability: **Low**

40. *Answer choices:*

(see index for correct answer)

- a. Customs racketeering
- b. Customs area
- c. Tariff
- d. Morrill Tariff

Guidance: level 1

:: Data analysis ::

In statistics, the _____ is a measure that is used to quantify the amount of variation or dispersion of a set of data values. A low _____ indicates that the data points tend to be close to the mean of the set, while a high _____ indicates that the data points are spread out over a wider range of values.

Exam Probability: **Medium**

41. *Answer choices:*

(see index for correct answer)

- a. Health care analytics
- b. Independent component analysis
- c. Data analysis
- d. Standard deviation

Guidance: level 1

:: Logistics ::

_____ is generally the detailed organization and implementation of a complex operation. In a general business sense, _____ is the management of the flow of things between the point of origin and the point of consumption in order to meet requirements of customers or corporations. The resources managed in _____ may include tangible goods such as materials, equipment, and supplies, as well as food and other consumable items. The _____ of physical items usually involves the integration of information flow, materials handling, production, packaging, inventory, transportation, warehousing, and often security.

Exam Probability: **Low**

42. *Answer choices:*

(see index for correct answer)

- a. Airbridge
- b. StarShipIt
- c. Logistics
- d. Clinical engineering

Guidance: level 1

:: Product management ::

_____ s, also known as Shewhart charts or process-behavior charts, are a statistical process control tool used to determine if a manufacturing or business process is in a state of control.

Exam Probability: **High**

43. *Answer choices:*

(see index for correct answer)

- a. Brand equity
- b. Control chart
- c. Brand extension
- d. Crossing the Chasm

Guidance: level 1

:: Market research ::

_____ is an organized effort to gather information about target markets or customers. It is a very important component of business strategy. The term is commonly interchanged with marketing research; however, expert practitioners may wish to draw a distinction, in that marketing research is concerned specifically about marketing processes, while _____ is concerned specifically with markets.

Exam Probability: **High**

44. *Answer choices:*

(see index for correct answer)

- a. Monroe Mendelsohn Research
- b. Market research
- c. Competitive intelligence
- d. Customer experience analytics

Guidance: level 1

:: Evaluation ::

_____ solving consists of using generic or ad hoc methods in an orderly manner to find solutions to _____ s. Some of the _____ -solving techniques developed and used in philosophy, artificial intelligence, computer science, engineering, mathematics, or medicine are related to mental _____ -solving techniques studied in psychology.

Exam Probability: **Low**

45. *Answer choices:*

(see index for correct answer)

- a. Problem
- b. Educational evaluation
- c. American Evaluation Association
- d. Career portfolio

Guidance: level 1

:: Majority–minority relations ::

_____ , also known as reservation in India and Nepal, positive discrimination / action in the United Kingdom, and employment equity in Canada and South Africa, is the policy of promoting the education and employment of members of groups that are known to have previously suffered from discrimination. Historically and internationally, support for _____ has sought to achieve goals such as bridging inequalities in employment and pay, increasing access to education, promoting diversity, and redressing apparent past wrongs, harms, or hindrances.

Exam Probability: **Medium**

46. *Answer choices:*

(see index for correct answer)

- a. positive discrimination
- b. Affirmative action
- c. cultural Relativism

Guidance: level 1

:: ::

An _____ is, most an organized examination or formal evaluation exercise. In engineering activities _____ involves the measurements, tests, and gauges applied to certain characteristics in regard to an object or activity. The results are usually compared to specified requirements and standards for determining whether the item or activity is in line with these targets, often with a Standard _____ Procedure in place to ensure consistent checking. _____ s are usually non-destructive.

Exam Probability: **Medium**

47. *Answer choices:*

(see index for correct answer)

- a. surface-level diversity
- b. cultural
- c. Sarbanes-Oxley act of 2002
- d. Inspection

Guidance: level 1

:: ::

_____ refers to the overall process of attracting, shortlisting, selecting and appointing suitable candidates for jobs within an organization. _____ can also refer to processes involved in choosing individuals for unpaid roles. Managers, human resource generalists and _____ specialists may be tasked with carrying out _____ , but in some cases public-sector employment agencies, commercial _____ agencies, or specialist search consultancies are used to undertake parts of the process. Internet-based technologies which support all aspects of _____ have become widespread.

Exam Probability: **Low**

48. *Answer choices:*

(see index for correct answer)

- a. Recruitment
- b. cultural
- c. interpersonal communication
- d. deep-level diversity

Guidance: level 1

:: Human resource management ::

_____ expands the capacity of individuals to perform in leadership roles within organizations. Leadership roles are those that facilitate execution of a company's strategy through building alignment, winning mindshare and growing the capabilities of others. Leadership roles may be formal, with the corresponding authority to make decisions and take responsibility, or they may be informal roles with little official authority .

Exam Probability: **Medium**

49. *Answer choices:*

(see index for correct answer)

- a. Formal organization
- b. Leadership development
- c. Kelly Services
- d. Employee relationship management

Guidance: level 1

:: Project management ::

A _____ is a team whose members usually belong to different groups, functions and are assigned to activities for the same project. A team can be divided into sub-teams according to need. Usually _____ s are only used for a defined period of time. They are disbanded after the project is deemed complete. Due to the nature of the specific formation and disbandment, _____ s are usually in organizations.

Exam Probability: **Medium**

50. *Answer choices:*

(see index for correct answer)

- a. Karol Adamiecki
- b. Trenegy Incorporated

- c. Project manager
- d. Elemental cost planning

Guidance: level 1

:: Evaluation methods ::

In social psychology, _____ is the process of looking at oneself in order to assess aspects that are important to one's identity. It is one of the motives that drive self-evaluation, along with self-verification and self-enhancement. Sedikides suggests that the _____ motive will prompt people to seek information to confirm their uncertain self-concept rather than their certain self-concept and at the same time people use _____ to enhance their certainty of their own self-knowledge. However, the _____ motive could be seen as quite different from the other two self-evaluation motives. Unlike the other two motives through _____ people are interested in the accuracy of their current self view, rather than improving their self-view. This makes _____ the only self-evaluative motive that may cause a person's self-esteem to be damaged.

Exam Probability: **Medium**

51. *Answer choices:*

(see index for correct answer)

- a. Fixtureless in-circuit test
- b. Reality TV confessional
- c. Design science
- d. Proof of concept

Guidance: level 1

:: Operations research ::

_____ is a method to achieve the best outcome in a mathematical model whose requirements are represented by linear relationships. _____ is a special case of mathematical programming.

Exam Probability: **Low**

52. *Answer choices:*

(see index for correct answer)

- a. Evidential reasoning approach
- b. Linear programming
- c. Integer programming
- d. Theory of two-level planning

Guidance: level 1

:: Management occupations ::

_____ ship is the process of designing, launching and running a new business, which is often initially a small business. The people who create these businesses are called _____ s.

Exam Probability: **Low**

53. *Answer choices:*

(see index for correct answer)

- a. Store manager
- b. Entrepreneur
- c. Chief design officer
- d. Corporate trainer

Guidance: level 1

:: Regression analysis ::

A _____ often refers to a set of documented requirements to be satisfied by a material, design, product, or service. A _____ is often a type of technical standard.

Exam Probability: **High**

54. *Answer choices:*

(see index for correct answer)

- a. Multivariate probit model
- b. Projection pursuit regression
- c. Scatterplot smoothing
- d. Specification

Guidance: level 1

:: ::

The _____ is a political and economic union of 28 member states that are located primarily in Europe. It has an area of 4,475,757 km2 and an estimated population of about 513 million. The EU has developed an internal single market through a standardised system of laws that apply in all member states in those matters, and only those matters, where members have agreed to act as one. EU policies aim to ensure the free movement of people, goods, services and capital within the internal market, enact legislation in justice and home affairs and maintain common policies on trade, agriculture, fisheries and regional development. For travel within the Schengen Area, passport controls have been abolished. A monetary union was established in 1999 and came into full force in 2002 and is composed of 19 EU member states which use the euro currency.

Exam Probability: **Low**

55. *Answer choices:*

(see index for correct answer)

- a. functional perspective
- b. interpersonal communication
- c. empathy
- d. European Union

Guidance: level 1

:: Social psychology ::

In social psychology, _____ is the phenomenon of a person exerting less effort to achieve a goal when he or she works in a group than when working alone. This is seen as one of the main reasons groups are sometimes less productive than the combined performance of their members working as individuals, but should be distinguished from the accidental coordination problems that groups sometimes experience.

Exam Probability: **Low**

56. *Answer choices:*

(see index for correct answer)

- a. Social penetration
- b. Social loafing
- c. Mutual engagement
- d. indoctrination

Guidance: level 1

:: Cognitive biases ::

The _____ is a type of immediate judgement discrepancy, or cognitive bias, where a person making an initial assessment of another person, place, or thing will assume ambiguous information based upon concrete information. A simplified example of the _____ is when an individual noticing that the person in the photograph is attractive, well groomed, and properly attired, assumes, using a mental heuristic, that the person in the photograph is a good person based upon the rules of that individual's social concept. This constant error in judgment is reflective of the individual's preferences, prejudices, ideology, aspirations, and social perception. The _____ is an evaluation by an individual and can affect the perception of a decision, action, idea, business, person, group, entity, or other whenever concrete data is generalized or influences ambiguous information.

Exam Probability: **High**

57. *Answer choices:*
(see index for correct answer)

- a. Positivity offset
- b. Hawthorne effect
- c. Overjustification effect
- d. Mistakes Were Made

Guidance: level 1

:: ::

_____ involves the development of an action plan designed to motivate and guide a person or group toward a goal. _____ can be guided by goal-setting criteria such as SMART criteria. _____ is a major component of personal-development and management literature.

Exam Probability: **Medium**

58. *Answer choices:*

(see index for correct answer)

- a. interpersonal communication
- b. co-culture
- c. corporate values
- d. surface-level diversity

Guidance: level 1

:: Game theory ::

_____ is the idea that rationality is limited when individuals make decisions: by the tractability of the decision problem, the cognitive limitations of the mind, and the time available to make the decision. Decision-makers, in this view, act as satisficers, seeking a satisfactory solution rather than an optimal one.

Exam Probability: **Low**

59. *Answer choices:*

(see index for correct answer)

- a. Ultimatum game
- b. Folk theorem
- c. Bounded rationality
- d. Metagaming

Guidance: level 1

Business law

Corporate law (also known as business law) is the body of law governing the rights, relations, and conduct of persons, companies, organizations and businesses. It refers to the legal practice relating to, or the theory of corporations. Corporate law often describes the law relating to matters which derive directly from the life-cycle of a corporation. It thus encompasses the formation, funding, governance, and death of a corporation.

:: Business law ::

A _____ is a form of partnership similar to a general partnership except that while a general partnership must have at least two general partners , a _____ must have at least one GP and at least one limited partner.

Exam Probability: **Medium**

1. *Answer choices:*

(see index for correct answer)

- a. Valuation using the Market Penetration Model
- b. Negative option billing
- c. Double ticketing
- d. Limited partnership

Guidance: level 1

:: ::

The _____ of 1933, also known as the 1933 Act, the _____ , the Truth in _____ , the Federal _____ , and the '33 Act, was enacted by the United States Congress on May 27, 1933, during the Great Depression, after the stock market crash of 1929. Legislated pursuant to the Interstate Commerce Clause of the Constitution, it requires every offer or sale of securities that uses the means and instrumentalities of interstate commerce to be registered with the SEC pursuant to the 1933 Act, unless an exemption from registration exists under the law. The term "means and instrumentalities of interstate commerce" is extremely broad and it is virtually impossible to avoid the operation of the statute by attempting to offer or sell a security without using an "instrumentality" of interstate commerce. Any use of a telephone, for example, or the mails would probably be enough to subject the transaction to the statute.

Exam Probability: **Medium**

2. *Answer choices:*

(see index for correct answer)

- a. hierarchical
- b. surface-level diversity

- c. process perspective
- d. empathy

Guidance: level 1

:: ::

_____ is property that is movable. In common law systems, _____ may also be called chattels or personalty. In civil law systems, _____ is often called movable property or movables – any property that can be moved from one location to another.

Exam Probability: **Medium**

3. *Answer choices:*
(see index for correct answer)

- a. Personal property
- b. process perspective
- c. surface-level diversity
- d. interpersonal communication

Guidance: level 1

:: Commercial crimes ::

_____ is the process of concealing the origins of money obtained illegally by passing it through a complex sequence of banking transfers or commercial transactions. The overall scheme of this process returns the money to the launderer in an obscure and indirect way.

Exam Probability: **Medium**

4. *Answer choices:*

(see index for correct answer)

- a. FATF blacklist
- b. Credit card hijacking
- c. The Informant
- d. Money laundering

Guidance: level 1

:: Parental leave ::

_____ is a type of employment discrimination that occurs when expectant women are fired, not hired, or otherwise discriminated against due to their pregnancy or intention to become pregnant. Common forms of _____ include not being hired due to visible pregnancy or likelihood of becoming pregnant, being fired after informing an employer of one's pregnancy, being fired after maternity leave, and receiving a pay dock due to pregnancy. Convention on the Elimination of All Forms of Discrimination against Women prohibits dismissal on the grounds of maternity or pregnancy and ensures right to maternity leave or comparable social benefits. The Maternity Protection Convention C 183 proclaims adequate protection for pregnancy as well. Though women have some protection in the United States because of the _____ Act of 1978, it has not completely curbed the incidence of _____ . The Equal Rights Amendment could ensure more robust sex equality ensuring that women and men could both work and have children at the same time.

Exam Probability: **Medium**

5. *Answer choices:*

(see index for correct answer)

- a. Parental leave economics
- b. Additional Paternity Leave Regulations 2010
- c. Pregnant Workers Directive
- d. Maternity and Parental Leave, etc Regulations 1999

Guidance: level 1

:: ::

A concept of English law, a _____ is an untrue or misleading statement of fact made during negotiations by one party to another, the statement then inducing that other party into the contract. The misled party may normally rescind the contract, and sometimes may be awarded damages as well.

Exam Probability: **High**

6. *Answer choices:*

(see index for correct answer)

- a. Misrepresentation
- b. open system
- c. interpersonal communication
- d. functional perspective

Guidance: level 1

:: Contract law ::

A _____ is an event or state of affairs that is required before something else will occur. In contract law, a _____ is an event which must occur, unless its non-occurrence is excused, before performance under a contract becomes due, i.e., before any contractual duty exists.

Exam Probability: **Low**

7. Answer choices:

(see index for correct answer)

- a. Condition precedent
- b. Escalator clause
- c. Rescission
- d. Time is of the essence

Guidance: level 1

:: ::

> Business is the activity of making one's living or making money by producing or buying and selling products. Simply put, it is "any activity or enterprise entered into for profit. It does not mean it is a company, a corporation, partnership, or have any such formal organization, but it can range from a street peddler to General Motors."

Exam Probability: **High**

8. Answer choices:

(see index for correct answer)

- a. surface-level diversity
- b. Firm
- c. levels of analysis
- d. cultural

Guidance: level 1

:: ::

A contract is a legally-binding agreement which recognises and governs the rights and duties of the parties to the agreement. A contract is legally enforceable because it meets the requirements and approval of the law. An agreement typically involves the exchange of goods, services, money, or promises of any of those. In the event of breach of contract, the law awards the injured party access to legal remedies such as damages and cancellation.

Exam Probability: **Medium**

9. *Answer choices:*

(see index for correct answer)

- a. hierarchical
- b. Contract law
- c. levels of analysis
- d. surface-level diversity

Guidance: level 1

:: Contract law ::

_____ are damages whose amount the parties designate during the formation of a contract for the injured party to collect as compensation upon a specific breach.

Exam Probability: **High**

10. *Answer choices:*

(see index for correct answer)

- a. Handshake deal
- b. Posting rule
- c. Liquidated damages
- d. Per minas

Guidance: level 1

:: Contract Clause case law ::

The _____ appears in the United States Constitution, Article I, section 10, clause 1. The clause prohibits a State from passing any law that "impairs the obligation of contracts" or "makes any thing but gold and silver coin a tender in payment of debts". It states.

Exam Probability: **Medium**

11. *Answer choices:*

(see index for correct answer)

- a. Charles River Bridge v. Warren Bridge
- b. Contract Clause
- c. Smyth v. Ames

Guidance: level 1

:: ::

_____ is a marketing communication that employs an openly sponsored, non-personal message to promote or sell a product, service or idea. Sponsors of _____ are typically businesses wishing to promote their products or services. _____ is differentiated from public relations in that an advertiser pays for and has control over the message. It differs from personal selling in that the message is non-personal, i.e., not directed to a particular individual. _____ is communicated through various mass media, including traditional media such as newspapers, magazines, television, radio, outdoor _____ or direct mail; and new media such as search results, blogs, social media, websites or text messages. The actual presentation of the message in a medium is referred to as an advertisement, or "ad" or advert for short.

Exam Probability: **High**

12. *Answer choices:*

(see index for correct answer)

- a. similarity-attraction theory
- b. cultural
- c. Advertising

- d. imperative

Guidance: level 1

According to the philosopher Piyush Mathur , "Tangibility is the property that a phenomenon exhibits if it has and/or transports mass and/or energy and/or momentum".

Exam Probability: **Low**

13. *Answer choices:*
(see index for correct answer)

- a. empathy
- b. deep-level diversity
- c. Tangible
- d. functional perspective

Guidance: level 1

An _____ is a criminal accusation that a person has committed a crime. In jurisdictions that use the concept of felonies, the most serious criminal offence is a felony; jurisdictions that do not use the felonies concept often use that of an indictable offence, an offence that requires an _____ .

Exam Probability: **High**

14. *Answer choices:*

(see index for correct answer)

- a. co-culture
- b. deep-level diversity
- c. surface-level diversity
- d. cultural

Guidance: level 1

:: ::

A _____ is a law passed by a legislative body in a common law system to set the maximum time after an event within which legal proceedings may be initiated.

Exam Probability: **Medium**

15. *Answer choices:*

(see index for correct answer)

- a. hierarchical
- b. levels of analysis
- c. Statute of limitations
- d. surface-level diversity

Guidance: level 1

:: Investment ::

In finance, the benefit from an _____ is called a return. The return may consist of a gain realised from the sale of property or an _____, unrealised capital appreciation, or _____ income such as dividends, interest, rental income etc., or a combination of capital gain and income. The return may also include currency gains or losses due to changes in foreign currency exchange rates.

Exam Probability: **Low**

16. *Answer choices:*

(see index for correct answer)

- a. Insurance bond
- b. Investment strategy
- c. Value averaging
- d. The Complete TurtleTrader

Guidance: level 1

:: Fraud ::

The _____ refers to the requirement that certain kinds of contracts be memorialized in writing, signed by the party to be charged, with sufficient content to evidence the contract.

Exam Probability: **Medium**

17. *Answer choices:*

(see index for correct answer)

- a. Statute of frauds
- b. Selling Hitler
- c. Pharma fraud
- d. Shell corporation

Guidance: level 1

:: ::

An _____ , commonly called an appeals court, court of appeals , appeal court , court of second instance or second instance court, is any court of law that is empowered to hear an appeal of a trial court or other lower tribunal. In most jurisdictions, the court system is divided into at least three levels: the trial court, which initially hears cases and reviews evidence and testimony to determine the facts of the case; at least one intermediate _____ ; and a supreme court which primarily reviews the decisions of the intermediate courts. A jurisdiction's supreme court is that jurisdiction's highest _____ . _____ s nationwide can operate under varying rules.

Exam Probability: **Low**

18. *Answer choices:*

(see index for correct answer)

- a. Appellate Court
- b. process perspective
- c. imperative
- d. Sarbanes-Oxley act of 2002

Guidance: level 1

:: Legal doctrines and principles ::

The _____ rule is a rule in the Anglo-American common law that governs what kinds of evidence parties to a contract dispute can introduce when trying to determine the specific terms of a contract. The rule also prevents parties who have reduced their agreement to a final written document from later introducing other evidence, such as the content of oral discussions from earlier in the negotiation process, as evidence of a different intent as to the terms of the contract. The rule provides that "extrinsic evidence is inadmissible to vary a written contract". The term "parol" derives from the Anglo-Norman French parol or parole, meaning "word of mouth" or "verbal", and in medieval times referred to oral pleadings in a court case.

Exam Probability: **Medium**

19. *Answer choices:*

(see index for correct answer)

- a. Proximate cause
- b. Parol evidence
- c. Mutual assent
- d. Acquiescence

Guidance: level 1

:: Contract law ::

_____ , also called an anticipatory breach, is a term in the law of contracts that describes a declaration by the promising party to a contract that he or she does not intend to live up to his or her obligations under the contract.

Exam Probability: **Low**

20. *Answer choices:*

(see index for correct answer)

- a. Peppercorn
- b. Substantial performance
- c. Pact ink
- d. Expectation damages

Guidance: level 1

:: Legal terms ::

An _____ is a legal and equitable remedy in the form of a special court order that compels a party to do or refrain from specific acts. "When a court employs the extraordinary remedy of _____ , it directs the conduct of a party, and does so with the backing of its full coercive powers." A party that fails to comply with an _____ faces criminal or civil penalties, including possible monetary sanctions and even imprisonment. They can also be charged with contempt of court. Counter _____ s are _____ s that stop or reverse the enforcement of another _____ .

Exam Probability: **Medium**

21. *Answer choices:*

(see index for correct answer)

- a. Call of duty
- b. Irreparable injury
- c. Injunction
- d. Continuing trespass

Guidance: level 1

:: ::

_____ , often abbreviated cert. in the United States, is a process for seeking judicial review and a writ issued by a court that agrees to review. A _____ is issued by a superior court, directing an inferior court, tribunal, or other public authority to send the record of a proceeding for review.

Exam Probability: **Low**

22. *Answer choices:*

(see index for correct answer)

- a. information systems assessment
- b. cultural
- c. Certiorari
- d. hierarchical perspective

Guidance: level 1

:: Legal procedure ::

An _____ is generally the first occasion that the trier of fact has to hear from a lawyer in a trial, aside possibly from questioning during voir dire. The _____ is generally constructed to serve as a "road map" for the fact-finder. This is especially essential, in many jury trials, since jurors know nothing at all about the case before the trial, . Though such statements may be dramatic and vivid, they must be limited to the evidence reasonably expected to be presented during the trial. Attorneys generally conclude _____ s with a reminder that at the conclusion of evidence, the attorney will return to ask the fact-finder to find in his or her client's favor.

Exam Probability: **Low**

23. *Answer choices:*

(see index for correct answer)

- a. Closing argument
- b. appellate
- c. Opening statement
- d. civil procedure

Guidance: level 1

:: ::

_____ is the study and management of exchange relationships. _____ is the business process of creating relationships with and satisfying customers. With its focus on the customer, _____ is one of the premier components of business management.

Exam Probability: **High**

24. *Answer choices:*

(see index for correct answer)

- a. imperative
- b. hierarchical perspective
- c. interpersonal communication
- d. Marketing

Guidance: level 1

:: Finance ::

A _____, in the law of the United States, is a contract that governs the relationship between the parties to a kind of financial transaction known as a secured transaction. In a secured transaction, the Grantor assigns, grants and pledges to the grantee a security interest in personal property which is referred to as the collateral. Examples of typical collateral are shares of stock, livestock, and vehicles. A _____ is not used to transfer any interest in real property, only personal property. The document used by lenders to obtain a lien on real property is a mortgage or deed of trust.

Exam Probability: **Low**

25. *Answer choices:*

(see index for correct answer)

- a. Style investing
- b. Security agreement
- c. Value investing
- d. Financial forecast

Guidance: level 1

:: Statutory law ::

_____ is a principal's approval of an act of its agent that lacked the authority to bind the principal legally. _____ defines the international act in which a state indicates its consent to be bound to a treaty if the parties intended to show their consent by such an act. In the case of bilateral treaties, _____ is usually accomplished by exchanging the requisite instruments, and in the case of multilateral treaties, the usual procedure is for the depositary to collect the _____ s of all states, keeping all parties informed of the situation.

Exam Probability: **Low**

26. *Answer choices:*

(see index for correct answer)

- a. Statutory law
- b. Statute of repose
- c. statute law
- d. incorporation by reference

Guidance: level 1

:: Meetings ::

A _____ is a body of one or more persons that is subordinate to a deliberative assembly. Usually, the assembly sends matters into a _____ as a way to explore them more fully than would be possible if the assembly itself were considering them. _____ s may have different functions and their type of work differ depending on the type of the organization and its needs.

Exam Probability: **Low**

27. *Answer choices:*
(see index for correct answer)

- a. Town hall meeting
- b. Chatham House Rule
- c. Committee
- d. Colloquy

Guidance: level 1

Punishment is the imposition of an undesirable or unpleasant outcome upon a group or individual, meted out by an authority—in contexts ranging from child discipline to criminal law—as a response and deterrent to a particular action or behaviour that is deemed undesirable or unacceptable. The reasoning may be to condition a child to avoid self-endangerment, to impose social conformity, to defend norms, to protect against future harms, and to maintain the law—and respect for rule of law—under which the social group is governed. Punishment may be self-inflicted as with self-flagellation and mortification of the flesh in the religious setting, but is most often a form of social coercion.

Exam Probability: **Low**

28. *Answer choices:*

(see index for correct answer)

- a. co-culture
- b. cultural
- c. Punitive
- d. empathy

Guidance: level 1

In financial markets, a share is a unit used as mutual funds, limited partnerships, and real estate investment trusts. The owner of _____ in the corporation/company is a shareholder of the corporation. A share is an indivisible unit of capital, expressing the ownership relationship between the company and the shareholder. The denominated value of a share is its face value, and the total of the face value of issued _____ represent the capital of a company, which may not reflect the market value of those _____ .

Exam Probability: **Low**

29. *Answer choices:*

(see index for correct answer)

- a. Shares
- b. open system
- c. personal values
- d. corporate values

Guidance: level 1

:: Business law ::

An _____ is a natural person, business, or corporation that provides goods or services to another entity under terms specified in a contract or within a verbal agreement. Unlike an employee, an _____ does not work regularly for an employer but works as and when required, during which time they may be subject to law of agency. _____ s are usually paid on a freelance basis. Contractors often work through a limited company or franchise, which they themselves own, or may work through an umbrella company.

Exam Probability: **Medium**

30. *Answer choices:*

(see index for correct answer)

- a. Agency in English law
- b. Independent contractor
- c. Board of directors
- d. Rules of origin

Guidance: level 1

:: ::

In law, a _____ is a coming together of parties to a dispute, to present information in a tribunal, a formal setting with the authority to adjudicate claims or disputes. One form of tribunal is a court. The tribunal, which may occur before a judge, jury, or other designated trier of fact, aims to achieve a resolution to their dispute.

Exam Probability: **Medium**

31. *Answer choices:*

(see index for correct answer)

- a. levels of analysis
- b. interpersonal communication
- c. Trial
- d. hierarchical perspective

Guidance: level 1

:: Legal terms ::

_____ is the set of laws that governs how members of a society are to behave. It is contrasted with procedural law, which is the set of procedures for making, administering, and enforcing _____ . _____ defines rights and responsibilities in civil law, and crimes and punishments in criminal law. It may be codified in statutes or exist through precedent in common law.

Exam Probability: **Medium**

32. *Answer choices:*

(see index for correct answer)

- a. Substantive law
- b. Error

- c. Cestui que
- d. Person of interest

Guidance: level 1

:: Labour relations ::

> _____ is a field of study that can have different meanings depending on the context in which it is used. In an international context, it is a subfield of labor history that studies the human relations with regard to work – in its broadest sense – and how this connects to questions of social inequality. It explicitly encompasses unregulated, historical, and non-Western forms of labor. Here, _____ define "for or with whom one works and under what rules. These rules determine the type of work, type and amount of remuneration, working hours, degrees of physical and psychological strain, as well as the degree of freedom and autonomy associated with the work."

Exam Probability: **Low**

33. *Answer choices:*
(see index for correct answer)

- a. Broad left
- b. Two-tier system
- c. Labor relations
- d. Jesse Simons

Guidance: level 1

:: Insurance terms ::

A _____ in the broadest sense is a natural person or other legal entity who receives money or other benefits from a benefactor. For example, the _____ of a life insurance policy is the person who receives the payment of the amount of insurance after the death of the insured.

Exam Probability: **Low**

34. *Answer choices:*
(see index for correct answer)

- a. Cash surrender value
- b. Omnibus clause
- c. Beneficiary
- d. Home warranty

Guidance: level 1

:: ::

_____ is the collection of mechanisms, processes and relations by which corporations are controlled and operated. Governance structures and principles identify the distribution of rights and responsibilities among different participants in the corporation and include the rules and procedures for making decisions in corporate affairs. _____ is necessary because of the possibility of conflicts of interests between stakeholders, primarily between shareholders and upper management or among shareholders.

Exam Probability: **Low**

35. *Answer choices:*

(see index for correct answer)

- a. deep-level diversity
- b. Corporate governance
- c. functional perspective
- d. cultural

Guidance: level 1

:: Project management ::

_____ is the right to exercise power, which can be formalized by a state and exercised by way of judges, appointed executives of government, or the ecclesiastical or priestly appointed representatives of a God or other deities.

Exam Probability: **Medium**

36. *Answer choices:*

(see index for correct answer)

- a. RationalPlan
- b. Authority
- c. Project sponsorship
- d. Hammock activity

Guidance: level 1

:: Competition law ::

In competition law, a _____ is a market in which a particular product or service is sold. It is the intersection of a relevant product market and a relevant geographic market. The European Commission defines a _____ and its product and geographic components as follows.

Exam Probability: **Medium**

37. *Answer choices:*

(see index for correct answer)

- a. Relevant market
- b. Merger control
- c. Block Exemption Regulation
- d. Vertical agreement

Guidance: level 1

:: Legal doctrines and principles ::

In law, a _____ is an event sufficiently related to an injury that the courts deem the event to be the cause of that injury. There are two types of causation in the law: cause-in-fact, and proximate cause. Cause-in-fact is determined by the "but for" test: But for the action, the result would not have happened. The action is a necessary condition, but may not be a sufficient condition, for the resulting injury. A few circumstances exist where the but for test is ineffective. Since but-for causation is very easy to show, a second test is used to determine if an action is close enough to a harm in a "chain of events" to be legally valid. This test is called _____ .
_____ is a key principle of Insurance and is concerned with how the loss or damage actually occurred. There are several competing theories of _____ . For an act to be deemed to cause a harm, both tests must be met; _____ is a legal limitation on cause-in-fact.

Exam Probability: **High**

38. *Answer choices:*
(see index for correct answer)

- a. Mutual mistake
- b. Act of state doctrine
- c. Proximate cause
- d. Unilateral mistake

Guidance: level 1

:: Anti-competitive behaviour ::

Restraints of trade is a common law doctrine relating to the enforceability of contractual restrictions on freedom to conduct business. It is a precursor of modern competition law. In an old leading case of Mitchel v Reynolds Lord Smith LC said,

Exam Probability: **High**

39. *Answer choices:*

(see index for correct answer)

- a. Pacman conjecture
- b. Ernest Varacalli
- c. Institute for Consumer Antitrust Studies
- d. Restraint of trade

Guidance: level 1

:: ::

A _____ is any person who contracts to acquire an asset in return for some form of consideration.

Exam Probability: **High**

40. *Answer choices:*

(see index for correct answer)

- a. hierarchical
- b. imperative
- c. levels of analysis
- d. similarity-attraction theory

Guidance: level 1

:: ::

> An _____ is a contingent motivator. Traditional _____ s are extrinsic motivators which reward actions to yield a desired outcome. The effectiveness of traditional _____ s has changed as the needs of Western society have evolved. While the traditional _____ model is effective when there is a defined procedure and goal for a task, Western society started to require a higher volume of critical thinkers, so the traditional model became less effective. Institutions are now following a trend in implementing strategies that rely on intrinsic motivations rather than the extrinsic motivations that the traditional _____ s foster.

Exam Probability: **Low**

41. *Answer choices:*

(see index for correct answer)

- a. hierarchical
- b. Incentive

- c. similarity-attraction theory
- d. hierarchical perspective

Guidance: level 1

:: ::

A _____ is monetary compensation paid by an employer to an employee in exchange for work done. Payment may be calculated as a fixed amount for each task completed, or at an hourly or daily rate, or based on an easily measured quantity of work done.

Exam Probability: **High**

42. *Answer choices:*

(see index for correct answer)

- a. Character
- b. functional perspective
- c. Wage
- d. similarity-attraction theory

Guidance: level 1

:: Contract law ::

In contract law, _____ is an excuse for the nonperformance of duties under a contract, based on a change in circumstances, the nonoccurrence of which was an underlying assumption of the contract, that makes performance of the contract literally impossible.

Exam Probability: **Low**

43. *Answer choices:*

(see index for correct answer)

- a. Impossibility
- b. Breach of contract
- c. Handshake deal
- d. Parent company guarantee

Guidance: level 1

:: Arbitration law ::

The United States Arbitration Act, more commonly referred to as the _____ or FAA, is an act of Congress that provides for judicial facilitation of private dispute resolution through arbitration. It applies in both state courts and federal courts, as was held constitutional in Southland Corp. v. Keating. It applies where the transaction contemplated by the parties "involves" interstate commerce and is predicated on an exercise of the Commerce Clause powers granted to Congress in the U.S. Constitution.

Exam Probability: **Low**

44. *Answer choices:*

(see index for correct answer)

- a. Convention on the Recognition and Enforcement of Foreign Arbitral Awards
- b. James A. Graham
- c. Title 9 of the United States Code
- d. UNCITRAL Model Law on International Commercial Arbitration

Guidance: level 1

:: Services management and marketing ::

A _____ or servicemark is a trademark used in the United States and several other countries to identify a service rather than a product.

Exam Probability: **Low**

45. *Answer choices:*

(see index for correct answer)

- a. Integrated customer management
- b. Backend as a service
- c. Internet hosting service
- d. Service mark

Guidance: level 1

:: ::

_____ Motor Company is an American multinational automaker that has its main headquarter in Dearborn, Michigan, a suburb of Detroit. It was founded by Henry _____ and incorporated on June 16, 1903. The company sells automobiles and commercial vehicles under the _____ brand and most luxury cars under the Lincoln brand. _____ also owns Brazilian SUV manufacturer Troller, an 8% stake in Aston Martin of the United Kingdom and a 32% stake in Jiangling Motors. It also has joint-ventures in China , Taiwan , Thailand , Turkey , and Russia . The company is listed on the New York Stock Exchange and is controlled by the _____ family; they have minority ownership but the majority of the voting power.

Exam Probability: **Low**

46. *Answer choices:*

(see index for correct answer)

- a. surface-level diversity
- b. hierarchical
- c. cultural
- d. Ford

Guidance: level 1

:: Finance ::

_____ is the investigation or exercise of care that a reasonable business or person is expected to take before entering into an agreement or contract with another party, or an act with a certain standard of care.

Exam Probability: **Low**

47. *Answer choices:*

(see index for correct answer)

- a. Structured settlement
- b. Securities market
- c. Revaluation of fixed assets
- d. Negative return

Guidance: level 1

:: False advertising law ::

The Lanham Act is the primary federal trademark statute of law in the United States. The Act prohibits a number of activities, including trademark infringement, trademark dilution, and false advertising.

Exam Probability: **Medium**

48. *Answer choices:*

(see index for correct answer)

- a. Lanham Act
- b. Rebecca Tushnet

Guidance: level 1

:: Insolvency ::

_____ is the state of being unable to pay the money owed, by a person or company, on time; those in a state of _____ are said to be insolvent. There are two forms: cash-flow _____ and balance-sheet _____ .

Exam Probability: **Low**

49. *Answer choices:*

(see index for correct answer)

- a. Personal Insolvency Arrangement
- b. George Samuel Ford
- c. Insolvency
- d. Bankruptcy

Guidance: level 1

:: Contract law ::

In jurisprudence, _____ is an equitable doctrine that involves one person taking advantage of a position of power over another person. This inequity in power between the parties can vitiate one party's consent as they are unable to freely exercise their independent will.

Exam Probability: **Low**

50. *Answer choices:*

(see index for correct answer)

- a. Unenforceable
- b. German contract law
- c. Complete contract
- d. Seal

Guidance: level 1

:: International relations ::

_____ is double mindedness or double heartedness in duplicity, fraud, or deception. It may involve intentional deceit of others, or self-deception.

Exam Probability: **Medium**

51. *Answer choices:*

(see index for correct answer)

- a. The Globalization of World Politics
- b. Bad faith
- c. Netpolitik
- d. Robin Niblett

Guidance: level 1

:: Business law ::

The _____ , first published in 1952, is one of a number of Uniform Acts that have been established as law with the goal of harmonizing the laws of sales and other commercial transactions across the United States of America through UCC adoption by all 50 states, the District of Columbia, and the Territories of the United States.

Exam Probability: **Low**

52. *Answer choices:*

(see index for correct answer)

- a. Whitewash waiver
- b. Uniform Commercial Code
- c. Leave of absence
- d. European Patent Convention

Guidance: level 1

:: Business law ::

An _____ is a clause in a contract that requires the parties to resolve their disputes through an arbitration process. Although such a clause may or may not specify that arbitration occur within a specific jurisdiction, it always binds the parties to a type of resolution outside the courts, and is therefore considered a kind of forum selection clause.

Exam Probability: **Medium**

53. *Answer choices:*

(see index for correct answer)

- a. Principal
- b. Turnkey
- c. Leave of absence
- d. Agency in English law

Guidance: level 1

:: Business models ::

A _____, _____ company or daughter company is a company that is owned or controlled by another company, which is called the parent company, parent, or holding company. The _____ can be a company, corporation, or limited liability company. In some cases it is a government or state-owned enterprise. In some cases, particularly in the music and book publishing industries, subsidiaries are referred to as imprints.

Exam Probability: **Low**

54. *Answer choices:*

(see index for correct answer)

- a. Gratis
- b. 70/20/10 Model
- c. Subsidiary
- d. Business-agile enterprise

Guidance: level 1

:: Business law ::

A _____ is a document guaranteeing the payment of a specific amount of money, either on demand, or at a set time, with the payer usually named on the document. More specifically, it is a document contemplated by or consisting of a contract, which promises the payment of money without condition, which may be paid either on demand or at a future date. The term can have different meanings, depending on what law is being applied and what country and context it is used in.

Exam Probability: **Low**

55. *Answer choices:*

(see index for correct answer)

- a. Registered agent

- b. Unfair business practices
- c. Power harassment
- d. Negotiable instrument

Guidance: level 1

:: Real estate ::

_____ , real estate, realty, or immovable property In English common law refers to landed properties belonging to some person. It include all structures, crops, buildings, machinery, wells, dams, ponds, mines, canals, and roads, among other things. The term is historic, arising from the now-discontinued form of action, which distinguish between _____ disputes and personal property disputes. Personal property was, and continues to refer to all properties that are not real properties.

Exam Probability: **High**

56. *Answer choices:*
(see index for correct answer)

- a. Home inspection
- b. Real property
- c. Pad site
- d. Affordable housing

Guidance: level 1

:: Writs ::

In common law, a _____ is a formal _____ ten order issued by a body with administrative or judicial jurisdiction; in modern usage, this body is generally a court. Warrants, prerogative _____ s, and subpoenas are common types of _____ , but many forms exist and have existed.

Exam Probability: **High**

57. *Answer choices:*

(see index for correct answer)

- a. Writ
- b. Writ of assistance
- c. Writ of execution

Guidance: level 1

:: ::

Competition arises whenever at least two parties strive for a goal which cannot be shared: where one's gain is the other's loss .

Exam Probability: **High**

58. *Answer choices:*

(see index for correct answer)

- a. functional perspective
- b. hierarchical
- c. corporate values
- d. Competitor

Guidance: level 1

:: ::

A _____ is the party who initiates a lawsuit before a court. By doing so, the _____ seeks a legal remedy; if this search is successful, the court will issue judgment in favor of the _____ and make the appropriate court order . "_____" is the term used in civil cases in most English-speaking jurisdictions, the notable exception being England and Wales, where a _____ has, since the introduction of the Civil Procedure Rules in 1999, been known as a "claimant", but that term also has other meanings. In criminal cases, the prosecutor brings the case against the defendant, but the key complaining party is often called the "complainant".

Exam Probability: **Medium**

59. *Answer choices:*

(see index for correct answer)

- a. co-culture
- b. process perspective
- c. Plaintiff

- d. information systems assessment

Guidance: level 1

Finance

Finance is a field that is concerned with the allocation (investment) of assets and liabilities over space and time, often under conditions of risk or uncertainty. Finance can also be defined as the science of money management. Participants in the market aim to price assets based on their risk level, fundamental value, and their expected rate of return. Finance can be split into three sub-categories: public finance, corporate finance and personal finance.

:: Finance ::

_____ , in finance and accounting, means stated value or face value. From this come the expressions at par , over par and under par .

Exam Probability: **Low**

1. *Answer choices:*

(see index for correct answer)

- a. Z-spread
- b. Ministry of Finance
- c. Financial Education Instructor of the Year
- d. Par value

Guidance: level 1

:: Management accounting ::

_____ is the process of recording, classifying, analyzing, summarizing, and allocating costs associated with a process, after that developing various courses of action to control the costs. Its goal is to advise the management on how to optimize business practices and processes based on cost efficiency and capability. _____ provides the detailed cost information that management needs to control current operations and plan for the future.

Exam Probability: **Medium**

2. *Answer choices:*

(see index for correct answer)

- a. Customer profitability
- b. Chartered Cost Accountant

- c. Construction accounting
- d. Institute of Management Accountants

Guidance: level 1

:: Bonds (finance) ::

An _____ is a legal contract that reflects or covers a debt or purchase obligation. It specifically refers to two types of practices: in historical usage, an _____ d servant status, and in modern usage, it is an instrument used for commercial debt or real estate transaction.

Exam Probability: **High**

3. *Answer choices:*
(see index for correct answer)

- a. Indenture
- b. Agency debt
- c. Eurobond
- d. Dim sum bond

Guidance: level 1

:: Economics terminology ::

A corporation's share capital or _____ is the portion of a corporation's equity that has been obtained by the issue of shares in the corporation to a shareholder, usually for cash. "Share capital" may also denote the number and types of shares that compose a corporation's share structure.

Exam Probability: **Medium**

4. *Answer choices:*

(see index for correct answer)

- a. External costs
- b. spillover effect
- c. Capital stock
- d. total revenue

Guidance: level 1

:: ::

_____ focuses on ratios, equities and debts. It is useful for portfolio management, distribution of dividend, capital raising, hedging and looking after fluctuations in foreign currency and product cycles. Financial managers are the people who will do research and based on the research, decide what sort of capital to obtain in order to fund the company's assets as well as maximizing the value of the firm for all the stakeholders. It also refers to the efficient and effective management of money in such a manner as to accomplish the objectives of the organization. It is the specialized function directly associated with the top management. The significance of this function is not seen in the `Line` but also in the capacity of the `Staff` in overall of a company. It has been defined differently by different experts in the field.

Exam Probability: **Low**

5. *Answer choices:*

(see index for correct answer)

- a. co-culture
- b. cultural
- c. similarity-attraction theory
- d. corporate values

Guidance: level 1

:: Loans ::

In finance, a _____ is the lending of money by one or more individuals, organizations, or other entities to other individuals, organizations etc. The recipient incurs a debt, and is usually liable to pay interest on that debt until it is repaid, and also to repay the principal amount borrowed.

Exam Probability: **High**

6. *Answer choices:*

(see index for correct answer)

- a. International lender of last resort
- b. Loan
- c. Government-backed loan
- d. Fixed interest

Guidance: level 1

:: Hazard analysis ::

Broadly speaking, a _____ is the combined effort of 1. identifying and analyzing potential events that may negatively impact individuals, assets, and/or the environment ; and 2. making judgments "on the tolerability of the risk on the basis of a risk analysis" while considering influencing factors . Put in simpler terms, a _____ analyzes what can go wrong, how likely it is to happen, what the potential consequences are, and how tolerable the identified risk is. As part of this process, the resulting determination of risk may be expressed in a quantitative or qualitative fashion. The _____ is an inherent part of an overall risk management strategy, which attempts to, after a _____ , "introduce control measures to eliminate or reduce" any potential risk-related consequences.

Exam Probability: **High**

7. *Answer choices:*

(see index for correct answer)

- a. Swiss cheese model
- b. Hazard
- c. Hazard identification
- d. Hazardous Materials Identification System

Guidance: level 1

:: Data analysis ::

In statistics, the _____ is a measure that is used to quantify the amount of variation or dispersion of a set of data values. A low _____ indicates that the data points tend to be close to the mean of the set, while a high _____ indicates that the data points are spread out over a wider range of values.

Exam Probability: **Medium**

8. *Answer choices:*
(see index for correct answer)

- a. Ariel Beresniak
- b. Standard deviation
- c. Training set
- d. Limited dependent variable

Guidance: level 1

:: ::

A tax is a compulsory financial charge or some other type of levy imposed upon a taxpayer by a governmental organization in order to fund various public expenditures. A failure to pay, along with evasion of or resistance to _____ , is punishable by law. Taxes consist of direct or indirect taxes and may be paid in money or as its labour equivalent.

Exam Probability: **High**

9. *Answer choices:*

(see index for correct answer)

- a. Taxation
- b. cultural
- c. functional perspective
- d. interpersonal communication

Guidance: level 1

:: ::

A _____ loan or, simply, _____ is used either by purchasers of real property to raise funds to buy real estate, or alternatively by existing property owners to raise funds for any purpose, while putting a lien on the property being _____ d. The loan is "secured" on the borrower's property through a process known as _____ origination. This means that a legal mechanism is put into place which allows the lender to take possession and sell the secured property to pay off the loan in the event the borrower defaults on the loan or otherwise fails to abide by its terms. The word _____ is derived from a Law French term used in Britain in the Middle Ages meaning "death pledge" and refers to the pledge ending when either the obligation is fulfilled or the property is taken through foreclosure. A _____ can also be described as "a borrower giving consideration in the form of a collateral for a benefit ".

Exam Probability: **Medium**

10. *Answer choices:*

(see index for correct answer)

- a. process perspective
- b. corporate values
- c. Character
- d. Mortgage

Guidance: level 1

:: Management accounting ::

In economics, _____ s, indirect costs or overheads are business expenses that are not dependent on the level of goods or services produced by the business. They tend to be time-related, such as interest or rents being paid per month, and are often referred to as overhead costs. This is in contrast to variable costs, which are volume-related and unknown at the beginning of the accounting year. For a simple example, such as a bakery, the monthly rent for the baking facilities, and the monthly payments for the security system and basic phone line are _____ s, as they do not change according to how much bread the bakery produces and sells. On the other hand, the wage costs of the bakery are variable, as the bakery will have to hire more workers if the production of bread increases. Economists reckon _____ as a entry barrier for new entrepreneurs.

Exam Probability: **Low**

11. *Answer choices:*

(see index for correct answer)

- a. Institute of Management Accountants
- b. Inventory valuation

- c. Fixed cost
- d. Direct material price variance

Guidance: level 1

:: Mereology ::

_____ , in the abstract, is what belongs to or with something, whether as an attribute or as a component of said thing. In the context of this article, it is one or more components , whether physical or incorporeal, of a person's estate; or so belonging to, as in being owned by, a person or jointly a group of people or a legal entity like a corporation or even a society. Depending on the nature of the _____ , an owner of _____ has the right to consume, alter, share, redefine, rent, mortgage, pawn, sell, exchange, transfer, give away or destroy it, or to exclude others from doing these things, as well as to perhaps abandon it; whereas regardless of the nature of the _____ , the owner thereof has the right to properly use it , or at the very least exclusively keep it.

Exam Probability: **Low**

12. *Answer choices:*
(see index for correct answer)

- a. Meronomy
- b. Mereological nihilism
- c. Simple
- d. Mereological essentialism

Guidance: level 1

:: ::

_____ is the consumption and saving opportunity gained by an entity within a specified timeframe, which is generally expressed in monetary terms. For households and individuals, " _____ is the sum of all the wages, salaries, profits, interest payments, rents, and other forms of earnings received in a given period of time."

Exam Probability: **Low**

13. *Answer choices:*

(see index for correct answer)

- a. personal values
- b. levels of analysis
- c. Income
- d. Sarbanes-Oxley act of 2002

Guidance: level 1

:: Taxation ::

In a tax system, the _____ is the ratio at which a business or person is taxed. There are several methods used to present a _____ : statutory, average, marginal, and effective. These rates can also be presented using different definitions applied to a tax base: inclusive and exclusive.

Exam Probability: **High**

14. *Answer choices:*

(see index for correct answer)

- a. Tax rate
- b. Paulette
- c. Fiscal burden of government
- d. Privilege tax

Guidance: level 1

:: Financial markets ::

A _____ is a financial market in which long-term debt or equity-backed securities are bought and sold. _____ s channel the wealth of savers to those who can put it to long-term productive use, such as companies or governments making long-term investments. Financial regulators like the Bank of England and the U.S. Securities and Exchange Commission oversee _____ s to protect investors against fraud, among other duties.

Exam Probability: **High**

15. *Answer choices:*

(see index for correct answer)

- a. Risk premium
- b. Forward market
- c. Ultra-low latency direct market access
- d. Capital market

Guidance: level 1

:: Finance ::

_____ is a field that is concerned with the allocation of assets and liabilities over space and time, often under conditions of risk or uncertainty. _____ can also be defined as the art of money management. Participants in the market aim to price assets based on their risk level, fundamental value, and their expected rate of return. _____ can be split into three sub-categories: public _____ , corporate _____ and personal _____ .

Exam Probability: **Low**

16. *Answer choices:*

(see index for correct answer)

- a. XBRL assurance
- b. Signature line of credit
- c. Finance

- d. Mohatra contract

Guidance: level 1

:: Scheduling (computing) ::

Ageing or _____ is the process of becoming older. The term refers especially to human beings, many animals, and fungi, whereas for example bacteria, perennial plants and some simple animals are potentially biologically immortal. In the broader sense, ageing can refer to single cells within an organism which have ceased dividing or to the population of a species.

Exam Probability: **Medium**

17. *Answer choices:*
(see index for correct answer)

- a. Multikernel
- b. Aging
- c. Notation for theoretic scheduling problems
- d. Affinity mask

Guidance: level 1

:: Financial risk ::

_____ is any of various types of risk associated with financing, including financial transactions that include company loans in risk of default. Often it is understood to include only downside risk, meaning the potential for financial loss and uncertainty about its extent.

Exam Probability: **Low**

18. *Answer choices:*

(see index for correct answer)

- a. Acceptance set
- b. Capital Requirements Directive
- c. Spectral risk measure
- d. Financial risk

Guidance: level 1

:: Public finance ::

_____ is the process by which the monetary authority of a country, typically the central bank or currency board, controls either the cost of very short-term borrowing or the money supply, often targeting inflation rate or interest rate to ensure price stability and general trust in the currency.

Exam Probability: **Medium**

19. *Answer choices:*

(see index for correct answer)

- a. Ways and means advances
- b. International Institute of Public Finance
- c. Monetary policy
- d. Budget Code of Russia

Guidance: level 1

:: Pension funds ::

_____ s typically have large amounts of money to invest and are the major investors in listed and private companies. They are especially important to the stock market where large institutional investors dominate. The largest 300 _____ s collectively hold about $6 trillion in assets. In January 2008, The Economist reported that Morgan Stanley estimates that _____ s worldwide hold over US$20 trillion in assets, the largest for any category of investor ahead of mutual funds, insurance companies, currency reserves, sovereign wealth funds, hedge funds, or private equity.

Exam Probability: **High**

20. *Answer choices:*

(see index for correct answer)

- a. Pension fund
- b. Pension buyout
- c. Pension led funding

Guidance: level 1

:: Accounting journals and ledgers ::

The subledger, or _____, provides details behind entries in the general ledger used in accounting. The subledger shows detail for part of the accounting records such as property and equipment, prepaid expenses, etc. The detail would include such items as date the item was purchased or expense incurred, a description of the item, the original balance, and the net book value. The total of the subledger would match the line item amount on the general ledger. This corresponding line item in the general ledger is referred to as the controlling account. The _____ balance is compared with its controlling account balance as part of the process of preparing a trial balance.

Exam Probability: **High**

21. *Answer choices:*
(see index for correct answer)

- a. Subledger
- b. Subsidiary ledger
- c. Sales journal
- d. Journal entry

Guidance: level 1

:: ::

A _____ is the period used by governments for accounting and budget purposes, which varies between countries. It is also used for financial reporting by business and other organizations. Laws in many jurisdictions require company financial reports to be prepared and published on an annual basis, but generally do not require the reporting period to align with the calendar year. Taxation laws generally require accounting records to be maintained and taxes calculated on an annual basis, which usually corresponds to the _____ used for government purposes. The calculation of tax on an annual basis is especially relevant for direct taxation, such as income tax. Many annual government fees—such as Council rates, licence fees, etc.—are also levied on a _____ basis, while others are charged on an anniversary basis.

Exam Probability: **Medium**

22. *Answer choices:*

(see index for correct answer)

- a. Sarbanes-Oxley act of 2002
- b. Fiscal year
- c. similarity-attraction theory
- d. empathy

Guidance: level 1

:: Fixed income market ::

The _____ is a financial market where participants can issue new debt, known as the primary market, or buy and sell debt securities, known as the secondary market. This is usually in the form of bonds, but it may include notes, bills, and so on.

Exam Probability: **Medium**

23. *Answer choices:*

(see index for correct answer)

- a. Bond market
- b. Basis point
- c. Fixed income
- d. Fixed-income attribution

Guidance: level 1

:: ::

The _____ is a private, non-profit organization standard-setting body whose primary purpose is to establish and improve Generally Accepted Accounting Principles within the United States in the public's interest. The Securities and Exchange Commission designated the FASB as the organization responsible for setting accounting standards for public companies in the US. The FASB replaced the American Institute of Certified Public Accountants' Accounting Principles Board on July 1, 1973.

Exam Probability: **Low**

24. *Answer choices:*

(see index for correct answer)

- a. imperative
- b. functional perspective
- c. open system
- d. Financial Accounting Standards Board

Guidance: level 1

:: Government bonds ::

A _____ , commonly known as a Muni Bond, is a bond issued by a local government or territory, or one of their agencies. It is generally used to finance public projects such as roads, schools, airports and seaports, and infrastructure-related repairs. The term _____ is commonly used in the United States, which has the largest market of such trade-able securities in the world. As of 2011, the _____ market was valued at $3.7 trillion. Potential issuers of _____ s include states, cities, counties, redevelopment agencies, special-purpose districts, school districts, public utility districts, publicly owned airports and seaports, and other governmental entities at or below the state level having more than a de minimis amount of one of the three sovereign powers: the power of taxation, the power of eminent domain or the police power.

Exam Probability: **Low**

25. *Answer choices:*

(see index for correct answer)

- a. Texas v. White
- b. GDP-linked bond
- c. Sovereign bond
- d. Government bond

Guidance: level 1

:: Money market instruments ::

_____ , in the global financial market, is an unsecured promissory note with a fixed maturity of not more than 270 days.

Exam Probability: **High**

26. *Answer choices:*
(see index for correct answer)

- a. Commercial paper
- b. Banker's acceptance

Guidance: level 1

:: ::

An _____, for United States federal income tax, is a closely held corporation that makes a valid election to be taxed under Subchapter S of Chapter 1 of the Internal Revenue Code. In general, _____s do not pay any income taxes. Instead, the corporation's income or losses are divided among and passed through to its shareholders. The shareholders must then report the income or loss on their own individual income tax returns.

Exam Probability: **Low**

27. *Answer choices:*

(see index for correct answer)

- a. surface-level diversity
- b. S corporation
- c. empathy
- d. Character

Guidance: level 1

:: Stock market ::

_____ or stock market launch is a type of public offering in which shares of a company are sold to institutional investors and usually also retail investors; an IPO is underwritten by one or more investment banks, who also arrange for the shares to be listed on one or more stock exchanges. Through this process, colloquially known as floating, or going public, a privately held company is transformed into a public company. _____ s can be used: to raise new equity capital for the company concerned; to monetize the investments of private shareholders such as company founders or private equity investors; and to enable easy trading of existing holdings or future capital raising by becoming publicly traded enterprises.

Exam Probability: **Low**

28. *Answer choices:*
(see index for correct answer)

- a. Yellow strip
- b. Initial public offering
- c. Next: The Future Just Happened
- d. Stop catching

Guidance: level 1

:: Options (finance) ::

A _____ , often simply labeled a "call", is a financial contract between two parties, the buyer and the seller of this type of option. The buyer of the _____ has the right, but not the obligation, to buy an agreed quantity of a particular commodity or financial instrument from the seller of the option at a certain time for a certain price . The seller is obligated to sell the commodity or financial instrument to the buyer if the buyer so decides. The buyer pays a fee for this right. The term "call" comes from the fact that the owner has the right to "call the stock away" from the seller.

Exam Probability: **High**

29. *Answer choices:*

(see index for correct answer)

- a. Interest rate guarantee
- b. Call option
- c. Chooser option
- d. Greenspan put

Guidance: level 1

:: Generally Accepted Accounting Principles ::

In accrual accounting, the revenue recognition principle states that expenses should be recorded during the period in which they are incurred, regardless of when the transfer of cash occurs. Conversely, cash basis accounting calls for the recognition of an expense when the cash is paid, regardless of when the expense was actually incurred.

Exam Probability: **Medium**

30. *Answer choices:*

(see index for correct answer)

- a. Insurance asset management
- b. Earnings before interest, taxes, depreciation, and amortization
- c. AICPA Statements of Position
- d. Matching principle

Guidance: level 1

:: ::

In financial markets, a share is a unit used as mutual funds, limited partnerships, and real estate investment trusts. The owner of _____ in the corporation/company is a shareholder of the corporation. A share is an indivisible unit of capital, expressing the ownership relationship between the company and the shareholder. The denominated value of a share is its face value, and the total of the face value of issued _____ represent the capital of a company, which may not reflect the market value of those _____ .

Exam Probability: **High**

31. *Answer choices:*

(see index for correct answer)

- a. deep-level diversity
- b. levels of analysis
- c. Shares
- d. empathy

Guidance: level 1

:: Generally Accepted Accounting Principles ::

_____ , also referred to as the bottom line, net income, or net earnings is a measure of the profitability of a venture after accounting for all costs and taxes. It is the actual profit, and includes the operating expenses that are excluded from gross profit.

Exam Probability: **High**

32. *Answer choices:*

(see index for correct answer)

- a. Net profit
- b. Consolidation
- c. Operating profit
- d. Generally accepted accounting principles

Guidance: level 1

:: Inventory ::

Costs are associated with particular goods using one of the several formulas, including specific identification, first-in first-out, or average cost. Costs include all costs of purchase, costs of conversion and other costs that are incurred in bringing the inventories to their present location and condition. Costs of goods made by the businesses include material, labor, and allocated overhead. The costs of those goods which are not yet sold are deferred as costs of inventory until the inventory is sold or written down in value.

Exam Probability: **Low**

33. *Answer choices:*

(see index for correct answer)

- a. LIFO
- b. Safety stock
- c. Inventory bounce
- d. Cost of goods sold

Guidance: level 1

:: Financial economics ::

A _____ is defined to include property of any kind held by an assessee, whether connected with their business or profession or not connected with their business or profession. It includes all kinds of property, movable or immovable, tangible or intangible, fixed or circulating. Thus, land and building, plant and machinery, motorcar, furniture, jewellery, route permits, goodwill, tenancy rights, patents, trademarks, shares, debentures, securities, units, mutual funds, zero-coupon bonds etc. are _____ s.

Exam Probability: **Medium**

34. *Answer choices:*

(see index for correct answer)

- a. Ask price
- b. Conditional variance swap
- c. Cyclical asymmetry
- d. Capital asset

Guidance: level 1

:: Generally Accepted Accounting Principles ::

_____ is a small amount of discretionary funds in the form of cash used for expenditures where it is not sensible to make any disbursement by cheque, because of the inconvenience and costs of writing, signing, and then cashing the cheque.

Exam Probability: **Low**

35. *Answer choices:*

(see index for correct answer)

- a. Deprival value
- b. Goodwill
- c. Petty cash
- d. Depreciation

Guidance: level 1

:: Budgets ::

A _____ is a financial plan for a defined period, often one year. It may also include planned sales volumes and revenues, resource quantities, costs and expenses, assets, liabilities and cash flows. Companies, governments, families and other organizations use it to express strategic plans of activities or events in measurable terms.

Exam Probability: **High**

36. *Answer choices:*

(see index for correct answer)

- a. Budgeted cost of work scheduled
- b. Budget
- c. Zero deficit budget
- d. Energy budget

Guidance: level 1

:: Costs ::

In economics, _____ is the total economic cost of production and is made up of variable cost, which varies according to the quantity of a good produced and includes inputs such as labour and raw materials, plus fixed cost, which is independent of the quantity of a good produced and includes inputs that cannot be varied in the short term: fixed costs such as buildings and machinery, including sunk costs if any. Since cost is measured per unit of time, it is a flow variable.

Exam Probability: **Low**

37. *Answer choices:*

(see index for correct answer)

- a. Sliding scale
- b. Joint cost
- c. Customer Cost
- d. Cost of products sold

Guidance: level 1

:: Financial markets ::

As money became a commodity, the _____ became a component of the financial market for assets involved in short-term borrowing, lending, buying and selling with original maturities of one year or less. Trading in _____ s is done over the counter and is wholesale.

Exam Probability: **High**

38. *Answer choices:*

(see index for correct answer)

- a. Money market in India
- b. Money market
- c. Index cohesive force
- d. Market depth

Guidance: level 1

:: ::

In business, economics or investment, market _____ is a market's feature whereby an individual or firm can quickly purchase or sell an asset without causing a drastic change in the asset's price. _____ is about how big the trade-off is between the speed of the sale and the price it can be sold for. In a liquid market, the trade-off is mild: selling quickly will not reduce the price much. In a relatively illiquid market, selling it quickly will require cutting its price by some amount.

Exam Probability: **Low**

39. Answer choices:

(see index for correct answer)

- a. empathy
- b. personal values
- c. deep-level diversity
- d. interpersonal communication

Guidance: level 1

:: ::

A _____ is an entity that owes a debt to another entity. The entity may be an individual, a firm, a government, a company or other legal person. The counterparty is called a creditor. When the counterpart of this debt arrangement is a bank, the _____ is more often referred to as a borrower.

Exam Probability: **High**

40. Answer choices:

(see index for correct answer)

- a. interpersonal communication
- b. Debtor
- c. Sarbanes-Oxley act of 2002
- d. Character

Guidance: level 1

:: Competition (economics) ::

_____ arises whenever at least two parties strive for a goal which cannot be shared: where one's gain is the other's loss.

Exam Probability: **Medium**

41. *Answer choices:*

(see index for correct answer)

- a. Level playing field
- b. Self-competition
- c. Category killer
- d. Wantrapreneur

Guidance: level 1

:: Global systemically important banks ::

_____ Inc. or Citi is an American multinational investment bank and financial services corporation headquartered in New York City. The company was formed by the merger of banking giant Citicorp and financial conglomerate Travelers Group in 1998; Travelers was subsequently spun off from the company in 2002. _____ owns Citicorp, the holding company for Citibank, as well as several international subsidiaries.

Exam Probability: **Medium**

42. *Answer choices:*

(see index for correct answer)

- a. Bank of America
- b. Banco Bilbao Vizcaya Argentaria
- c. The Bank of New York Mellon
- d. Citigroup

Guidance: level 1

:: Accounting in the United States ::

_____ is the title of qualified accountants in numerous countries in the English-speaking world. In the United States, the CPA is a license to provide accounting services to the public. It is awarded by each of the 50 states for practice in that state. Additionally, almost every state has passed mobility laws to allow CPAs from other states to practice in their state. State licensing requirements vary, but the minimum standard requirements include passing the Uniform _____ Examination, 150 semester units of college education, and one year of accounting related experience.

Exam Probability: **High**

43. *Answer choices:*

(see index for correct answer)

- a. Governmental Accounting Standards Board
- b. Certified Government Financial Manager
- c. Clean Energy Bank
- d. Association of Certified Fraud Examiners

Guidance: level 1

:: Investment ::

_____ , and investment appraisal, is the planning process used to determine whether an organization's long term investments such as new machinery, replacement of machinery, new plants, new products, and research development projects are worth the funding of cash through the firm's capitalization structure . It is the process of allocating resources for major capital, or investment, expenditures. One of the primary goals of _____ investments is to increase the value of the firm to the shareholders.

Exam Probability: **High**

44. *Answer choices:*

(see index for correct answer)

- a. Foreign portfolio investment

- b. Institutional investor
- c. Investment wine
- d. Media Development Investment Fund

Guidance: level 1

:: Accounting terminology ::

A _____ contains all the accounts for recording transactions relating to a company's assets, liabilities, owners' equity, revenue, and expenses. In modern accounting software or ERP, the _____ works as a central repository for accounting data transferred from all subledgers or modules like accounts payable, accounts receivable, cash management, fixed assets, purchasing and projects. The _____ is the backbone of any accounting system which holds financial and non-financial data for an organization. The collection of all accounts is known as the _____ . Each account is known as a ledger account. In a manual or non-computerized system this may be a large book.The statement of financial position and the statement of income and comprehensive income are both derived from the _____ . Each account in the _____ consists of one or more pages. The _____ is where posting to the accounts occurs. Posting is the process of recording amounts as credits , and amounts as debits , in the pages of the _____ . Additional columns to the right hold a running activity total .

Exam Probability: **Medium**

45. *Answer choices:*
(see index for correct answer)

- a. General ledger

- b. Statement of financial position
- c. Accrual
- d. Chart of accounts

Guidance: level 1

:: Accounting in the United States ::

The _____ is a private-sector, nonprofit corporation created by the Sarbanes–Oxley Act of 2002 to oversee the audits of public companies and other issuers in order to protect the interests of investors and further the public interest in the preparation of informative, accurate and independent audit reports. The PCAOB also oversees the audits of broker-dealers, including compliance reports filed pursuant to federal securities laws, to promote investor protection. All PCAOB rules and standards must be approved by the U.S. Securities and Exchange Commission .

Exam Probability: **Low**

46. *Answer choices:*

(see index for correct answer)

- a. Public Company Accounting Oversight Board
- b. Institute of Internal Auditors
- c. American Institute of Certified Public Accountants
- d. Positive assurance

Guidance: level 1

:: ::

An _____ is a comprehensive report on a company's activities throughout the preceding year. _____ s are intended to give shareholders and other interested people information about the company's activities and financial performance. They may be considered as grey literature. Most jurisdictions require companies to prepare and disclose _____ s, and many require the _____ to be filed at the company's registry. Companies listed on a stock exchange are also required to report at more frequent intervals.

Exam Probability: **High**

47. *Answer choices:*

(see index for correct answer)

- a. Annual report
- b. empathy
- c. hierarchical
- d. surface-level diversity

Guidance: level 1

:: Derivatives (finance) ::

A _____ or _____ row is a line of closely spaced shrubs and sometimes trees, planted and trained to form a barrier or to mark the boundary of an area, such as between neighbouring properties. _____ s used to separate a road from adjoining fields or one field from another, and of sufficient age to incorporate larger trees, are known as _____ rows. Often they serve as windbreaks to improve conditions for the adjacent crops, as in bocage country. When clipped and maintained, _____ s are also a simple form of topiary.

Exam Probability: **High**

48. *Answer choices:*

(see index for correct answer)

- a. Texas hedge
- b. Hedge
- c. Constant maturity swap
- d. Cashflow matching

Guidance: level 1

:: Costs ::

The _____ is computed by dividing the total cost of goods available for sale by the total units available for sale. This gives a weighted-average unit cost that is applied to the units in the ending inventory.

Exam Probability: **Low**

49. Answer choices:

(see index for correct answer)

- a. Incremental cost-effectiveness ratio
- b. Average Cost
- c. Khozraschyot
- d. Implicit cost

Guidance: level 1

:: Banking ::

A _____ is a financial account maintained by a bank for a customer. A _____ can be a deposit account, a credit card account, a current account, or any other type of account offered by a financial institution, and represents the funds that a customer has entrusted to the financial institution and from which the customer can make withdrawals. Alternatively, accounts may be loan accounts in which case the customer owes money to the financial institution.

Exam Probability: **Low**

50. Answer choices:

(see index for correct answer)

- a. Gold key
- b. Savings account
- c. Standing order
- d. Discount policy

Guidance: level 1

:: Interest rates ::

An _____ is the amount of interest due per period, as a proportion of the amount lent, deposited or borrowed. The total interest on an amount lent or borrowed depends on the principal sum, the _____ , the compounding frequency, and the length of time over which it is lent, deposited or borrowed.

Exam Probability: **Low**

51. *Answer choices:*

(see index for correct answer)

- a. Zero interest-rate policy
- b. Interest rate
- c. EURONIA
- d. Official cash rate

Guidance: level 1

:: Banking ::

_____ refers to a broad area of finance involving the collection, handling, and usage of cash. It involves assessing market liquidity, cash flow, and investments.

Exam Probability: **Medium**

52. *Answer choices:*

(see index for correct answer)

- a. Excess reserves
- b. Cash management
- c. Tier 2 capital
- d. Discount window

Guidance: level 1

:: Fixed income analysis ::

The _____ , book yield or redemption yield of a bond or other fixed-interest security, such as gilts, is the internal rate of return earned by an investor who buys the bond today at the market price, assuming that the bond is held until maturity, and that all coupon and principal payments are made on schedule. _____ is the discount rate at which the sum of all future cash flows from the bond is equal to the current price of the bond. The YTM is often given in terms of Annual Percentage Rate , but more often market convention is followed. In a number of major markets the convention is to quote annualized yields with semi-annual compounding ; thus, for example, an annual effective yield of 10.25% would be quoted as 10.00%, because 1.05 × 1.05 = 1.1025 and 2 × 5 = 10.

Exam Probability: **Low**

53. *Answer choices:*

(see index for correct answer)

- a. Bond convexity
- b. Embedded option
- c. Yield to maturity
- d. Chen model

Guidance: level 1

:: Debt ::

_____ , in finance and economics, is payment from a borrower or deposit-taking financial institution to a lender or depositor of an amount above repayment of the principal sum , at a particular rate. It is distinct from a fee which the borrower may pay the lender or some third party. It is also distinct from dividend which is paid by a company to its shareholders from its profit or reserve, but not at a particular rate decided beforehand, rather on a pro rata basis as a share in the reward gained by risk taking entrepreneurs when the revenue earned exceeds the total costs.

Exam Probability: **Low**

54. *Answer choices:*

(see index for correct answer)

- a. Interest
- b. Terminal debt
- c. Crown debt
- d. Zombie company

Guidance: level 1

:: Generally Accepted Accounting Principles ::

The first published description of the process is found in Luca Pacioli's 1494 work Summa de arithmetica, in the section titled Particularis de Computis et Scripturis. Although he did not use the term, he essentially prescribed a technique similar to a post-closing _____ .

Exam Probability: **High**

55. *Answer choices:*

(see index for correct answer)

- a. Write-off
- b. Treasury stock
- c. Trial balance
- d. Cost principle

Guidance: level 1

:: Banking ::

A _____ is a financial institution that accepts deposits from the public and creates credit. Lending activities can be performed either directly or indirectly through capital markets. Due to their importance in the financial stability of a country, _____ s are highly regulated in most countries. Most nations have institutionalized a system known as fractional reserve _____ ing under which _____ s hold liquid assets equal to only a portion of their current liabilities. In addition to other regulations intended to ensure liquidity, _____ s are generally subject to minimum capital requirements based on an international set of capital standards, known as the Basel Accords.

Exam Probability: **High**

56. *Answer choices:*

(see index for correct answer)

- a. Narrow banking
- b. Retail banking
- c. Joint account
- d. Bank

Guidance: level 1

:: International trade ::

In finance, an _____ is the rate at which one currency will be exchanged for another. It is also regarded as the value of one country's currency in relation to another currency. For example, an interbank _____ of 114 Japanese yen to the United States dollar means that ¥114 will be exchanged for each US$1 or that US$1 will be exchanged for each ¥114. In this case it is said that the price of a dollar in relation to yen is ¥114, or equivalently that the price of a yen in relation to dollars is $1/114.

Exam Probability: **Medium**

57. *Answer choices:*

(see index for correct answer)

- a. Lee Byung-chul
- b. Intra-industry trade
- c. Business English
- d. Exchange rate

Guidance: level 1

:: Financial markets ::

For an individual, a _____ is the minimum amount of money by which the expected return on a risky asset must exceed the known return on a risk-free asset in order to induce an individual to hold the risky asset rather than the risk-free asset. It is positive if the person is risk averse. Thus it is the minimum willingness to accept compensation for the risk.

Exam Probability: **Low**

58. *Answer choices:*

(see index for correct answer)

- a. Market data
- b. Risk premium
- c. Price-weighted
- d. Long/short equity

Guidance: level 1

:: Subprime mortgage crisis ::

The _____ Group, Inc., is an American multinational investment bank and financial services company headquartered in New York City. It offers services in investment management, securities, asset management, prime brokerage, and securities underwriting.

Exam Probability: **Medium**

59. *Answer choices:*

(see index for correct answer)

- a. Home Affordable Modification Program
- b. Hope Now Alliance
- c. Goldman Sachs

- d. California Bureau of Real Estate Appraisers

Guidance: level 1

Human resource management

Human resource (HR) management is the strategic approach to the effective management of organization workers so that they help the business gain a competitive advantage. It is designed to maximize employee performance in service of an employer's strategic objectives. HR is primarily concerned with the management of people within organizations, focusing on policies and on systems. HR departments are responsible for overseeing employee-benefits design, employee recruitment, training and development, performance appraisal, and rewarding (e.g., managing pay and benefit systems). HR also concerns itself with organizational change and industrial relations, that is, the balancing of organizational practices with requirements arising from collective bargaining and from governmental laws.

_____ is the withdrawal from one's position or occupation or from one's active working life. A person may also semi-retire by reducing work hours.

Exam Probability: **High**

1. *Answer choices:*

(see index for correct answer)

- a. cultural
- b. interpersonal communication
- c. surface-level diversity
- d. deep-level diversity

Guidance: level 1

:: Cognitive biases ::

The _____ is a type of immediate judgement discrepancy, or cognitive bias, where a person making an initial assessment of another person, place, or thing will assume ambiguous information based upon concrete information. A simplified example of the _____ is when an individual noticing that the person in the photograph is attractive, well groomed, and properly attired, assumes, using a mental heuristic, that the person in the photograph is a good person based upon the rules of that individual's social concept. This constant error in judgment is reflective of the individual's preferences, prejudices, ideology, aspirations, and social perception. The _____ is an evaluation by an individual and can affect the perception of a decision, action, idea, business, person, group, entity, or other whenever concrete data is generalized or influences ambiguous information.

2. Answer choices:

(see index for correct answer)

- a. Halo effect
- b. Ostrich effect
- c. Self-fulfilling prophecy
- d. Conjunction fallacy

Guidance: level 1

:: ::

_____ is the combination of structured planning and the active management choice of one's own professional career. _____ was first defined in a social work doctoral thesis by Mary Valentich as the implementation of a career strategy through application of career tactics in relation to chosen career orientation. Career orientation referred to the overall design or pattern of one's career, shaped by particular goals and interests and identifiable by particular positions that embody these goals and interests. Career strategy pertains to the individual's general approach to the realization of career goals, and to the specificity of the goals themselves. Two general strategy approaches are adaptive and planned. Career tactics are actions to maintain oneself in a satisfactory employment situation. Tactics may be more or less assertive, with assertiveness in the work situation referring to actions taken to advance one's career interests or to exercise one's legitimate rights while respecting the rights of others.

3. *Answer choices:*

(see index for correct answer)

- a. hierarchical
- b. functional perspective
- c. Career management
- d. personal values

Guidance: level 1

:: Employment ::

A flat organization has an organizational structure with few or no levels of middle management between staff and executives. An organization's structure refers to the nature of the distribution of the units and positions within it, also to the nature of the relationships among those units and positions. Tall and flat organizations differ based on how many levels of management are present in the organization, and how much control managers are endowed with.

Exam Probability: **Medium**

4. *Answer choices:*

(see index for correct answer)

- a. Virtual Student Foreign Service
- b. Ethical job
- c. Extreme careerism
- d. Employment Development Department

Guidance: level 1

:: Industrial engineering ::

_____ is the formal process that sits alongside Requirements analysis and focuses on the human elements of the requirements.

Exam Probability: **Low**

5. *Answer choices:*

(see index for correct answer)

- a. Society for Health Systems
- b. Flow process chart
- c. Needs analysis
- d. Work Measurement

Guidance: level 1

:: ::

A _____ is a research instrument consisting of a series of questions for the purpose of gathering information from respondents. The _____ was invented by the Statistical Society of London in 1838.

Exam Probability: **Low**

6. *Answer choices:*

(see index for correct answer)

- a. empathy
- b. process perspective
- c. co-culture
- d. Questionnaire

Guidance: level 1

:: ::

An _____ is a person temporarily or permanently residing in a country other than their native country. In common usage, the term often refers to professionals, skilled workers, or artists taking positions outside their home country, either independently or sent abroad by their employers, who can be companies, universities, governments, or non-governmental organisations. Effectively migrant workers, they usually earn more than they would at home, and less than local employees. However, the term ` _____ ` is also used for retirees and others who have chosen to live outside their native country. Historically, it has also referred to exiles.

Exam Probability: **Medium**

7. *Answer choices:*

(see index for correct answer)

- a. empathy
- b. surface-level diversity
- c. deep-level diversity
- d. Expatriate

Guidance: level 1

:: Income ::

A _____ is a unit in systems of monetary compensation for employment. It is commonly used in public service, both civil and military, but also for companies of the private sector. _____ s facilitate the employment process by providing a fixed framework of salary ranges, as opposed to a free negotiation. Typically, _____ s encompass two dimensions: a "vertical" range where each level corresponds to the responsibility of, and requirements needed for a certain position; and a "horizontal" range within this scale to allow for monetary incentives rewarding the employee's quality of performance or length of service. Thus, an employee progresses within the horizontal and vertical ranges upon achieving positive appraisal on a regular basis. In most cases, evaluation is done annually and encompasses more than one method.

Exam Probability: **Medium**

8. *Answer choices:*

(see index for correct answer)

- a. bottom line
- b. Gratuity
- c. Pay grade

- d. Independent income

Guidance: level 1

:: Labour relations ::

A _____, also known as a post-entry closed shop, is a form of a union security clause. Under this, the employer agrees to either only hire labor union members or to require that any new employees who are not already union members become members within a certain amount of time. Use of the _____ varies widely from nation to nation, depending on the level of protection given trade unions in general.

Exam Probability: **Low**

9. *Answer choices:*

(see index for correct answer)

- a. Big labor
- b. Global union federation
- c. Union shop
- d. Two-tier system

Guidance: level 1

:: Organizational behavior ::

Greenberg introduced the concept of _____ with regard to how an employee judges the behaviour of the organization and the employee's resulting attitude and behaviour. .

Exam Probability: **Low**

10. *Answer choices:*

(see index for correct answer)

- a. Administrative Behavior
- b. Organizational retaliatory behavior
- c. Behavioral systems analysis
- d. Organizational justice

Guidance: level 1

:: Learning methods ::

_____ is an approach to problem solving. It involves taking action and reflecting upon the results. This helps improve the problem-solving process as well as simplify the solutions developed by the team.

Exam Probability: **Medium**

11. *Answer choices:*

(see index for correct answer)

- a. Action learning
- b. double loop learning
- c. Collaborative learning
- d. Double-loop learning

Guidance: level 1

:: Financial accounting ::

_____ is the intangible value of a business, covering its people, the value relating to its relationships, and everything that is left when the employees go home, of which intellectual property is but one component. It is the sum of everything everybody in a company knows that gives it a competitive edge. The term is used in academia in an attempt to account for the value of intangible assets not listed explicitly on a company's balance sheets. On a national level _____ refers to national intangible capital, NIC.A second meaning that is used in academia and was adopted in large corporations is focused on the recycling of knowledge via knowledge management and _____ management . Creating, shaping and updating the stock of _____ requires the formulation of a strategic vision, which blends together all three dimensions of _____ within the organisational context through exploration, exploitation, measurement, and disclosure. _____ is used in the context of assessing the wealth of organizations. A metric for the value of _____ is the amount by which the enterprise value of a firm exceeds the value of its tangible assets. Directly visible on corporate books is capital embodied in its physical assets and financial capital; however all three make up the value of an enterprise. Measuring the real value and the total performance of _____ 's components is a critical part of running a company in the knowledge economy and Information Age. Understanding the _____ in an enterprise allows leveraging of its intellectual assets. For a corporation, the result will optimize its stock price.

Exam Probability: **Low**

12. *Answer choices:*

(see index for correct answer)

- a. Intangibles
- b. Money measurement concept
- c. Accelerated depreciation
- d. Intellectual capital

Guidance: level 1

:: Job interview ::

An _____ is a survey conducted with an individual who is separating from an organization or relationship. Most commonly, this occurs between an employee and an organization, a student and an educational institution, or a member and an association. An organization can use the information gained from an _____ to assess what should be improved, changed, or remain intact. More so, an organization can use the results from _____ s to reduce employee, student, or member turnover and increase productivity and engagement, thus reducing the high costs associated with turnover. Some examples of the value of conducting _____ s include shortening the recruiting and hiring process, reducing absenteeism, improving innovation, sustaining performance, and reducing possible litigation if issues mentioned in the _____ are addressed. It is important for each organization to customize its own _____ in order to maintain the highest levels of survey validity and reliability.

Exam Probability: High

13. *Answer choices:*

(see index for correct answer)

- a. Exit interview
- b. Mock interview
- c. SOARA
- d. Informational interview

Guidance: level 1

:: Ethically disputed business practices ::

An _____ in US labor law refers to certain actions taken by employers or unions that violate the National Labor Relations Act of 1935 29 U.S.C. § 151–169 and other legislation. Such acts are investigated by the National Labor Relations Board.

Exam Probability: **Low**

14. *Answer choices:*

(see index for correct answer)

- a. Off-label use
- b. Constructive dismissal
- c. Patent troll
- d. Black market

Guidance: level 1

:: Self ::

_____ is a term that has been used in various psychology theories, often in different ways. The term was originally introduced by the organismic theorist Kurt Goldstein for the motive to realize one's full potential. In Goldstein's view, it is the organism's master motive, the only real motive: "the tendency to actualize itself as fully as possible is the basic drive ... the drive of _____ ." Carl Rogers similarly wrote of "the curative force in psychotherapy man's tendency to actualize himself, to become his potentialities ... to express and activate all the capacities of the organism." The concept was brought most fully to prominence in Abraham Maslow's hierarchy of needs theory as the final level of psychological development that can be achieved when all basic and mental needs are essentially fulfilled and the "actualization" of the full personal potential takes place, although he adapted this viewpoint later on in life to be more flexible.

Exam Probability: **Low**

15. *Answer choices:*

(see index for correct answer)

- a. Egocentrism
- b. Self-presentation
- c. Narcissism
- d. Self-actualization

Guidance: level 1

:: Employment compensation ::

A _____ is an agreement between a company and an employee specifying that the employee will receive certain significant benefits if employment is terminated. Most definitions specify the employment termination is as a result of a merger or takeover, also known as "Change-in-control benefits", but more recently the term has been used to describe perceived excessive CEO severance packages unrelated to change in ownership. The benefits may include severance pay, cash bonuses, stock options, or other benefits.

Exam Probability: **Medium**

16. *Answer choices:*
(see index for correct answer)

- a. Basic Income Earth Network
- b. Golden parachute
- c. Workers Compensation Act 1987
- d. Compensation of employees

Guidance: level 1

:: Employment ::

_____ is a relationship between two parties, usually based on a contract where work is paid for, where one party, which may be a corporation, for profit, not-for-profit organization, co-operative or other entity is the employer and the other is the employee. Employees work in return for payment, which may be in the form of an hourly wage, by piecework or an annual salary, depending on the type of work an employee does or which sector she or he is working in. Employees in some fields or sectors may receive gratuities, bonus payment or stock options. In some types of _____ , employees may receive benefits in addition to payment. Benefits can include health insurance, housing, disability insurance or use of a gym. _____ is typically governed by _____ laws, regulations or legal contracts.

Exam Probability: **High**

17. *Answer choices:*

(see index for correct answer)

- a. Employment
- b. Temporary duty assignment
- c. Personal chef
- d. Job shadow

Guidance: level 1

:: Employee relations ::

_____ ownership, or employee share ownership, is an ownership interest in a company held by the company's workforce. The ownership interest may be facilitated by the company as part of employees' remuneration or incentive compensation for work performed, or the company itself may be employee owned.

Exam Probability: **Low**

18. *Answer choices:*

(see index for correct answer)

- a. Industry Federation of the State of Rio de Janeiro
- b. Fringe benefit
- c. Employee surveys
- d. Employee handbook

Guidance: level 1

:: Survey methodology ::

An _____ is a conversation where questions are asked and answers are given. In common parlance, the word "_____" refers to a one-on-one conversation between an _____ er and an _____ ee. The _____ er asks questions to which the _____ ee responds, usually so information may be transferred from _____ ee to _____ er . Sometimes, information can be transferred in both directions. It is a communication, unlike a speech, which produces a one-way flow of information.

Exam Probability: **High**

19. *Answer choices:*

(see index for correct answer)

- a. Administrative error
- b. American Association for Public Opinion Research
- c. Public opinion
- d. Self-report

Guidance: level 1

:: Employment compensation ::

A _____ is a type of employee benefit plan offered in the United States pursuant to Section 125 of the Internal Revenue Code. Its name comes from the earliest such plans that allowed employees to choose between different types of benefits, similar to the ability of a customer to choose among available items in a cafeteria. Qualified _____ s are excluded from gross income. To qualify, a _____ must allow employees to choose from two or more benefits consisting of cash or qualified benefit plans. The Internal Revenue Code explicitly excludes deferred compensation plans from qualifying as a _____ subject to a gross income exemption. Section 125 also provides two exceptions.

Exam Probability: **Medium**

20. *Answer choices:*

(see index for correct answer)

- a. WorkCover Authority of New South Wales

- b. Corporate child care
- c. Cafeteria plan
- d. Family wage

Guidance: level 1

:: Trade unions in the United States ::

The _____ is an American labor union representing over 670,000 employees of the federal government, about 5,000 employees of the District of Columbia, and a few hundred private sector employees, mostly in and around federal facilities. AFGE is the largest union for civilian, non-postal federal employees and the largest union for District of Columbia employees who report directly to the mayor. It is affiliated with the AFL-CIO.

Exam Probability: **Medium**

21. *Answer choices:*
(see index for correct answer)

- a. Allied Pilots Association
- b. United Brotherhood of Carpenters and Joiners of America
- c. Operation Dixie
- d. American Federation of Government Employees

Guidance: level 1

:: ::

A _____ is a technical analysis of a biological specimen, for example urine, hair, blood, breath, sweat, and/or oral fluid/saliva—to determine the presence or absence of specified parent drugs or their metabolites. Major applications of _____ ing include detection of the presence of performance enhancing steroids in sport, employers and parole/probation officers screening for drugs prohibited by law and police officers testing for the presence and concentration of alcohol in the blood commonly referred to as BAC . BAC tests are typically administered via a breathalyzer while urinalysis is used for the vast majority of _____ ing in sports and the workplace. Numerous other methods with varying degrees of accuracy, sensitivity , and detection periods exist.

Exam Probability: **Medium**

22. *Answer choices:*

(see index for correct answer)

- a. Character
- b. levels of analysis
- c. hierarchical perspective
- d. information systems assessment

Guidance: level 1

:: Human resource management ::

_____ expands the capacity of individuals to perform in leadership roles within organizations. Leadership roles are those that facilitate execution of a company's strategy through building alignment, winning mindshare and growing the capabilities of others. Leadership roles may be formal, with the corresponding authority to make decisions and take responsibility, or they may be informal roles with little official authority.

Exam Probability: **Low**

23. *Answer choices:*
(see index for correct answer)

- a. Job description management
- b. E-HRM
- c. Leadership development
- d. Succession planning

Guidance: level 1

:: Self ::

_____ is a conscious or subconscious process in which people attempt to influence the perceptions of other people about a person, object or event. They do so by regulating and controlling information in social interaction. It was first conceptualized by Erving Goffman in 1959 in The Presentation of Self in Everyday Life, and then was expanded upon in 1967. An example of _____ theory in play is in sports such as soccer. At an important game, a player would want to showcase themselves in the best light possible, because there are college recruiters watching. This person would have the flashiest pair of cleats and try and perform their best to show off their skills. Their main goal may be to impress the college recruiters in a way that maximizes their chances of being chosen for a college team rather than winning the game.

Exam Probability: **Medium**

24. *Answer choices:*

(see index for correct answer)

- a. Impression management
- b. Narcissism
- c. Self-actualization
- d. Self-presentation

Guidance: level 1

:: ::

_____ are interactive computer-mediated technologies that facilitate the creation and sharing of information, ideas, career interests and other forms of expression via virtual communities and networks. The variety of stand-alone and built-in _____ services currently available introduces challenges of definition; however, there are some common features.

Exam Probability: **High**

25. *Answer choices:*

(see index for correct answer)

- a. Social media
- b. Character
- c. information systems assessment
- d. Sarbanes-Oxley act of 2002

Guidance: level 1

:: Management ::

The _____ is a strategy performance management tool – a semi-standard structured report, that can be used by managers to keep track of the execution of activities by the staff within their control and to monitor the consequences arising from these actions.

Exam Probability: **Medium**

26. *Answer choices:*

(see index for correct answer)

- a. Balanced scorecard
- b. Six phases of a big project
- c. Wireless informatics
- d. Commercial management

Guidance: level 1

:: ::

_____ is the extraction of valuable minerals or other geological materials from the earth, usually from an ore body, lode, vein, seam, reef or placer deposit. These deposits form a mineralized package that is of economic interest to the miner.

Exam Probability: **Low**

27. *Answer choices:*

(see index for correct answer)

- a. interpersonal communication
- b. Mining
- c. hierarchical perspective
- d. similarity-attraction theory

Guidance: level 1

:: Psychometrics ::

In statistics and research, _____ is typically a measure based on the correlations between different items on the same test. It measures whether several items that propose to measure the same general construct produce similar scores. For example, if a respondent expressed agreement with the statements "I like to ride bicycles" and "I've enjoyed riding bicycles in the past", and disagreement with the statement "I hate bicycles", this would be indicative of good _____ of the test.

Exam Probability: **Low**

28. *Answer choices:*
(see index for correct answer)

- a. Sequential probability ratio test
- b. Differential item functioning
- c. Psychometric function
- d. Visual analogue scale

Guidance: level 1

:: Human resource management ::

_____ is a method of job analysis that was developed by the Employment and Training Administration of the United States Department of Labor. FJA produces standardized occupational information specific to the performance of the work and the performer.

Exam Probability: **Low**

29. *Answer choices:*

(see index for correct answer)

- a. Randstad Holding
- b. Functional job analysis
- c. Talascend
- d. Employee value proposition

Guidance: level 1

:: Management ::

_____ or executive pay is composed of the financial compensation and other non-financial awards received by an executive from their firm for their service to the organization. It is typically a mixture of salary, bonuses, shares of or call options on the company stock, benefits, and perquisites, ideally configured to take into account government regulations, tax law, the desires of the organization and the executive, and rewards for performance.

Exam Probability: **Low**

30. *Answer choices:*

(see index for correct answer)

- a. Economic production quantity
- b. Linear scheduling method
- c. Executive compensation
- d. Continuous-flow manufacturing

Guidance: level 1

:: ::

_____ is the formal act of giving up or quitting one's office or position. A _____ can occur when a person holding a position gained by election or appointment steps down, but leaving a position upon the expiration of a term, or choosing not to seek an additional term, is not considered _____ .

Exam Probability: **Medium**

31. *Answer choices:*

(see index for correct answer)

- a. imperative
- b. surface-level diversity
- c. hierarchical
- d. Resignation

Guidance: level 1

:: Offshoring ::

Outsourcing is an agreement in which one company hires another company to be responsible for a planned or existing activity that is or could be done internally, and sometimes involves transferring employees and assets from one firm to another.

Exam Probability: **Medium**

32. *Answer choices:*

(see index for correct answer)

- a. Offshore custom software development
- b. Antex
- c. Nearshoring
- d. Offshoring Research Network

Guidance: level 1

:: ::

_____ is the process of two or more people or organizations working together to complete a task or achieve a goal. _____ is similar to cooperation. Most _____ requires leadership, although the form of leadership can be social within a decentralized and egalitarian group. Teams that work collaboratively often access greater resources, recognition and rewards when facing competition for finite resources.

Exam Probability: **Low**

33. *Answer choices:*

(see index for correct answer)

- a. Collaboration
- b. imperative
- c. interpersonal communication
- d. levels of analysis

Guidance: level 1

:: Employment compensation ::

_____, merit increase or pay for performance, is performance-related pay, most frequently in the context of educational reform or government civil service reform. It provides bonuses for workers who perform their jobs effectively, according to easily measurable criteria. In the United States, policy makers are divided on whether _____ should be offered to public school teachers, and other public employees, as is commonly the case in the United Kingdom.

Exam Probability: **Low**

34. *Answer choices:*

(see index for correct answer)

- a. ADP, LLC
- b. Dearness allowance
- c. Merit pay
- d. Employee benefit

Guidance: level 1

:: ::

_____, also known as drug abuse, is a patterned use of a drug in which the user consumes the substance in amounts or with methods which are harmful to themselves or others, and is a form of substance-related disorder. Widely differing definitions of drug abuse are used in public health, medical and criminal justice contexts. In some cases criminal or anti-social behaviour occurs when the person is under the influence of a drug, and long term personality changes in individuals may occur as well. In addition to possible physical, social, and psychological harm, use of some drugs may also lead to criminal penalties, although these vary widely depending on the local jurisdiction.

Exam Probability: **Medium**

35. *Answer choices:*

(see index for correct answer)

- a. information systems assessment
- b. deep-level diversity
- c. personal values
- d. empathy

Guidance: level 1

:: Labour law ::

In law, _____ is to give an immediately secured right of present or future deployment. One has a vested right to an asset that cannot be taken away by any third party, even though one may not yet possess the asset. When the right, interest, or title to the present or future possession of a legal estate can be transferred to any other party, it is termed a vested interest.

Exam Probability: **Low**

36. *Answer choices:*

(see index for correct answer)

- a. Caselex
- b. Undue hardship
- c. Vesting
- d. Conditional dismissal

Guidance: level 1

:: Socialism ::

In sociology, _____ is the process of internalizing the norms and ideologies of society. _____ encompasses both learning and teaching and is thus "the means by which social and cultural continuity are attained".

Exam Probability: **Low**

37. *Answer choices:*

(see index for correct answer)

- a. To the Finland Station
- b. Socialization
- c. Tory socialism
- d. Socialist Studies

Guidance: level 1

:: ::

_____ is a common standard in United States labor law arbitration that is used in labor union contracts in the United States as a form of job security.

Exam Probability: **Low**

38. Answer choices:

(see index for correct answer)

- a. information systems assessment
- b. similarity-attraction theory
- c. Just cause
- d. interpersonal communication

Guidance: level 1

:: Recruitment ::

_____ is a recruitment strategy that uses mobile technology to attract, engage and convert candidates. Common _____ tactics include mobile career sites, _____ by text, _____ apps and social recruiting. _____ is often cited as a growing opportunity for recruiters to connect with candidates more efficiently with "over 89% of job seekers saying their mobile device will be an important tool and resource for their job search." Traditionally, recruiters have used emails and phone calls to engage candidates, but the increase in mobile usage among job seekers has contributed to _____'s rising popularity.

Exam Probability: **Low**

39. Answer choices:

(see index for correct answer)

- a. Labour brokering
- b. Association of Graduate Recruiters

- c. Mobile recruiting
- d. The Select Family of Staffing Companies

Guidance: level 1

:: Telecommuting ::

_____, also called telework, teleworking, working from home, mobile work, remote work, and flexible workplace, is a work arrangement in which employees do not commute or travel to a central place of work, such as an office building, warehouse, or store. Teleworkers in the 21st century often use mobile telecommunications technology such as Wi-Fi-equipped laptop or tablet computers and smartphones to work from coffee shops; others may use a desktop computer and a landline phone at their home. According to a Reuters poll, approximately "one in five workers around the globe, particularly employees in the Middle East, Latin America and Asia, telecommute frequently and nearly 10 percent work from home every day." In the 2000s, annual leave or vacation in some organizations was seen as absence from the workplace rather than ceasing work, and some office employees used telework to continue to check work e-mails while on vacation.

Exam Probability: **Low**

40. *Answer choices:*

(see index for correct answer)

- a. contracting out
- b. IvanAnywhere
- c. VenueGen
- d. Telecommuting

Guidance: level 1

:: Human resource management ::

_____ means increasing the scope of a job through extending the range of its job duties and responsibilities generally within the same level and periphery. _____ involves combining various activities at the same level in the organization and adding them to the existing job. It is also called the horizontal expansion of job activities. This contradicts the principles of specialisation and the division of labour whereby work is divided into small units, each of which is performed repetitively by an individual worker and the responsibilities are always clear. Some motivational theories suggest that the boredom and alienation caused by the division of labour can actually cause efficiency to fall. Thus, _____ seeks to motivate workers through reversing the process of specialisation. A typical approach might be to replace assembly lines with modular work; instead of an employee repeating the same step on each product, they perform several tasks on a single item. In order for employees to be provided with _____ they will need to be retrained in new fields to understand how each field works.

Exam Probability: **Low**

41. *Answer choices:*
(see index for correct answer)

- a. Randstad Holding
- b. Human resource management
- c. Skill mix
- d. Job enlargement

Guidance: level 1

:: Analysis ::

_____ is the process of breaking a complex topic or substance into smaller parts in order to gain a better understanding of it. The technique has been applied in the study of mathematics and logic since before Aristotle, though _____ as a formal concept is a relatively recent development.

Exam Probability: **Low**

42. *Answer choices:*

(see index for correct answer)

- a. Analysis
- b. SWOQe
- c. Deviation analysis
- d. Analytical quality control

Guidance: level 1

:: Organizational behavior ::

_____ is the act of matching attitudes, beliefs, and behaviors to group norms or politics. Norms are implicit, specific rules, shared by a group of individuals, that guide their interactions with others. People often choose to conform to society rather than to pursue personal desires because it is often easier to follow the path others have made already, rather than creating a new one. This tendency to conform occurs in small groups and/or society as a whole, and may result from subtle unconscious influences , or direct and overt social pressure. _____ can occur in the presence of others, or when an individual is alone. For example, people tend to follow social norms when eating or watching television, even when alone.

Exam Probability: **Low**

43. *Answer choices:*
(see index for correct answer)

- a. Organizational behavior management
- b. Group behaviour
- c. Conformity
- d. Micro-initiative

Guidance: level 1

:: Management education ::

_____ is the implementation of government policy and also an academic discipline that studies this implementation and prepares civil servants for working in the public service. As a "field of inquiry with a diverse scope" whose fundamental goal is to "advance management and policies so that government can function". Some of the various definitions which have been offered for the term are: "the management of public programs"; the "translation of politics into the reality that citizens see every day"; and "the study of government decision making, the analysis of the policies themselves, the various inputs that have produced them, and the inputs necessary to produce alternative policies."

Exam Probability: **Low**

44. *Answer choices:*

(see index for correct answer)

- a. Open management education
- b. EABIS
- c. Human systems engineering
- d. Business simulation

Guidance: level 1

:: Sexual harassment in the United States ::

In law, a _____, reasonable man, or the man on the Clapham omnibus is a hypothetical person of legal fiction crafted by the courts and communicated through case law and jury instructions.

Exam Probability: **Medium**

45. *Answer choices:*

(see index for correct answer)

- a. Reasonable person
- b. War Zone
- c. Sandy Gallin
- d. Charol Shakeshaft

Guidance: level 1

:: Employment of foreign-born ::

_____ refers to the international labor pool of workers, including those employed by multinational companies and connected through a global system of networking and production, immigrant workers, transient migrant workers, telecommuting workers, those in export-oriented employment, contingent work or other precarious employment. As of 2012, the global labor pool consisted of approximately 3 billion workers, around 200 million unemployed.

Exam Probability: **Low**

46. *Answer choices:*

(see index for correct answer)

- a. Global workforce
- b. H-2B visa

- c. Human capital flight
- d. Foreign born

Guidance: level 1

:: Business ethics ::

A _____ is a person who exposes any kind of information or activity that is deemed illegal, unethical, or not correct within an organization that is either private or public. The information of alleged wrongdoing can be classified in many ways: violation of company policy/rules, law, regulation, or threat to public interest/national security, as well as fraud, and corruption. Those who become _____ s can choose to bring information or allegations to surface either internally or externally. Internally, a _____ can bring his/her accusations to the attention of other people within the accused organization such as an immediate supervisor. Externally, a _____ can bring allegations to light by contacting a third party outside of an accused organization such as the media, government, law enforcement, or those who are concerned. _____ s, however, take the risk of facing stiff reprisal and retaliation from those who are accused or alleged of wrongdoing.

Exam Probability: **Medium**

47. *Answer choices:*

(see index for correct answer)

- a. Center for Adult Development
- b. Interfaith Center on Corporate Responsibility
- c. Sustainability Accounting Standards Board
- d. CUC International

Guidance: level 1

:: Human resource management ::

_____ is athletic training in sports other than the athlete's usual sport. The goal is improving overall performance. It takes advantage of the particular effectiveness of one training method to negate the shortcomings of another.

Exam Probability: **High**

48. *Answer choices:*

(see index for correct answer)

- a. Fresh tracks
- b. Simultaneous recruiting of new graduates
- c. Reward management
- d. Cross-functional team

Guidance: level 1

:: Human resource management ::

A _____ is a group of people with different functional expertise working toward a common goal. It may include people from finance, marketing, operations, and human resources departments. Typically, it includes employees from all levels of an organization. Members may also come from outside an organization .

Exam Probability: **Medium**

49. *Answer choices:*

(see index for correct answer)

- a. Cross-functional team
- b. Voluntary redundancy
- c. Human relations movement
- d. Leadership development

Guidance: level 1

:: Human resource management ::

_____ is an institutional process that maximizes performance levels and competency for an organization. The process includes all the activities needed to maintain a productive workforce, such as field service management, human resource management, performance and training management, data collection, recruiting, budgeting, forecasting, scheduling and analytics.

Exam Probability: **High**

50. *Answer choices:*

(see index for correct answer)

- a. Performance domain
- b. Workforce management
- c. Workplace mentoring
- d. Broadbanding

Guidance: level 1

:: Labour law ::

A _____ is a legal contract that is meant to limit the liability of an employer whose employees are romantically involved. An employer may choose to require a _____ when a romantic relationship within the company becomes known, in order to indemnify the company in case the employees' romantic relationship fails, primarily so that one party can't bring a sexual harassment lawsuit against the company. To that end, the _____ states that the relationship is consensual, and both parties of the relationship must sign it. The _____ may also stipulate rules for acceptable romantic behavior in the workplace.

Exam Probability: **Low**

51. *Answer choices:*

(see index for correct answer)

- a. Undue hardship
- b. Conditional dismissal

- c. Love contract
- d. Bharat Forge Co Ltd v Uttam Manohar Nakate

Guidance: level 1

:: ::

_____ involves the development of an action plan designed to motivate and guide a person or group toward a goal. _____ can be guided by goal-setting criteria such as SMART criteria. _____ is a major component of personal-development and management literature.

Exam Probability: **Medium**

52. *Answer choices:*

(see index for correct answer)

- a. corporate values
- b. interpersonal communication
- c. personal values
- d. Goal setting

Guidance: level 1

:: United States employment discrimination case law ::

_____ , 641 F.2d 934 , was a D.C. Circuit opinion, written by Judge Skelly Wright, that held that workplace sexual harassment could constitute employment discrimination under the Civil Rights Act of 1964.

Exam Probability: **Low**

53. *Answer choices:*

(see index for correct answer)

- a. Bundy v. Jackson
- b. Shyamala Rajender v. University of Minnesota
- c. Glenn v. Brumby
- d. Price Waterhouse v. Hopkins

Guidance: level 1

:: Bankruptcy ::

_____ is the concept of a person or group of people taking precedence over another person or group because the former is either older than the latter or has occupied a particular position longer than the latter. _____ is present between parents and children and may be present in other common relationships, such as among siblings of different ages or between workers and their managers.

Exam Probability: **High**

54. Answer choices:

(see index for correct answer)

- a. Seniority
- b. Pre-packaged insolvency
- c. Enforcement of foreign judgments
- d. Insolvency Service

Guidance: level 1

:: Human resource management ::

_____ is the application of information technology for both networking and supporting at least two individual or collective actors in their shared performing of HR activities.

Exam Probability: **Low**

55. Answer choices:

(see index for correct answer)

- a. The war for talent
- b. Salary
- c. Resource-based view
- d. TPI-theory

Guidance: level 1

:: Business law ::

A pre-entry _____ is a form of union security agreement under which the employer agrees to hire union members only, and employees must remain members of the union at all times in order to remain employed. This is different from a post-entry _____ , which is an agreement requiring all employees to join the union if they are not already members. In a union shop, the union must accept as a member any person hired by the employer.

Exam Probability: **High**

56. *Answer choices:*

(see index for correct answer)

- a. Enhanced use lease
- b. Starting a Business Index
- c. Managed service company
- d. Secret rebate

Guidance: level 1

:: Management ::

In business, a _____ is the attribute that allows an organization to outperform its competitors. A _____ may include access to natural resources, such as high-grade ores or a low-cost power source, highly skilled labor, geographic location, high entry barriers, and access to new technology.

Exam Probability: **Medium**

57. *Answer choices:*

(see index for correct answer)

- a. Infrastructure asset management
- b. Main Street Manager
- c. IT performance management
- d. Competitive advantage

Guidance: level 1

:: Survey methodology ::

A _____ is the procedure of systematically acquiring and recording information about the members of a given population. The term is used mostly in connection with national population and housing _____ es; other common _____ es include agriculture, business, and traffic _____ es. The United Nations defines the essential features of population and housing _____ es as "individual enumeration, universality within a defined territory, simultaneity and defined periodicity", and recommends that population _____ es be taken at least every 10 years. United Nations recommendations also cover _____ topics to be collected, official definitions, classifications and other useful information to co-ordinate international practice.

Exam Probability: **Low**

58. *Answer choices:*

(see index for correct answer)

- a. Census
- b. Group concept mapping
- c. Scale analysis
- d. American Association for Public Opinion Research

Guidance: level 1

:: Employment compensation ::

An _____ is an employee benefit program that assists employees with personal problems and/or work-related problems that may impact their job performance, health, mental and emotional well-being. EAPs generally offer free and confidential assessments, short-term counseling, referrals, and follow-up services for employees and their household members. EAP counselors also work in a consultative role with managers and supervisors to address employee and organizational challenges and needs. Many corporations, academic institution and/or government agencies are active in helping organizations prevent and cope with workplace violence, trauma, and other emergency response situations. There is a variety of support programs offered for employees. Even though EAPs are mainly aimed at work-related problems, there are a variety of programs that can assist with problems outside of the workplace. EAPs have grown over the years, and are more desirable economically and socially.

Exam Probability: **High**

59. *Answer choices:*

(see index for correct answer)

- a. Agency Workers Regulations 2010
- b. Salary cap
- c. Cafeteria plan
- d. Corporate child care

Guidance: level 1

Information systems

Information systems (IS) are formal, sociotechnical, organizational systems designed to collect, process, store, and distribute information. In a sociotechnical perspective Information Systems are composed by four components: technology, process, people and organizational structure.

:: Computing input devices ::

In computing, an _____ is a piece of computer hardware equipment used to provide data and control signals to an information processing system such as a computer or information appliance. Examples of _____ s include keyboards, mouse, scanners, digital cameras and joysticks. Audio _____ s may be used for purposes including speech recognition. Many companies are utilizing speech recognition to help assist users to use their device.

Exam Probability: **Medium**

1. *Answer choices:*

(see index for correct answer)

- a. Film scanner
- b. Griffin PowerMate
- c. Input device
- d. Motion capture

Guidance: level 1

:: Information systems ::

An _____ , or a group of such silos, is an insular management system in which one information system or subsystem is incapable of reciprocal operation with others that are, or should be, related. Thus information is not adequately shared but rather remains sequestered within each system or subsystem, figuratively trapped within a container like grain is trapped within a silo: there may be a lot of it, and it may be stacked quite high and freely available within those limits, but it has no effect outside those limits. Such data silos are proving to be an obstacle for businesses wishing to use data mining to make productive use of their data.

Exam Probability: **Medium**

2. *Answer choices:*

(see index for correct answer)

- a. UK Academy for Information Systems
- b. Self-service software vendors
- c. Information engineering
- d. Information silo

Guidance: level 1

:: Google services ::

A blog is a discussion or informational website published on the World Wide Web consisting of discrete, often informal diary-style text entries . Posts are typically displayed in reverse chronological order, so that the most recent post appears first, at the top of the web page. Until 2009, blogs were usually the work of a single individual, occasionally of a small group, and often covered a single subject or topic. In the 2010s, "multi-author blogs" emerged, featuring the writing of multiple authors and sometimes professionally edited. MABs from newspapers, other media outlets, universities, think tanks, advocacy groups, and similar institutions account for an increasing quantity of blog traffic. The rise of Twitter and other "microblogging" systems helps integrate MABs and single-author blogs into the news media. Blog can also be used as a verb, meaning to maintain or add content to a blog.

Exam Probability: **High**

3. *Answer choices:*

(see index for correct answer)

- a. Blogger
- b. Google Flights

- c. Google Translator Toolkit
- d. Google Takeout

Guidance: level 1

:: Cloud storage ::

_____ was an online backup service for both Windows and macOS users. Linux support was made available in Q3, 2014. In 2007 _____ was acquired by EMC, and in 2013 _____ was included in the EMC Backup Recovery Systems division's product list. On September 7, 2016, Dell Inc. acquired EMC Corporation to form Dell Technologies, restructuring the original Dell Inc. as a subsidiary of Dell Technologies.. On March 19, 2018 Carbonite acquired _____ from Dell for $148.5 million in cash and in 2019 shut down the service, incorporating _____ 's clients into its own online backup service programs.

Exam Probability: **Medium**

4. *Answer choices:*
(see index for correct answer)

- a. HP Cloud
- b. Mozy
- c. Gluster
- d. Windows Live Devices

Guidance: level 1

:: Human–machine interaction ::

In electrical engineering, a _____ is an electrical component that can "make" or "break" an electrical circuit, interrupting the current or diverting it from one conductor to another. The mechanism of a _____ removes or restores the conducting path in a circuit when it is operated. It may be operated manually, for example, a light _____ or a keyboard button, may be operated by a moving object such as a door, or may be operated by some sensing element for pressure, temperature or flow. A _____ will have one or more sets of contacts, which may operate simultaneously, sequentially, or alternately. _____ es in high-powered circuits must operate rapidly to prevent destructive arcing, and may include special features to assist in rapidly interrupting a heavy current. Multiple forms of actuators are used for operation by hand or to sense position, level, temperature or flow. Special types are used, for example, for control of machinery, to reverse electric motors, or to sense liquid level. Many specialized forms exist. A common use is control of lighting, where multiple _____ es may be wired into one circuit to allow convenient control of light fixtures.

Exam Probability: **High**

5. *Answer choices:*
(see index for correct answer)

- a. Pistol grip
- b. Key
- c. Grip
- d. Switch

Guidance: level 1

A _____ is a research instrument consisting of a series of questions for the purpose of gathering information from respondents. The _____ was invented by the Statistical Society of London in 1838.

Exam Probability: **Low**

6. *Answer choices:*

(see index for correct answer)

- a. open system
- b. information systems assessment
- c. surface-level diversity
- d. Questionnaire

Guidance: level 1

Sustainability is the process of people maintaining change in a balanced environment, in which the exploitation of resources, the direction of investments, the orientation of technological development and institutional change are all in harmony and enhance both current and future potential to meet human needs and aspirations. For many in the field, sustainability is defined through the following interconnected domains or pillars: environment, economic and social, which according to Fritjof Capra is based on the principles of Systems Thinking. Sub-domains of _____ development have been considered also: cultural, technological and political. While _____ development may be the organizing principle for sustainability for some, for others, the two terms are paradoxical . _____ development is the development that meets the needs of the present without compromising the ability of future generations to meet their own needs. Brundtland Report for the World Commission on Environment and Development introduced the term of _____ development.

Exam Probability: **Low**

7. *Answer choices:*

(see index for correct answer)

- a. deep-level diversity
- b. similarity-attraction theory
- c. Sustainable
- d. process perspective

Guidance: level 1

:: Systems theory ::

A _____ is a group of interacting or interrelated entities that form a unified whole. A _____ is delineated by its spatial and temporal boundaries, surrounded and influenced by its environment, described by its structure and purpose and expressed in its functioning.

Exam Probability: **Low**

8. *Answer choices:*

(see index for correct answer)

- a. process system
- b. steady state
- c. management system
- d. subsystem

Guidance: level 1

:: ::

_____ Holdings, Inc. is an American company operating a worldwide online payments system that supports online money transfers and serves as an electronic alternative to traditional paper methods like checks and money orders. The company operates as a payment processor for online vendors, auction sites, and many other commercial users, for which it charges a fee in exchange for benefits such as one-click transactions and password memory. _____'s payment system, also called _____, is considered a type of payment rail.

Exam Probability: **Low**

9. Answer choices:

(see index for correct answer)

- a. imperative
- b. PayPal
- c. empathy
- d. corporate values

Guidance: level 1

:: Sensitivity analysis ::

_____ is the study of how the uncertainty in the output of a mathematical model or system can be divided and allocated to different sources of uncertainty in its inputs. A related practice is uncertainty analysis, which has a greater focus on uncertainty quantification and propagation of uncertainty; ideally, uncertainty and _____ should be run in tandem.

Exam Probability: **Medium**

10. Answer choices:

(see index for correct answer)

- a. Elementary effects method
- b. Tornado diagram
- c. Variance-based sensitivity analysis
- d. Sensitivity analysis

Guidance: level 1

:: Monopoly (economics) ::

A _____ exists when a specific person or enterprise is the only supplier of a particular commodity. This contrasts with a monopsony which relates to a single entity's control of a market to purchase a good or service, and with oligopoly which consists of a few sellers dominating a market. Monopolies are thus characterized by a lack of economic competition to produce the good or service, a lack of viable substitute goods, and the possibility of a high _____ price well above the seller's marginal cost that leads to a high _____ profit. The verb monopolise or monopolize refers to the process by which a company gains the ability to raise prices or exclude competitors. In economics, a _____ is a single seller. In law, a _____ is a business entity that has significant market power, that is, the power to charge overly high prices. Although monopolies may be big businesses, size is not a characteristic of a _____. A small business may still have the power to raise prices in a small industry.

Exam Probability: **High**

11. *Answer choices:*
(see index for correct answer)

- a. History of monopoly
- b. Monopoly
- c. Complementary monopoly
- d. Concentration ratio

Guidance: level 1

:: ::

A _____ is a knowledge base website on which users collaboratively modify content and structure directly from the web browser. In a typical _____ , text is written using a simplified markup language and often edited with the help of a rich-text editor.

Exam Probability: **Medium**

12. *Answer choices:*

(see index for correct answer)

- a. co-culture
- b. empathy
- c. process perspective
- d. corporate values

Guidance: level 1

:: E-commerce ::

Electronic governance or e-governance is the application of information and communication technology for delivering government services, exchange of information, communication transactions, integration of various stand-alone systems and services between _____ , government-to-business , government-to-government , government-to-employees as well as back-office processes and interactions within the entire government framework. Through e-governance, government services are made available to citizens in a convenient, efficient, and transparent manner. The three main target groups that can be distinguished in governance concepts are government, citizens, andbusinesses/interest groups. In e-governance, there are no distinct boundaries.

Exam Probability: **Low**

13. *Answer choices:*

(see index for correct answer)

- a. TRANZ 330
- b. Rising Tide Studios
- c. Government-to-citizen
- d. Associate-O-Matic

Guidance: level 1

:: Marketing ::

_____ is a business model in which consumers create value and businesses consume that value. For example, when a consumer writes reviews or when a consumer gives a useful idea for new product development then that consumer is creating value for the business if the business adopts the input.
In the C2B model, a reverse auction or demand collection model, enables buyers to name or demand their own price, which is often binding, for a specific good or service. Inside of a consumer to business market the roles involved in the transaction must be established and the consumer must offer something of value to the business.

Exam Probability: **High**

14. *Answer choices:*

(see index for correct answer)

- a. Landing page
- b. Consumer-to-business
- c. Industrial marketing
- d. Buy one, get one free

Guidance: level 1

:: Google services ::

_____ is a discontinued image organizer and image viewer for organizing and editing digital photos, plus an integrated photo-sharing website, originally created by a company named Lifescape in 2002. In July 2004, Google acquired _____ from Lifescape and began offering it as freeware. "_____" is a blend of the name of Spanish painter Pablo Picasso, the phrase mi casa and "pic" for pictures.

Exam Probability: **Medium**

15. *Answer choices:*

(see index for correct answer)

- a. Google Apps Script
- b. App Inventor for Android
- c. Google Translate
- d. Picasa

Guidance: level 1

:: Policy ::

A _____ is a statement or a legal document that discloses some or all of the ways a party gathers, uses, discloses, and manages a customer or client's data. It fulfills a legal requirement to protect a customer or client's privacy. Personal information can be anything that can be used to identify an individual, not limited to the person's name, address, date of birth, marital status, contact information, ID issue, and expiry date, financial records, credit information, medical history, where one travels, and intentions to acquire goods and services. In the case of a business it is often a statement that declares a party's policy on how it collects, stores, and releases personal information it collects. It informs the client what specific information is collected, and whether it is kept confidential, shared with partners, or sold to other firms or enterprises. Privacy policies typically represent a broader, more generalized treatment, as opposed to data use statements, which tend to be more detailed and specific.

Exam Probability: **Medium**

16. *Answer choices:*

(see index for correct answer)

- a. Policy studies
- b. Privacy policy
- c. Multifunctionality in agriculture
- d. Policy Monitoring

Guidance: level 1

:: Information systems ::

_____ are formal, sociotechnical, organizational systems designed to collect, process, store, and distribute information. In a sociotechnical perspective, _____ are composed by four components: task, people, structure, and technology.

Exam Probability: **Medium**

17. *Answer choices:*

(see index for correct answer)

- a. Digital firm
- b. Information systems
- c. Mi-Case
- d. Personal knowledge management

Guidance: level 1

:: Computer access control ::

_____ is the act of confirming the truth of an attribute of a single piece of data claimed true by an entity. In contrast with identification, which refers to the act of stating or otherwise indicating a claim purportedly attesting to a person or thing's identity, _____ is the process of actually confirming that identity. It might involve confirming the identity of a person by validating their identity documents, verifying the authenticity of a website with a digital certificate, determining the age of an artifact by carbon dating, or ensuring that a product is what its packaging and labeling claim to be. In other words, _____ often involves verifying the validity of at least one form of identification.

Exam Probability: **Low**

18. *Answer choices:*

(see index for correct answer)

- a. HTTP cookie
- b. Software token
- c. Authentication
- d. Mobilegov

Guidance: level 1

:: Business models ::

_____ , a portmanteau of the words "free" and "premium", is a pricing strategy by which a product or service is provided free of charge, but money is charged for additional features, services, or virtual or physical goods. The business model has been in use by the software industry since the 1980s as a licensing scheme. A subset of this model used by the video game industry is called free-to-play.

Exam Probability: **Medium**

19. *Answer choices:*

(see index for correct answer)

- a. Copy to China
- b. Lawyers on Demand

- c. Entreship
- d. Co-operative Wholesale Society

Guidance: level 1

:: Business process ::

_____ is a discipline in operations management in which people use various methods to discover, model, analyze, measure, improve, optimize, and automate business processes. BPM focuses on improving corporate performance by managing business processes. Any combination of methods used to manage a company's business processes is BPM. Processes can be structured and repeatable or unstructured and variable. Though not required, enabling technologies are often used with BPM.

Exam Probability: **Medium**

20. *Answer choices:*
(see index for correct answer)

- a. Desktop outsourcing
- b. Business process management
- c. Bizagi
- d. Knowledge process outsourcing

Guidance: level 1

:: Data analysis ::

_____, also referred to as text data mining, roughly equivalent to text analytics, is the process of deriving high-quality information from text. High-quality information is typically derived through the devising of patterns and trends through means such as statistical pattern learning. _____ usually involves the process of structuring the input text , deriving patterns within the structured data, and finally evaluation and interpretation of the output. 'High quality' in _____ usually refers to some combination of relevance, novelty, and interest. Typical _____ tasks include text categorization, text clustering, concept/entity extraction, production of granular taxonomies, sentiment analysis, document summarization, and entity relation modeling .

Exam Probability: **Low**

21. *Answer choices:*

(see index for correct answer)

- a. Lulu smoothing
- b. Synqera
- c. Text mining
- d. Limited dependent variable

Guidance: level 1

:: Data management ::

In computing, a _____, also known as an enterprise _____, is a system used for reporting and data analysis, and is considered a core component of business intelligence. DWs are central repositories of integrated data from one or more disparate sources. They store current and historical data in one single place that are used for creating analytical reports for workers throughout the enterprise.

Exam Probability: **High**

22. *Answer choices:*

(see index for correct answer)

- a. SQL/PSM
- b. Automatic data processing equipment
- c. Metadirectory
- d. Data warehouse

Guidance: level 1

:: Internet advertising ::

_____ is software that aims to gather information about a person or organization, sometimes without their knowledge, that may send such information to another entity without the consumer's consent, that asserts control over a device without the consumer's knowledge, or it may send such information to another entity with the consumer's consent, through cookies.

Exam Probability: **High**

23. Answer choices:

(see index for correct answer)

- a. Spyware
- b. Digital marketing engineer
- c. Domain name speculation
- d. Ad rotation

Guidance: level 1

:: Asset ::

In financial accounting, an _____ is any resource owned by the business. Anything tangible or intangible that can be owned or controlled to produce value and that is held by a company to produce positive economic value is an _____ . Simply stated, _____ s represent value of ownership that can be converted into cash . The balance sheet of a firm records the monetary value of the _____ s owned by that firm. It covers money and other valuables belonging to an individual or to a business.

Exam Probability: **Medium**

24. Answer choices:

(see index for correct answer)

- a. Asset
- b. Fixed asset

Guidance: level 1

:: History of human–computer interaction ::

_____ is a line of motion sensing input devices produced by Microsoft. Initially, the _____ was developed as a gaming accessory for Xbox 360 and Xbox One video game consoles and Microsoft Windows PCs. Based around a webcam-style add-on peripheral, it enabled users to control and interact with their console/computer without the need for a game controller, through a natural user interface using gestures and spoken commands. While the gaming line did not gain much traction and eventually discontinued, third-party developers and researches found several after-market uses for _____ 's advanced low-cost sensor features, leading Microsoft to drive the product line towards more application-neutral uses, including integrating the device with Microsoft's cloud computing platform Azure.

Exam Probability: **High**

25. *Answer choices:*

(see index for correct answer)

- a. Kinect
- b. IBM 3270
- c. Trackball
- d. IRCF360

Guidance: level 1

:: Payment systems ::

_____ s are part of a payment system issued by financial institutions, such as a bank, to a customer that enables its owner to access the funds in the customer's designated bank accounts, or through a credit account and make payments by electronic funds transfer and access automated teller machines .
Such cards are known by a variety of names including bank cards, ATM cards, MAC , client cards, key cards or cash cards.

Exam Probability: **Medium**

26. *Answer choices:*

(see index for correct answer)

- a. Chase Paymentech
- b. CyberCash, Inc.
- c. Bad check restitution program
- d. Argentum album

Guidance: level 1

:: Information technology ::

_____ is the use of computers to store, retrieve, transmit, and manipulate data, or information, often in the context of a business or other enterprise. IT is considered to be a subset of information and communications technology. An _____ system is generally an information system, a communications system or, more specifically speaking, a computer system – including all hardware, software and peripheral equipment – operated by a limited group of users.

Exam Probability: **Low**

27. *Answer choices:*

(see index for correct answer)

- a. Henry Bakis
- b. Information Technology Institute
- c. Software-defined storage
- d. Enumerate

Guidance: level 1

:: ::

_____ LLC is an American multinational technology company that specializes in Internet-related services and products, which include online advertising technologies, search engine, cloud computing, software, and hardware. It is considered one of the Big Four technology companies, alongside Amazon, Apple and Facebook.

Exam Probability: **Low**

28. *Answer choices:*

(see index for correct answer)

- a. interpersonal communication
- b. functional perspective
- c. Google
- d. Sarbanes-Oxley act of 2002

Guidance: level 1

:: Geographic information systems ::

_____ is the computational process of transforming a physical address description to a location on the Earth's surface. Reverse _____, on the other hand, converts geographic coordinates to a description of a location, usually the name of a place or an addressable location. _____ relies on a computer representation of address points, the street / road network, together with postal and administrative boundaries.

Exam Probability: **Medium**

29. *Answer choices:*

(see index for correct answer)

- a. At-location mapping
- b. Toponym Resolution

- c. Geocoding
- d. Android Tactical Assault Kit

Guidance: level 1

:: E-commerce ::

_____ , and its now-deprecated predecessor, Secure Sockets Layer , are cryptographic protocols designed to provide communications security over a computer network. Several versions of the protocols find widespread use in applications such as web browsing, email, instant messaging, and voice over IP . Websites can use TLS to secure all communications between their servers and web browsers.

Exam Probability: **Medium**

30. *Answer choices:*

(see index for correct answer)

- a. Electronic Commerce Directive
- b. GamersGate
- c. Transport Layer Security
- d. Loppi

Guidance: level 1

:: E-commerce ::

A _____ is a plastic payment card that can be used instead of cash when making purchases. It is similar to a credit card, but unlike a credit card, the money is immediately transferred directly from the cardholder's bank account when performing a transaction.

Exam Probability: **High**

31. *Answer choices:*

(see index for correct answer)

- a. Zingiri
- b. Public eProcurement
- c. Maritime E-Commerce Association
- d. Private label rights

Guidance: level 1

:: Industrial design ::

Across the many fields concerned with _____, including information science, computer science, human-computer interaction, communication, and industrial design, there is little agreement over the meaning of the term "_____", although all are related to interaction with computers and other machines with a user interface.

Exam Probability: **Medium**

32. *Answer choices:*

(see index for correct answer)

- a. Sustainable furniture design
- b. Tokujin Yoshioka
- c. Humanscale
- d. Aerospike engine

Guidance: level 1

:: E-commerce ::

_____ is a subset of electronic commerce that involves social media, online media that supports social interaction, and user contributions to assist online buying and selling of products and services.

Exam Probability: **Low**

33. *Answer choices:*

(see index for correct answer)

- a. Feefighters
- b. Wildcard certificate
- c. Social commerce
- d. E-commerce

Guidance: level 1

:: Enterprise architecture ::

Enterprise software, also known as _____ software, is computer software used to satisfy the needs of an organization rather than individual users. Such organizations include businesses, schools, interest-based user groups, clubs, charities, and governments. Enterprise software is an integral part of a information system.

Exam Probability: **High**

34. *Answer choices:*

(see index for correct answer)

- a. Architecture domain
- b. Enterprise application
- c. INgage Networks
- d. Orbus Software

Guidance: level 1

:: Market structure and pricing ::

_____ is a term denoting that a product includes permission to use its source code, design documents, or content. It most commonly refers to the open-source model, in which open-source software or other products are released under an open-source license as part of the open-source-software movement. Use of the term originated with software, but has expanded beyond the software sector to cover other open content and forms of open collaboration.

Exam Probability: **High**

35. *Answer choices:*

(see index for correct answer)

- a. Open source
- b. Liberalization
- c. Market structure
- d. Installed base

Guidance: level 1

:: Product testing ::

_____ is a characteristic of a product or system, whose interfaces are completely understood, to work with other products or systems, at present or in the future, in either implementation or access, without any restrictions.

Exam Probability: **High**

36. *Answer choices:*

(see index for correct answer)

- a. Destructive testing
- b. Beer tasting
- c. Product testing
- d. Interoperability

Guidance: level 1

:: Fault tolerance ::

_____ is the property that enables a system to continue operating properly in the event of the failure of some of its components. If its operating quality decreases at all, the decrease is proportional to the severity of the failure, as compared to a naively designed system, in which even a small failure can cause total breakdown. _____ is particularly sought after in high-availability or life-critical systems. The ability of maintaining functionality when portions of a system break down is referred to as graceful degradation.

Exam Probability: **Low**

37. *Answer choices:*

(see index for correct answer)

- a. Fault tolerance
- b. Dual modular redundancy

- c. Random fault
- d. Fly-by-wire

Guidance: level 1

:: Information technology management ::

_____ concerns a cycle of organizational activity: the acquisition of information from one or more sources, the custodianship and the distribution of that information to those who need it, and its ultimate disposition through archiving or deletion.

Exam Probability: **High**

38. *Answer choices:*
(see index for correct answer)

- a. IQuate
- b. Speech analytics
- c. Microsoft Customer Care Framework
- d. Information management

Guidance: level 1

:: Data management ::

Given organizations' increasing dependency on information technology to run their operations, Business continuity planning covers the entire organization, and Disaster recovery focuses on IT.

Exam Probability: **High**

39. *Answer choices:*

(see index for correct answer)

- a. Ontology merging
- b. Data custodian
- c. Retention period
- d. Disaster recovery plan

Guidance: level 1

:: Web security exploits ::

A _____ is a baked or cooked food that is small, flat and sweet. It usually contains flour, sugar and some type of oil or fat. It may include other ingredients such as raisins, oats, chocolate chips, nuts, etc.

Exam Probability: **Low**

40. *Answer choices:*

(see index for correct answer)

- a. Cookie
- b. Metasploit Project
- c. XML external entity
- d. Reflected DOM Injection

Guidance: level 1

:: Knowledge engineering ::

The _____ is an extension of the World Wide Web through standards by the World Wide Web Consortium. The standards promote common data formats and exchange protocols on the Web, most fundamentally the Resource Description Framework. According to the W3C, "The _____ provides a common framework that allows data to be shared and reused across application, enterprise, and community boundaries". The _____ is therefore regarded as an integrator across different content, information applications and systems.

Exam Probability: **Low**

41. *Answer choices:*

(see index for correct answer)

- a. Artificial architecture
- b. Knowledge Acquisition and Documentation Structuring
- c. Subject-matter expert
- d. Collaborative innovation network

Guidance: level 1

:: Infographics ::

A _____ is a symbolic representation of information according to visualization technique. _____ s have been used since ancient times, but became more prevalent during the Enlightenment. Sometimes, the technique uses a three-dimensional visualization which is then projected onto a two-dimensional surface. The word graph is sometimes used as a synonym for _____ .

Exam Probability: **Medium**

42. *Answer choices:*

(see index for correct answer)

- a. Walam Olum
- b. DOT pictograms
- c. Vis5D
- d. Diagram

Guidance: level 1

:: E-commerce ::

_____ , cybersecurity or information technology security is the protection of computer systems from theft or damage to their hardware, software or electronic data, as well as from disruption or misdirection of the services they provide.

Exam Probability: **Low**

43. *Answer choices:*

(see index for correct answer)

- a. Wanelo
- b. IBill
- c. Multichannel retailing
- d. Computer security

Guidance: level 1

:: Internet governance ::

A _____ is one of the domains at the highest level in the hierarchical Domain Name System of the Internet. The _____ names are installed in the root zone of the name space. For all domains in lower levels, it is the last part of the domain name, that is, the last label of a fully qualified domain name. For example, in the domain name www.example.com, the _____ is com. Responsibility for management of most _____ s is delegated to specific organizations by the Internet Corporation for Assigned Names and Numbers , which operates the Internet Assigned Numbers Authority , and is in charge of maintaining the DNS root zone.

Exam Probability: **High**

44. *Answer choices:*

(see index for correct answer)

- a. PKNIC
- b. Digital citizen
- c. Top-level domain
- d. Domain name registry

Guidance: level 1

:: Information technology management ::

The term _____ is used to refer to periods when a system is unavailable. _____ or outage duration refers to a period of time that a system fails to provide or perform its primary function. Reliability, availability, recovery, and unavailability are related concepts. The unavailability is the proportion of a time-span that a system is unavailable or offline. This is usually a result of the system failing to function because of an unplanned event, or because of routine maintenance.

Exam Probability: **Low**

45. *Answer choices:*

(see index for correct answer)

- a. IT Interaction Model

- b. ESCM-CL
- c. Storage hypervisor
- d. Information management

Guidance: level 1

:: Information systems ::

A _____ manages the creation and modification of digital content. It typically supports multiple users in a collaborative environment.

Exam Probability: **High**

46. *Answer choices:*
(see index for correct answer)

- a. Information filtering system
- b. Self-service software
- c. CGA
- d. Content management system

Guidance: level 1

:: Data quality ::

_____ is the maintenance of, and the assurance of the accuracy and consistency of, data over its entire life-cycle, and is a critical aspect to the design, implementation and usage of any system which stores, processes, or retrieves data. The term is broad in scope and may have widely different meanings depending on the specific context even under the same general umbrella of computing. It is at times used as a proxy term for data quality, while data validation is a pre-requisite for _____ . _____ is the opposite of data corruption. The overall intent of any _____ technique is the same: ensure data is recorded exactly as intended and upon later retrieval, ensure the data is the same as it was when it was originally recorded. In short, _____ aims to prevent unintentional changes to information. _____ is not to be confused with data security, the discipline of protecting data from unauthorized parties.

Exam Probability: **Medium**

47. *Answer choices:*

(see index for correct answer)

- a. Information quality
- b. Data integrity
- c. Data Quality Firewall
- d. Referential integrity

Guidance: level 1

:: Human–computer interaction ::

_____ is a database query language for relational databases. It was devised by Moshé M. Zloof at IBM Research during the mid-1970s, in parallel to the development of SQL. It is the first graphical query language, using visual tables where the user would enter commands, example elements and conditions. Many graphical front-ends for databases use the ideas from QBE today. Originally limited only for the purpose of retrieving data, QBE was later extended to allow other operations, such as inserts, deletes and updates, as well as creation of temporary tables.

Exam Probability: **High**

48. *Answer choices:*

(see index for correct answer)

- a. Query by Example
- b. Bodystorming
- c. Sketch recognition
- d. Computer Graphics International

Guidance: level 1

:: Payment systems ::

_____ is a mobile phone-based money transfer, financing and microfinancing service, launched in 2007 by Vodafone for Safaricom and Vodacom, the largest mobile network operators in Kenya and Tanzania. It has since expanded to Afghanistan, South Africa, India and in 2014 to Romania and in 2015 to Albania. _____ allows users to deposit, withdraw, transfer money and pay for goods and services easily with a mobile device.

Exam Probability: **Low**

49. *Answer choices:*

(see index for correct answer)

- a. Official Payments Corporation
- b. M-Pesa
- c. BIPS
- d. Argentum album

Guidance: level 1

:: Identity management ::

_____ is the ability of an individual or group to seclude themselves, or information about themselves, and thereby express themselves selectively. The boundaries and content of what is considered private differ among cultures and individuals, but share common themes. When something is private to a person, it usually means that something is inherently special or sensitive to them. The domain of _____ partially overlaps with security, which can include the concepts of appropriate use, as well as protection of information. _____ may also take the form of bodily integrity.

Exam Probability: **High**

50. *Answer choices:*

(see index for correct answer)

- a. Oracle Identity Management
- b. Common Indexing Protocol
- c. Privacy
- d. Mobile Signature Roaming

Guidance: level 1

:: Intrusion detection systems ::

An _____ is a device or software application that monitors a network or systems for malicious activity or policy violations. Any malicious activity or violation is typically reported either to an administrator or collected centrally using a security information and event management system. A SIEM system combines outputs from multiple sources, and uses alarm filtering techniques to distinguish malicious activity from false alarms.

Exam Probability: **High**

51. *Answer choices:*

(see index for correct answer)

- a. Intrusion detection system
- b. Boundaries of Security Report
- c. Security Device Event Exchange
- d. Network tap

Guidance: level 1

:: Sound recording ::

_____ is a medium for magnetic recording, made of a thin, magnetizable coating on a long, narrow strip of plastic film. It was developed in Germany in 1928, based on magnetic wire recording. Devices that record and play back audio and video using _____ are tape recorders and video tape recorders respectively. A device that stores computer data on _____ is known as a tape drive.

Exam Probability: **Low**

52. *Answer choices:*

(see index for correct answer)

- a. Experimental Talking Clock
- b. Waterfall plot
- c. Magnetic tape
- d. Home recording

Guidance: level 1

:: Data security ::

In information technology, a _____ , or data _____ , or the process of backing up, refers to the copying into an archive file of computer data that is already in secondary storage—so that it may be used to restore the original after a data loss event. The verb form is "back up", whereas the noun and adjective form is "_____".

Exam Probability: **Low**

53. *Answer choices:*

(see index for correct answer)

- a. Jericho Forum
- b. Backup
- c. Single loss expectancy
- d. Information sensitivity

Guidance: level 1

:: Network analyzers ::

A _____ , meaning "meat eater" , is an organism that derives its energy and nutrient requirements from a diet consisting mainly or exclusively of animal tissue, whether through predation or scavenging. Animals that depend solely on animal flesh for their nutrient requirements are called obligate _____ s while those that also consume non-animal food are called facultative _____ s. Omnivores also consume both animal and non-animal food, and, apart from the more general definition, there is no clearly defined ratio of plant to animal material that would distinguish a facultative _____ from an omnivore. A _____ at the top of the food chain, not preyed upon by other animals, is termed an apex predator.

Exam Probability: **High**

54. *Answer choices:*

(see index for correct answer)

- a. Security Administrator Tool for Analyzing Networks
- b. Nessus
- c. Carnivore
- d. AirSnort

Guidance: level 1

:: Data management ::

_____ is a set of processes and technologies that supports the collection, managing, and publishing of information in any form or medium. When stored and accessed via computers, this information may be more specifically referred to as digital content, or simply as content.

Exam Probability: **High**

55. *Answer choices:*

(see index for correct answer)

- a. Modular serializability
- b. Data migration
- c. Long-lived transaction
- d. Content management

Guidance: level 1

:: E-commerce ::

_____ is the activity of buying or selling of products on online services or over the Internet. Electronic commerce draws on technologies such as mobile commerce, electronic funds transfer, supply chain management, Internet marketing, online transaction processing, electronic data interchange, inventory management systems, and automated data collection systems.

Exam Probability: **Medium**

56. *Answer choices:*

(see index for correct answer)

- a. Spamvertising
- b. GS1 US
- c. Online wallet
- d. The iBridge Network

Guidance: level 1

:: Finance ::

_____ is a financial estimate intended to help buyers and owners determine the direct and indirect costs of a product or system. It is a management accounting concept that can be used in full cost accounting or even ecological economics where it includes social costs.

Exam Probability: **Low**

57. *Answer choices:*

(see index for correct answer)

- a. Day trader
- b. Total cost of ownership
- c. Currency converter
- d. NOPAT

Guidance: level 1

:: Information technology management ::

B2B is often contrasted with business-to-consumer. In B2B commerce, it is often the case that the parties to the relationship have comparable negotiating power, and even when they do not, each party typically involves professional staff and legal counsel in the negotiation of terms, whereas B2C is shaped to a far greater degree by economic implications of information asymmetry. However, within a B2B context, large companies may have many commercial, resource and information advantages over smaller businesses. The United Kingdom government, for example, created the post of Small Business Commissioner under the Enterprise Act 2016 to "enable small businesses to resolve disputes" and "consider complaints by small business suppliers about payment issues with larger businesses that they supply."

Exam Probability: **High**

58. *Answer choices:*

(see index for correct answer)

- a. Business transaction performance
- b. Novo Solutions
- c. Shadow system
- d. IQuate

Guidance: level 1

:: Information technology ::

_____ is the reorientation of product and service designs to focus on the end user as an individual consumer, in contrast with an earlier era of only organization-oriented offerings . Technologies whose first commercialization was at the inter-organization level thus have potential for later _____ . The emergence of the individual consumer as the primary driver of product and service design is most commonly associated with the IT industry, as large business and government organizations dominated the early decades of computer usage and development. Thus the microcomputer revolution, in which electronic computing moved from exclusively enterprise and government use to include personal computing, is a cardinal example of _____ . But many technology-based products, such as calculators and mobile phones, have also had their origins in business markets, and only over time did they become dominated by high-volume consumer usage, as these products commoditized and prices fell. An example of enterprise software that became consumer software is optical character recognition software, which originated with banks and postal systems but eventually became personal productivity software.

Exam Probability: **High**

59. *Answer choices:*

(see index for correct answer)

- a. Digital transformation
- b. ISO/IEC JTC 1/WG 7
- c. Local Government ICT Network
- d. Consumerization

Guidance: level 1

Marketing

Marketing is the study and management of exchange relationships. Marketing is the business process of creating relationships with and satisfying customers. With its focus on the customer, marketing is one of the premier components of business management.

Marketing is defined by the American Marketing Association as "the activity, set of institutions, and processes for creating, communicating, delivering, and exchanging offerings that have value for customers, clients, partners, and society at large."

Market segmentation is the activity of dividing a broad consumer or business market, normally consisting of existing and potential customers, into sub-groups of consumers based on some type of shared characteristics. In dividing or segmenting markets, researchers typically look for common characteristics such as shared needs, common interests, similar lifestyles or even similar demographic profiles. The overall aim of segmentation is to identify high yield segments – that is, those segments that are likely to be the most profitable or that have growth potential – so that these can be selected for special attention .

Exam Probability: **Medium**

1. *Answer choices:*

(see index for correct answer)

- a. levels of analysis
- b. personal values
- c. co-culture
- d. Market segments

Guidance: level 1

:: Data management ::

In computing, a _____ , also known as an enterprise _____ , is a system used for reporting and data analysis, and is considered a core component of business intelligence. DWs are central repositories of integrated data from one or more disparate sources. They store current and historical data in one single place that are used for creating analytical reports for workers throughout the enterprise.

Exam Probability: **Medium**

2. *Answer choices:*

(see index for correct answer)

- a. Atomicity
- b. Data warehouse
- c. Automatic data processing equipment
- d. Data room

Guidance: level 1

:: Data collection ::

A _____ is an utterance which typically functions as a request for information. _____ s can thus be understood as a kind of illocutionary act in the field of pragmatics or as special kinds of propositions in frameworks of formal semantics such as alternative semantics or inquisitive semantics. The information requested is expected to be provided in the form of an answer. _____ s are often conflated with interrogatives, which are the grammatical forms typically used to achieve them. Rhetorical _____ s, for example, are interrogative in form but may not be considered true _____ s as they are not expected to be answered. Conversely, non-interrogative grammatical structures may be considered _____ s as in the case of the imperative sentence "tell me your name".

Exam Probability: **Medium**

3. *Answer choices:*

(see index for correct answer)

- a. Interpellation
- b. Question
- c. Surveylab
- d. Crude Oil Data Exchange

Guidance: level 1

:: ::

In law, a _____ is a coming together of parties to a dispute, to present information in a tribunal, a formal setting with the authority to adjudicate claims or disputes. One form of tribunal is a court. The tribunal, which may occur before a judge, jury, or other designated trier of fact, aims to achieve a resolution to their dispute.

Exam Probability: **Low**

4. *Answer choices:*

(see index for correct answer)

- a. Trial
- b. levels of analysis
- c. hierarchical perspective
- d. deep-level diversity

Guidance: level 1

:: Generally Accepted Accounting Principles ::

Expenditure is an outflow of money to another person or group to pay for an item or service, or for a category of costs. For a tenant, rent is an _____ . For students or parents, tuition is an _____ . Buying food, clothing, furniture or an automobile is often referred to as an _____ . An _____ is a cost that is "paid" or "remitted", usually in exchange for something of value. Something that seems to cost a great deal is "expensive". Something that seems to cost little is "inexpensive". " _____ s of the table" are _____ s of dining, refreshments, a feast, etc.

Exam Probability: **Medium**

5. *Answer choices:*

(see index for correct answer)

- a. Access to finance
- b. Expense
- c. Earnings before interest, taxes and depreciation
- d. Historical cost

Guidance: level 1

:: International trade ::

_____ or globalisation is the process of interaction and integration among people, companies, and governments worldwide. As a complex and multifaceted phenomenon, _____ is considered by some as a form of capitalist expansion which entails the integration of local and national economies into a global, unregulated market economy. _____ has grown due to advances in transportation and communication technology. With the increased global interactions comes the growth of international trade, ideas, and culture. _____ is primarily an economic process of interaction and integration that`s associated with social and cultural aspects. However, conflicts and diplomacy are also large parts of the history of _____ , and modern _____ .

Exam Probability: **High**

6. *Answer choices:*

(see index for correct answer)

- a. Market access
- b. Globalization
- c. Bureau de change
- d. Export-led growth

Guidance: level 1

:: Marketing ::

> _____ is a growth strategy that identifies and develops new market segments for current products. A _____ strategy targets non-buying customers in currently targeted segments. It also targets new customers in new segments.

Exam Probability: **High**

7. *Answer choices:*

(see index for correct answer)

- a. Mandatory labelling
- b. Local store marketing
- c. Market development
- d. National brand

Guidance: level 1

:: ::

_____ is a means of protection from financial loss. It is a form of risk management, primarily used to hedge against the risk of a contingent or uncertain loss

Exam Probability: **Low**

8. *Answer choices:*

(see index for correct answer)

- a. Insurance
- b. open system
- c. Sarbanes-Oxley act of 2002
- d. levels of analysis

Guidance: level 1

:: Business ::

In commerce, _____ is the product of an interaction between an organization and a customer over the duration of their relationship. This interaction is made up of three parts: the customer journey, the brand touchpoints the customer interacts with, and the environments the _____ s during their experience. A good _____ means that the individual's experience during all points of contact matches the individual's expectations. Gartner asserts the importance of managing the customer's experience.

Exam Probability: **Medium**

9. *Answer choices:*

(see index for correct answer)

- a. Business
- b. Retail design
- c. E-lancing
- d. Organizational life cycle

Guidance: level 1

:: Credit cards ::

The _____ Company, also known as Amex, is an American multinational financial services corporation headquartered in Three World Financial Center in New York City. The company was founded in 1850 and is one of the 30 components of the Dow Jones Industrial Average. The company is best known for its charge card, credit card, and traveler's cheque businesses.

Exam Probability: **Medium**

10. *Answer choices:*

(see index for correct answer)

- a. Medi Script
- b. SBI Cards
- c. Centurion Card
- d. American Express

Guidance: level 1

:: ::

In sales, commerce and economics, a _____ is the recipient of a good, service, product or an idea - obtained from a seller, vendor, or supplier via a financial transaction or exchange for money or some other valuable consideration.

Exam Probability: **High**

11. *Answer choices:*

(see index for correct answer)

- a. interpersonal communication
- b. hierarchical perspective
- c. levels of analysis

- d. co-culture

Guidance: level 1

:: ::

In international relations, _____ is – from the perspective of governments – a voluntary transfer of resources from one country to another.

Exam Probability: **Low**

12. *Answer choices:*

(see index for correct answer)

- a. co-culture
- b. process perspective
- c. imperative
- d. corporate values

Guidance: level 1

:: ::

A _____ is a discussion or informational website published on the World Wide Web consisting of discrete, often informal diary-style text entries . Posts are typically displayed in reverse chronological order, so that the most recent post appears first, at the top of the web page. Until 2009, _____ s were usually the work of a single individual, occasionally of a small group, and often covered a single subject or topic. In the 2010s, "multi-author _____ s" emerged, featuring the writing of multiple authors and sometimes professionally edited. MABs from newspapers, other media outlets, universities, think tanks, advocacy groups, and similar institutions account for an increasing quantity of _____ traffic. The rise of Twitter and other "micro _____ ging" systems helps integrate MABs and single-author _____ s into the news media. _____ can also be used as a verb, meaning to maintain or add content to a _____ .

Exam Probability: **Medium**

13. *Answer choices:*

(see index for correct answer)

- a. open system
- b. Blog
- c. imperative
- d. functional perspective

Guidance: level 1

:: ::

_____ is a process whereby a person assumes the parenting of another, usually a child, from that person's biological or legal parent or parents.
Legal _____ s permanently transfers all rights and responsibilities, along with filiation, from the biological parent or parents.

Exam Probability: **Low**

14. *Answer choices:*

(see index for correct answer)

- a. empathy
- b. interpersonal communication
- c. Adoption
- d. cultural

Guidance: level 1

:: ::

_____ refers to a business or organization attempting to acquire goods or services to accomplish its goals. Although there are several organizations that attempt to set standards in the _____ process, processes can vary greatly between organizations. Typically the word "_____" is not used interchangeably with the word "procurement", since procurement typically includes expediting, supplier quality, and transportation and logistics in addition to _____ .

Exam Probability: **Low**

15. *Answer choices:*

(see index for correct answer)

- a. Purchasing
- b. surface-level diversity
- c. interpersonal communication
- d. empathy

Guidance: level 1

:: Reputation management ::

A _____ is an astronomical object consisting of a luminous spheroid of plasma held together by its own gravity. The nearest _____ to Earth is the Sun. Many other _____ s are visible to the naked eye from Earth during the night, appearing as a multitude of fixed luminous points in the sky due to their immense distance from Earth. Historically, the most prominent _____ s were grouped into constellations and asterisms, the brightest of which gained proper names. Astronomers have assembled _____ catalogues that identify the known _____ s and provide standardized stellar designations. However, most of the estimated 300 sextillion _____ s in the Universe are invisible to the naked eye from Earth, including all _____ s outside our galaxy, the Milky Way.

Exam Probability: **Medium**

16. *Answer choices:*

(see index for correct answer)

- a. Whuffie
- b. Sybil attack
- c. Conversocial
- d. Star

Guidance: level 1

:: Management accounting ::

_____ s are costs that change as the quantity of the good or service that a business produces changes. _____ s are the sum of marginal costs over all units produced. They can also be considered normal costs. Fixed costs and _____ s make up the two components of total cost. Direct costs are costs that can easily be associated with a particular cost object. However, not all _____ s are direct costs. For example, variable manufacturing overhead costs are _____ s that are indirect costs, not direct costs. _____ s are sometimes called unit-level costs as they vary with the number of units produced.

Exam Probability: **Low**

17. *Answer choices:*

(see index for correct answer)

- a. Activity-based management
- b. Relevant cost
- c. Bridge life-cycle cost analysis
- d. Cost driver

Guidance: level 1

:: Marketing ::

_____ is a market strategy in which a firm decides to ignore market segment differences and appeal the whole market with one offer or one strategy, which supports the idea of broadcasting a message that will reach the largest number of people possible. Traditionally _____ has focused on radio, television and newspapers as the media used to reach this broad audience. By reaching the largest audience possible, exposure to the product is maximized, and in theory this would directly correlate with a larger number of sales or buys into the product.

Exam Probability: **High**

18. *Answer choices:*
(see index for correct answer)

- a. Mass marketing
- b. Impulse purchase
- c. Customer franchise
- d. Fourth screen

Guidance: level 1

:: ::

The _____ is an agreement signed by Canada, Mexico, and the United States, creating a trilateral trade bloc in North America. The agreement came into force on January 1, 1994, and superseded the 1988 Canada–United States Free Trade Agreement between the United States and Canada. The NAFTA trade bloc is one of the largest trade blocs in the world by gross domestic product.

Exam Probability: **Medium**

19. *Answer choices:*

(see index for correct answer)

- a. surface-level diversity
- b. open system
- c. hierarchical perspective
- d. Sarbanes-Oxley act of 2002

Guidance: level 1

:: ::

In regulatory jurisdictions that provide for it, _____ is a group of laws and organizations designed to ensure the rights of consumers as well as fair trade, competition and accurate information in the marketplace. The laws are designed to prevent the businesses that engage in fraud or specified unfair practices from gaining an advantage over competitors. They may also provides additional protection for those most vulnerable in society. _____ laws are a form of government regulation that aim to protect the rights of consumers. For example, a government may require businesses to disclose detailed information about products—particularly in areas where safety or public health is an issue, such as food.

Exam Probability: **High**

20. *Answer choices:*

(see index for correct answer)

- a. process perspective
- b. Character
- c. hierarchical
- d. personal values

Guidance: level 1

:: ::

An _____ is an area of the production, distribution, or trade, and consumption of goods and services by different agents. Understood in its broadest sense, 'The _____ is defined as a social domain that emphasize the practices, discourses, and material expressions associated with the production, use, and management of resources'. Economic agents can be individuals, businesses, organizations, or governments. Economic transactions occur when two parties agree to the value or price of the transacted good or service, commonly expressed in a certain currency. However, monetary transactions only account for a small part of the economic domain.

Exam Probability: **Low**

21. *Answer choices:*

(see index for correct answer)

- a. corporate values
- b. imperative
- c. process perspective
- d. Sarbanes-Oxley act of 2002

Guidance: level 1

:: Legal terms ::

A _____ is a person who is called upon to issue a response to a communication made by another. The term is used in legal contexts, in survey methodology, and in psychological conditioning.

Exam Probability: **Medium**

22. *Answer choices:*

(see index for correct answer)

- a. Respondent
- b. Injunction
- c. Legal district
- d. Collateral estoppel

Guidance: level 1

:: Marketing ::

_____ , in marketing, manufacturing, call centres and management, is the use of flexible computer-aided manufacturing systems to produce custom output. Such systems combine the low unit costs of mass production processes with the flexibility of individual customization.

Exam Probability: **High**

23. *Answer choices:*

(see index for correct answer)

- a. Free Comic Book Day
- b. Electronic money
- c. Postmodern communication

- d. Inbound marketing

Guidance: level 1

:: Logistics ::

_____ is generally the detailed organization and implementation of a complex operation. In a general business sense, _____ is the management of the flow of things between the point of origin and the point of consumption in order to meet requirements of customers or corporations. The resources managed in _____ may include tangible goods such as materials, equipment, and supplies, as well as food and other consumable items. The _____ of physical items usually involves the integration of information flow, materials handling, production, packaging, inventory, transportation, warehousing, and often security.

Exam Probability: **Low**

24. *Answer choices:*

(see index for correct answer)

- a. Terminal Operating System
- b. Medical logistics
- c. ISO/IEC 18000-3
- d. Logistics

Guidance: level 1

:: Industry ::

_____ describes various measures of the efficiency of production. Often, a _____ measure is expressed as the ratio of an aggregate output to a single input or an aggregate input used in a production process, i.e. output per unit of input. Most common example is the labour _____ measure, e.g., such as GDP per worker. There are many different definitions of _____ and the choice among them depends on the purpose of the _____ measurement and/or data availability. The key source of difference between various _____ measures is also usually related to how the outputs and the inputs are aggregated into scalars to obtain such a ratio-type measure of _____ .

Exam Probability: **Low**

25. *Answer choices:*
(see index for correct answer)

- a. Recommended exposure limit
- b. Thomson Reuters Business Classification
- c. Productivity
- d. Metalworking

Guidance: level 1

:: Supply chain management ::

_____ is the removal of intermediaries in economics from a supply chain, or cutting out the middlemen in connection with a transaction or a series of transactions. Instead of going through traditional distribution channels, which had some type of intermediary, companies may now deal with customers directly, for example via the Internet. Hence, the use of factory direct and direct from the factory to mean the same thing.

Exam Probability: **Medium**

26. *Answer choices:*

(see index for correct answer)

- a. Retalix
- b. Disintermediation
- c. Design for logistics
- d. TXT e-solutions

Guidance: level 1

:: Organizational structure ::

An _____ defines how activities such as task allocation, coordination, and supervision are directed toward the achievement of organizational aims.

Exam Probability: **High**

27. *Answer choices:*

(see index for correct answer)

- a. Organization of the New York City Police Department
- b. The Starfish and the Spider
- c. Automated Bureaucracy
- d. Followership

Guidance: level 1

:: Production and manufacturing ::

_____ consists of organization-wide efforts to "install and make permanent climate where employees continuously improve their ability to provide on demand products and services that customers will find of particular value." "Total" emphasizes that departments in addition to production are obligated to improve their operations; "management" emphasizes that executives are obligated to actively manage quality through funding, training, staffing, and goal setting. While there is no widely agreed-upon approach, TQM efforts typically draw heavily on the previously developed tools and techniques of quality control. TQM enjoyed widespread attention during the late 1980s and early 1990s before being overshadowed by ISO 9000, Lean manufacturing, and Six Sigma.

Exam Probability: **High**

28. *Answer choices:*
(see index for correct answer)

- a. Positive recall
- b. Total Quality Management

- c. Woodworking machine
- d. Wireless DNC

Guidance: level 1

:: Library science ::

_____ refers to data which is collected by someone who is someone other than the user. Common sources of _____ for social science include censuses, information collected by government departments, organizational records and data that was originally collected for other research purposes. Primary data, by contrast, are collected by the investigator conducting the research.

Exam Probability: **Medium**

29. *Answer choices:*

(see index for correct answer)

- a. Secondary data
- b. Preservation of meaning
- c. Frances E. Henne
- d. Library

Guidance: level 1

:: Marketing ::

_____ is the marketing of products that are presumed to be environmentally safe. It incorporates a broad range of activities, including product modification, changes to the production process, sustainable packaging, as well as modifying advertising. Yet defining _____ is not a simple task where several meanings intersect and contradict each other; an example of this will be the existence of varying social, environmental and retail definitions attached to this term. Other similar terms used are environmental marketing and ecological marketing.

Exam Probability: **Medium**

30. *Answer choices:*

(see index for correct answer)

- a. Bass diffusion model
- b. Existing visitor optimisation
- c. Online ethnography
- d. Product marketing

Guidance: level 1

:: Marketing ::

_____ or stock is the goods and materials that a business holds for the ultimate goal of resale.

Exam Probability: **Medium**

31. *Answer choices:*

(see index for correct answer)

- a. Audience segmentation
- b. Enterprise marketing management
- c. Inventory
- d. Demand signal repository

Guidance: level 1

:: Manufacturing ::

A _____ is a building for storing goods. _____s are used by manufacturers, importers, exporters, wholesalers, transport businesses, customs, etc. They are usually large plain buildings in industrial parks on the outskirts of cities, towns or villages.

Exam Probability: **High**

32. *Answer choices:*

(see index for correct answer)

- a. Nails
- b. Warehouse
- c. Closed loop manufacturing
- d. Factory tour

Guidance: level 1

:: Direct selling ::

_____ consists of two main business models: single-level marketing, in which a direct seller makes money by buying products from a parent organization and selling them directly to customers, and multi-level marketing , in which the direct seller may earn money from both direct sales to customers and by sponsoring new direct sellers and potentially earning a commission from their efforts.

Exam Probability: **High**

33. *Answer choices:*

(see index for correct answer)

- a. Direct selling
- b. The Longaberger Company
- c. Direct Selling Association
- d. Direct Selling News

Guidance: level 1

:: ::

_____ is the process whereby a business sets the price at which it will sell its products and services, and may be part of the business's marketing plan. In setting prices, the business will take into account the price at which it could acquire the goods, the manufacturing cost, the market place, competition, market condition, brand, and quality of product.

Exam Probability: **High**

34. *Answer choices:*

(see index for correct answer)

- a. Pricing
- b. co-culture
- c. cultural
- d. hierarchical

Guidance: level 1

:: Brand management ::

_____ is defined as positive feelings towards a brand and dedication to purchase the same product or service repeatedly now and in the future from the same brand, regardless of a competitor's actions or changes in the environment. It can also be demonstrated with other behaviors such as positive word-of-mouth advocacy. _____ is where an individual buys products from the same manufacturer repeatedly rather than from other suppliers. Businesses whose financial and ethical values, for example ESG responsibilities, rest in large part on their _____ are said to use the loyalty business model.

Exam Probability: **Low**

35. *Answer choices:*

(see index for correct answer)

- a. Brand loyalty
- b. MoonScoop Group
- c. Brand legacy
- d. Entertainment Rights

Guidance: level 1

:: ::

Distribution is one of the four elements of the marketing mix. Distribution is the process of making a product or service available for the consumer or business user who needs it. This can be done directly by the producer or service provider, or using indirect channels with distributors or intermediaries. The other three elements of the marketing mix are product, pricing, and promotion.

Exam Probability: **High**

36. *Answer choices:*

(see index for correct answer)

- a. similarity-attraction theory
- b. surface-level diversity

- c. Sarbanes-Oxley act of 2002
- d. open system

Guidance: level 1

:: Management ::

A _____ is a comprehensive document or blueprint that outlines the advertising and marketing efforts for the coming year. It describes business activities involved in accomplishing specific marketing objectives within a set time frame. A _____ also includes a description of the current marketing position of a business, a discussion of the target market and a description of the marketing mix that a business will use to achieve their marketing goals. A _____ has a formal structure, but can be used as a formal or informal document which makes it very flexible. It contains some historical data, future predictions, and methods or strategies to achieve the marketing objectives. _____ s start with the identification of customer needs through a market research and how the business can satisfy these needs while generating an acceptable return. This includes processes such as market situation analysis, action programs, budgets, sales forecasts, strategies and projected financial statements. A _____ can also be described as a technique that helps a business to decide on the best use of its resources to achieve corporate objectives. It can also contain a full analysis of the strengths and weaknesses of a company, its organization and its products.

Exam Probability: **Low**

37. *Answer choices:*

(see index for correct answer)

- a. Pomodoro Technique

- b. Management by exception
- c. Narcissistic leadership
- d. Marketing plan

Guidance: level 1

:: Strategic alliances ::

A _____ is an agreement between two or more parties to pursue a set of agreed upon objectives needed while remaining independent organizations. A _____ will usually fall short of a legal partnership entity, agency, or corporate affiliate relationship. Typically, two companies form a _____ when each possesses one or more business assets or have expertise that will help the other by enhancing their businesses. _____ s can develop in outsourcing relationships where the parties desire to achieve long-term win-win benefits and innovation based on mutually desired outcomes.

Exam Probability: **Medium**

38. *Answer choices:*
(see index for correct answer)

- a. Management contract
- b. Bridge Alliance
- c. Defensive termination
- d. Strategic alliance

Guidance: level 1

:: Services management and marketing ::

_____ is a specialised branch of marketing. _____ emerged as a separate field of study in the early 1980s, following the recognition that the unique characteristics of services required different strategies compared with the marketing of physical goods.

Exam Probability: **Low**

39. *Answer choices:*

(see index for correct answer)

- a. Service delivery framework
- b. Automated attendant
- c. Services marketing
- d. The Experience Economy

Guidance: level 1

:: ::

_____ is the collection of techniques, skills, methods, and processes used in the production of goods or services or in the accomplishment of objectives, such as scientific investigation. _____ can be the knowledge of techniques, processes, and the like, or it can be embedded in machines to allow for operation without detailed knowledge of their workings. Systems applying _____ by taking an input, changing it according to the system's use, and then producing an outcome are referred to as _____ systems or technological systems.

Exam Probability: **Low**

40. *Answer choices:*

(see index for correct answer)

- a. corporate values
- b. Technology
- c. co-culture
- d. levels of analysis

Guidance: level 1

:: Marketing ::

_____ comes from the Latin neg and otsia referring to businessmen who, unlike the patricians, had no leisure time in their industriousness; it held the meaning of business until the 17th century when it took on the diplomatic connotation as a dialogue between two or more people or parties intended to reach a beneficial outcome over one or more issues where a conflict exists with respect to at least one of these issues. Thus, _____ is a process of combining divergent positions into a joint agreement under a decision rule of unanimity.

Exam Probability: **Low**

41. *Answer choices:*

(see index for correct answer)

- a. Negotiation
- b. Macromarketing
- c. Mass affluent
- d. Marketing communications planning framework

Guidance: level 1

:: Management ::

In business, a _____ is the attribute that allows an organization to outperform its competitors. A _____ may include access to natural resources, such as high-grade ores or a low-cost power source, highly skilled labor, geographic location, high entry barriers, and access to new technology.

Exam Probability: **High**

42. *Answer choices:*

(see index for correct answer)

- a. Competitive advantage
- b. Downstream
- c. Evidence-based management
- d. Decentralized decision-making

Guidance: level 1

:: ::

In financial markets, a share is a unit used as mutual funds, limited partnerships, and real estate investment trusts. The owner of _____ in the corporation/company is a shareholder of the corporation. A share is an indivisible unit of capital, expressing the ownership relationship between the company and the shareholder. The denominated value of a share is its face value, and the total of the face value of issued _____ represent the capital of a company, which may not reflect the market value of those _____ .

Exam Probability: **Low**

43. *Answer choices:*

(see index for correct answer)

- a. Sarbanes-Oxley act of 2002
- b. Shares
- c. functional perspective
- d. process perspective

Guidance: level 1

:: ::

_____ is the act of conveying meanings from one entity or group to another through the use of mutually understood signs, symbols, and semiotic rules.

Exam Probability: **Medium**

44. *Answer choices:*

(see index for correct answer)

- a. corporate values
- b. cultural
- c. surface-level diversity
- d. Communication

Guidance: level 1

:: Brand management ::

In marketing, _____ is the analysis and planning on how a brand is perceived in the market. Developing a good relationship with the target market is essential for _____. Tangible elements of _____ include the product itself; its look, price, and packaging, etc. The intangible elements are the experiences that the consumers share with the brand, and also the relationships they have with the brand. A brand manager would oversee all aspects of the consumer's brand association as well as relationships with members of the supply chain.

Exam Probability: **High**

45. *Answer choices:*

(see index for correct answer)

- a. Boomerang Media
- b. E3 Agency Network
- c. Imation
- d. The Co-operative brand

Guidance: level 1

:: Management ::

The term _____ refers to measures designed to increase the degree of autonomy and self-determination in people and in communities in order to enable them to represent their interests in a responsible and self-determined way, acting on their own authority. It is the process of becoming stronger and more confident, especially in controlling one's life and claiming one's rights. _____ as action refers both to the process of self-_____ and to professional support of people, which enables them to overcome their sense of powerlessness and lack of influence, and to recognize and use their resources. To do work with power.

Exam Probability: **Low**

46. *Answer choices:*
(see index for correct answer)

- a. Decentralized decision-making
- b. Enterprise decision management
- c. Value migration
- d. Crisis management

Guidance: level 1

:: ::

_____ is the means to see, hear, or become aware of something or someone through our fundamental senses. The term _____ derives from the Latin word perceptio, and is the organization, identification, and interpretation of sensory information in order to represent and understand the presented information, or the environment.

Exam Probability: **High**

47. *Answer choices:*

(see index for correct answer)

- a. deep-level diversity
- b. functional perspective
- c. Perception
- d. process perspective

Guidance: level 1

:: Advertising ::

A _____ is a document used by creative professionals and agencies to develop creative deliverables: visual design, copy, advertising, web sites, etc. The document is usually developed by the requestor and approved by the creative team of designers, writers, and project managers. In some cases, the project's _____ may need creative director approval before work will commence.

Exam Probability: **Low**

48. *Answer choices:*

(see index for correct answer)

- a. Advertising elasticity of demand
- b. Sponsor

- c. Cost per acquisition
- d. Social classifieds

Guidance: level 1

:: Monopoly (economics) ::

The _____ of 1890 was a United States antitrust law that regulates competition among enterprises, which was passed by Congress under the presidency of Benjamin Harrison.

Exam Probability: **Medium**

49. *Answer choices:*

(see index for correct answer)

- a. Privatization
- b. Ramsey problem
- c. Sherman Antitrust Act
- d. Herfindahl index

Guidance: level 1

:: Marketing ::

_____ is based on a marketing concept which can be adopted by an organization as a strategy for business expansion. Where implemented, a franchisor licenses its know-how, procedures, intellectual property, use of its business model, brand, and rights to sell its branded products and services to a franchisee. In return the franchisee pays certain fees and agrees to comply with certain obligations, typically set out in a Franchise Agreement.

Exam Probability: **High**

50. *Answer choices:*

(see index for correct answer)

- a. Osborne effect
- b. Franchising
- c. Pitching engine
- d. Packshot

Guidance: level 1

:: ::

_____ , known in Europe as research and technological development , refers to innovative activities undertaken by corporations or governments in developing new services or products, or improving existing services or products. _____ constitutes the first stage of development of a potential new service or the production process.

Exam Probability: **High**

51. *Answer choices:*

(see index for correct answer)

- a. interpersonal communication
- b. similarity-attraction theory
- c. Character
- d. Research and development

Guidance: level 1

:: ::

A _____ is a graphic mark, emblem, or symbol used to aid and promote public identification and recognition. It may be of an abstract or figurative design or include the text of the name it represents as in a wordmark.

Exam Probability: **Medium**

52. *Answer choices:*

(see index for correct answer)

- a. hierarchical perspective
- b. Character
- c. corporate values
- d. interpersonal communication

Guidance: level 1

:: Product management ::

_____ is a phrase used in the marketing industry which describes the value of having a well-known brand name, based on the idea that the owner of a well-known brand name can generate more revenue simply from brand recognition; that is from products with that brand name than from products with a less well known name, as consumers believe that a product with a well-known name is better than products with less well-known names.

Exam Probability: **Low**

53. *Answer choices:*

(see index for correct answer)

- a. Brand equity
- b. Scarcity Development Cycle
- c. Obsolescence
- d. Product manager

Guidance: level 1

:: Types of marketing ::

_____ is "marketing on a worldwide scale reconciling or taking commercial advantage of global operational differences, similarities and opportunities in order to meet global objectives".

Exam Probability: **Medium**

54. *Answer choices:*

(see index for correct answer)

- a. Global marketing
- b. Ethical marketing
- c. Influencer marketing
- d. Alliance marketing

Guidance: level 1

:: Management ::

_____ is the process of thinking about the activities required to achieve a desired goal. It is the first and foremost activity to achieve desired results. It involves the creation and maintenance of a plan, such as psychological aspects that require conceptual skills. There are even a couple of tests to measure someone's capability of _____ well. As such, _____ is a fundamental property of intelligent behavior. An important further meaning, often just called " _____ " is the legal context of permitted building developments.

Exam Probability: **Low**

55. *Answer choices:*

(see index for correct answer)

- a. Supply management
- b. Planning
- c. Control
- d. Shrinkage

Guidance: level 1

:: Television terminology ::

A _____ organization, also known as a non-business entity, not-for-profit organization, or _____ institution, is dedicated to furthering a particular social cause or advocating for a shared point of view. In economic terms, it is an organization that uses its surplus of the revenues to further achieve its ultimate objective, rather than distributing its income to the organization's shareholders, leaders, or members. _____ s are tax exempt or charitable, meaning they do not pay income tax on the money that they receive for their organization. They can operate in religious, scientific, research, or educational settings.

Exam Probability: **High**

56. *Answer choices:*

(see index for correct answer)

- a. multiplexing
- b. Nonprofit
- c. distance learning
- d. Satellite television

Guidance: level 1

:: ::

_____ s are formal, sociotechnical, organizational systems designed to collect, process, store, and distribute information. In a sociotechnical perspective, _____ s are composed by four components: task, people, structure, and technology.

Exam Probability: **Medium**

57. *Answer choices:*

(see index for correct answer)

- a. Information system
- b. interpersonal communication
- c. process perspective
- d. surface-level diversity

Guidance: level 1

:: Product management ::

_____ or brand stretching is a marketing strategy in which a firm marketing a product with a well-developed image uses the same brand name in a different product category. The new product is called a spin-off. Organizations use this strategy to increase and leverage brand equity. An example of a _____ is Jello-gelatin creating Jello pudding pops. It increases awareness of the brand name and increases profitability from offerings in more than one product category.

Exam Probability: **Low**

58. *Answer choices:*

(see index for correct answer)

- a. Brand extension
- b. Product cost management
- c. Trademark look
- d. Crossing the Chasm

Guidance: level 1

:: Health promotion ::

_____, as defined by the World _____ Organization, is "a state of complete physical, mental and social well-being and not merely the absence of disease or infirmity." This definition has been subject to controversy, as it may have limited value for implementation. _____ may be defined as the ability to adapt and manage physical, mental and social challenges throughout life.

Exam Probability: **Low**

59. *Answer choices:*

(see index for correct answer)

- a. Hopkins Center for Health Disparities Solutions
- b. Myokine
- c. Transtheoretical model
- d. Health risk assessment

Guidance: level 1

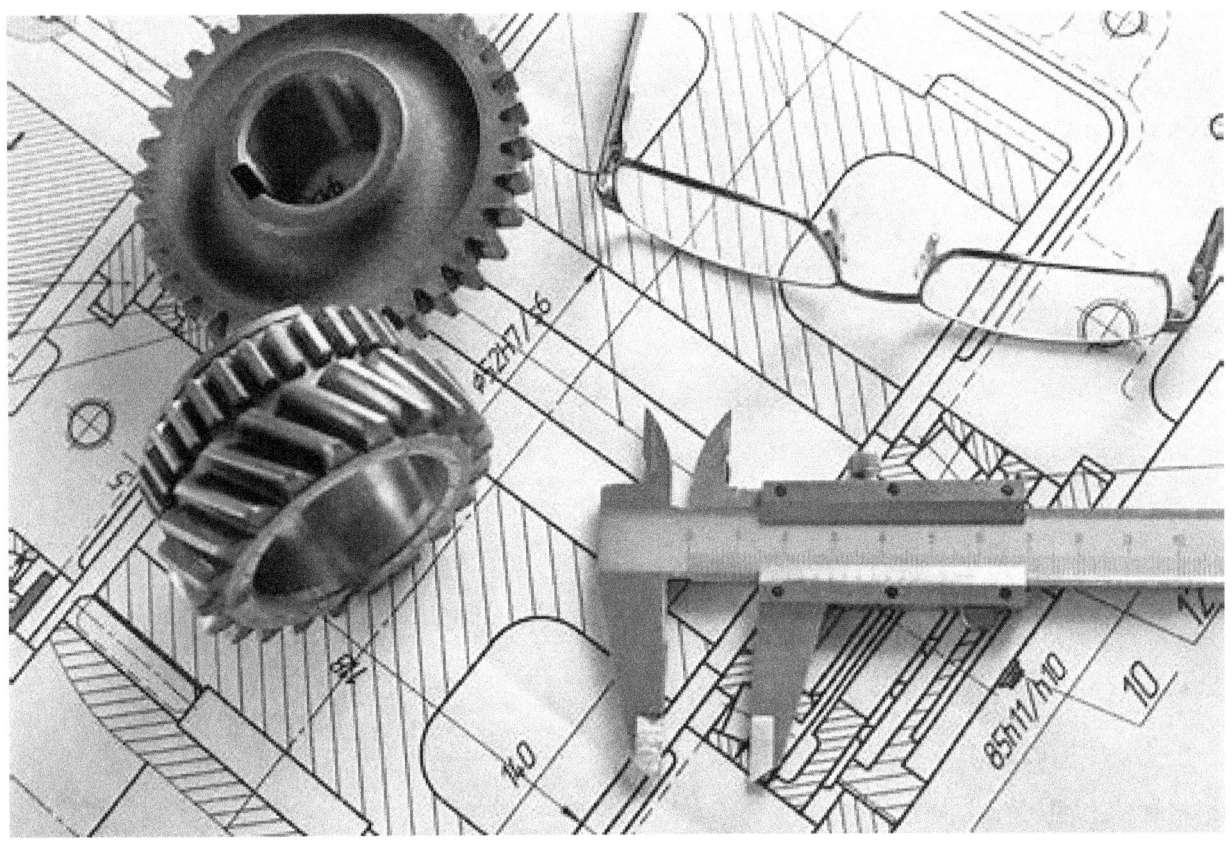

Manufacturing

Manufacturing is the production of merchandise for use or sale using labor and machines, tools, chemical and biological processing, or formulation. The term may refer to a range of human activity, from handicraft to high tech, but is most commonly applied to industrial design, in which raw materials are transformed into finished goods on a large scale. Such finished goods may be sold to other manufacturers for the production of other, more complex products, such as aircraft, household appliances, furniture, sports equipment or automobiles, or sold to wholesalers, who in turn sell them to retailers, who then sell them to end users and consumers.

:: Data management ::

_____ refers to a data-driven improvement cycle used for improving, optimizing and stabilizing business processes and designs. The _____ improvement cycle is the core tool used to drive Six Sigma projects. However, _____ is not exclusive to Six Sigma and can be used as the framework for other improvement applications.

Exam Probability: **High**

1. *Answer choices:*
(see index for correct answer)

- a. Online analytical processing
- b. Copyright
- c. Uniform data access
- d. Semantic integration

Guidance: level 1

:: Management ::

A process is a unique combination of tools, materials, methods, and people engaged in producing a measurable output; for example a manufacturing line for machine parts. All processes have inherent statistical variability which can be evaluated by statistical methods.

Exam Probability: **High**

2. Answer choices:

(see index for correct answer)

- a. Purchasing management
- b. Process capability
- c. Process management
- d. Marketing management

Guidance: level 1

:: Supply chain management terms ::

In business and finance, _____ is a system of organizations, people, activities, information, and resources involved in moving a product or service from supplier to customer. _____ activities involve the transformation of natural resources, raw materials, and components into a finished product that is delivered to the end customer. In sophisticated _____ systems, used products may re-enter the _____ at any point where residual value is recyclable. _____ s link value chains.

Exam Probability: **High**

3. Answer choices:

(see index for correct answer)

- a. Last mile
- b. Work in process
- c. Most valuable customers

- d. Direct shipment

Guidance: level 1

:: Waste ::

_____ are unwanted or unusable materials. _____ is any substance which is discarded after primary use, or is worthless, defective and of no use. A by-product by contrast is a joint product of relatively minor economic value. A _____ product may become a by-product, joint product or resource through an invention that raises a _____ product's value above zero.

Exam Probability: **Low**

4. *Answer choices:*
(see index for correct answer)

- a. Commercial waste
- b. Clinker
- c. Waste
- d. Wood ash

Guidance: level 1

:: Lean manufacturing ::

_____ is a scheduling system for lean manufacturing and just-in-time manufacturing. Taiichi Ohno, an industrial engineer at Toyota, developed _____ to improve manufacturing efficiency. _____ is one method to achieve JIT. The system takes its name from the cards that track production within a factory. For many in the automotive sector, _____ is known as the "Toyota nameplate system" and as such the term is not used by some other automakers.

Exam Probability: **Low**

5. *Answer choices:*

(see index for correct answer)

- a. Lean services
- b. Kanban
- c. Setsuban Kanri
- d. Statistical thinking

Guidance: level 1

:: Production and manufacturing ::

_____ is the process of determining the production capacity needed by an organization to meet changing demands for its products. In the context of _____, design capacity is the maximum amount of work that an organization is capable of completing in a given period. Effective capacity is the maximum amount of work that an organization is capable of completing in a given period due to constraints such as quality problems, delays, material handling, etc.

Exam Probability: **Medium**

6. *Answer choices:*

(see index for correct answer)

- a. Production
- b. Piece work
- c. ERPNEXT
- d. Capacity planning

Guidance: level 1

:: Project management ::

Some scenarios associate "this kind of planning" with learning "life skills". _____s are necessary, or at least useful, in situations where individuals need to know what time they must be at a specific location to receive a specific service, and where people need to accomplish a set of goals within a set time period.

Exam Probability: **High**

7. *Answer choices:*

(see index for correct answer)

- a. Stages of project finance
- b. Schedule

- c. Level of Effort
- d. Scrumedge

Guidance: level 1

:: Quality ::

_____ is a concept first outlined by quality expert Joseph M. Juran in publications, most notably Juran on _____. Designing for quality and innovation is one of the three universal processes of the Juran Trilogy, in which Juran describes what is required to achieve breakthroughs in new products, services, and processes. Juran believed that quality could be planned, and that most quality crises and problems relate to the way in which quality was planned.

Exam Probability: **Low**

8. *Answer choices:*

(see index for correct answer)

- a. European Organization for Quality
- b. Diamond clarity
- c. Market Driven Quality
- d. Robustification

Guidance: level 1

:: Project management ::

A _____ is a team whose members usually belong to different groups, functions and are assigned to activities for the same project. A team can be divided into sub-teams according to need. Usually _____ s are only used for a defined period of time. They are disbanded after the project is deemed complete. Due to the nature of the specific formation and disbandment, _____ s are usually in organizations.

Exam Probability: **Medium**

9. *Answer choices:*

(see index for correct answer)

- a. Project engineering
- b. Responsibility assignment matrix
- c. Project cycle management
- d. Project team

Guidance: level 1

:: Management ::

A _____ is an idea of the future or desired result that a person or a group of people envisions, plans and commits to achieve. People endeavor to reach _____ s within a finite time by setting deadlines.

Exam Probability: **High**

10. *Answer choices:*

(see index for correct answer)

- a. Risk appetite
- b. Scenario planning
- c. Success trap
- d. Dynamic enterprise modeling

Guidance: level 1

:: Management ::

_____ is the practice of initiating, planning, executing, controlling, and closing the work of a team to achieve specific goals and meet specific success criteria at the specified time.

Exam Probability: **Low**

11. *Answer choices:*

(see index for correct answer)

- a. Information excellence
- b. Innovation leadership
- c. Project management
- d. Evidence-based management

Guidance: level 1

:: Quality assurance ::

The _____ is a United States-based nonprofit tax-exempt 501 organization that accredits more than 21,000 US health care organizations and programs. The international branch accredits medical services from around the world. A majority of US state governments recognize _____ accreditation as a condition of licensure for the receipt of Medicaid and Medicare reimbursements.

Exam Probability: **Low**

12. *Answer choices:*

(see index for correct answer)

- a. Health tourism provider
- b. Joint Commission
- c. HP Quality Center
- d. Software quality assurance

Guidance: level 1

:: Management ::

_____ , also known as natural process limits, are horizontal lines drawn on a statistical process control chart, usually at a distance of ±3 standard deviations of the plotted statistic from the statistic's mean.

Exam Probability: **High**

13. *Answer choices:*

(see index for correct answer)

- a. Earned value management
- b. Control limits
- c. Outrage constraint
- d. Business process improvement

Guidance: level 1

:: Production and manufacturing ::

_____ is a concept in purchasing and project management for securing the quality and timely delivery of goods and components.

Exam Probability: **High**

14. *Answer choices:*

(see index for correct answer)

- a. International Automotive Task Force
- b. Managed services
- c. Scientific management
- d. Reverse engineering

Guidance: level 1

:: Industrial processes ::

_____ is a technique involving the condensation of vapors and the return of this condensate to the system from which it originated. It is used in industrial and laboratory distillations. It is also used in chemistry to supply energy to reactions over a long period of time.

Exam Probability: **Low**

15. *Answer choices:*

(see index for correct answer)

- a. Reflux
- b. Scoring
- c. Photonic curing
- d. Liquid air

Guidance: level 1

:: Costs ::

In economics, _____ is the total economic cost of production and is made up of variable cost, which varies according to the quantity of a good produced and includes inputs such as labour and raw materials, plus fixed cost, which is independent of the quantity of a good produced and includes inputs that cannot be varied in the short term: fixed costs such as buildings and machinery, including sunk costs if any. Since cost is measured per unit of time, it is a flow variable.

Exam Probability: **Low**

16. *Answer choices:*

(see index for correct answer)

- a. Khozraschyot
- b. Total cost
- c. Incremental cost-effectiveness ratio
- d. labor cost

Guidance: level 1

:: Accounting source documents ::

A _____ is a commercial document and first official offer issued by a buyer to a seller indicating types, quantities, and agreed prices for products or services. It is used to control the purchasing of products and services from external suppliers. _____s can be an essential part of enterprise resource planning system orders.

Exam Probability: **Medium**

17. *Answer choices:*

(see index for correct answer)

- a. Credit memo
- b. Purchase order
- c. Credit memorandum
- d. Air waybill

Guidance: level 1

:: Non-parametric statistics ::

A _____ is an accurate representation of the distribution of numerical data. It is an estimate of the probability distribution of a continuous variable and was first introduced by Karl Pearson. It differs from a bar graph, in the sense that a bar graph relates two variables, but a _____ relates only one. To construct a _____, the first step is to "bin" the range of values—that is, divide the entire range of values into a series of intervals—and then count how many values fall into each interval. The bins are usually specified as consecutive, non-overlapping intervals of a variable. The bins must be adjacent, and are often of equal size.

Exam Probability: **Low**

18. *Answer choices:*

(see index for correct answer)

- a. Mantel test
- b. Friedman test
- c. Kernel smoother
- d. Histogram

Guidance: level 1

:: Retailing ::

_____ is the process of selling consumer goods or services to customers through multiple channels of distribution to earn a profit. _____ ers satisfy demand identified through a supply chain. The term "_____ er" is typically applied where a service provider fills the small orders of a large number of individuals, who are end-users, rather than large orders of a small number of wholesale, corporate or government clientele. Shopping generally refers to the act of buying products. Sometimes this is done to obtain final goods, including necessities such as food and clothing; sometimes it takes place as a recreational activity. Recreational shopping often involves window shopping and browsing: it does not always result in a purchase.

Exam Probability: **Low**

19. *Answer choices:*

(see index for correct answer)

- a. Retail
- b. Gold Souq
- c. Moratorium
- d. Hobby shop

Guidance: level 1

:: Data management ::

_____ is the ability of a physical product to remain functional, without requiring excessive maintenance or repair, when faced with the challenges of normal operation over its design lifetime. There are several measures of _____ in use, including years of life, hours of use, and number of operational cycles. In economics, goods with a long usable life are referred to as durable goods.

Exam Probability: **High**

20. *Answer choices:*

(see index for correct answer)

- a. Processor data transfer
- b. Network transparency
- c. Durability
- d. Tuple

Guidance: level 1

:: Management ::

_____ is a method of quality control which employs statistical methods to monitor and control a process. This helps to ensure that the process operates efficiently, producing more specification-conforming products with less waste. SPC can be applied to any process where the "conforming product" output can be measured. Key tools used in SPC include run charts, control charts, a focus on continuous improvement, and the design of experiments. An example of a process where SPC is applied is manufacturing lines.

Exam Probability: **Low**

21. *Answer choices:*

(see index for correct answer)

- a. Planning fallacy
- b. Sensemaking
- c. Stovepipe
- d. Statistical process control

Guidance: level 1

:: Industrial processes ::

A _____ is a device used for high-temperature heating. The name derives from Latin word fornax, which means oven. The heat energy to fuel a _____ may be supplied directly by fuel combustion, by electricity such as the electric arc _____ , or through induction heating in induction _____ s.

Exam Probability: **Medium**

22. *Answer choices:*

(see index for correct answer)

- a. Perforation
- b. Furnace
- c. Sinter Plant
- d. Frasch process

Guidance: level 1

:: Commercial item transport and distribution ::

_____ in logistics and supply chain management is an organization's use of third-party businesses to outsource elements of its distribution, warehousing, and fulfillment services.

Exam Probability: **High**

23. *Answer choices:*

(see index for correct answer)

- a. Haulage
- b. Third-party logistics
- c. Straddle carrier
- d. Incoterms

Guidance: level 1

:: Business ::

The seller, or the provider of the goods or services, completes a sale in response to an acquisition, appropriation, requisition or a direct interaction with the buyer at the point of sale. There is a passing of title of the item, and the settlement of a price, in which agreement is reached on a price for which transfer of ownership of the item will occur. The seller, not the purchaser typically executes the sale and it may be completed prior to the obligation of payment. In the case of indirect interaction, a person who sells goods or service on behalf of the owner is known as a _____ man or _____ woman or _____ person, but this often refers to someone selling goods in a store/shop, in which case other terms are also common, including _____ clerk, shop assistant, and retail clerk.

Exam Probability: **Low**

24. *Answer choices:*
(see index for correct answer)

- a. Viability study

- b. Sustainopreneurship
- c. Door-to-door
- d. Business sector

Guidance: level 1

:: Quality control tools ::

A _____ is a type of diagram that represents an algorithm, workflow or process. _____ can also be defined as a diagramatic representation of an algorithm.

Exam Probability: **High**

25. *Answer choices:*

(see index for correct answer)

- a. Flowchart
- b. EWMA chart
- c. Run chart
- d. Robustness validation

Guidance: level 1

:: Quality awards ::

The _____ recognizes U.S. organizations in the business, health care, education, and nonprofit sectors for performance excellence. The Baldrige Award is the only formal recognition of the performance excellence of both public and private U.S. organizations given by the President of the United States. It is administered by the Baldrige Performance Excellence Program, which is based at and managed by the National Institute of Standards and Technology , an agency of the U.S. Department of Commerce.

Exam Probability: **Medium**

26. *Answer choices:*

(see index for correct answer)

- a. Malcolm Baldrige National Quality Award
- b. EFQM Excellence Award
- c. Rajiv Gandhi National Quality Award
- d. Philippine Quality Award

Guidance: level 1

:: Metal forming ::

_____ is a type of motion that combines rotation and translation of that object with respect to a surface , such that, if ideal conditions exist, the two are in contact with each other without sliding.

Exam Probability: **High**

27. *Answer choices:*

(see index for correct answer)

- a. Induction forging
- b. Steckel mill
- c. Stamping
- d. Hubbing

Guidance: level 1

:: Packaging materials ::

_____ is a non-crystalline, amorphous solid that is often transparent and has widespread practical, technological, and decorative uses in, for example, window panes, tableware, and optoelectronics. The most familiar, and historically the oldest, types of manufactured _____ are "silicate _____ es" based on the chemical compound silica , the primary constituent of sand. The term _____ , in popular usage, is often used to refer only to this type of material, which is familiar from use as window _____ and in _____ bottles. Of the many silica-based _____ es that exist, ordinary glazing and container _____ is formed from a specific type called soda-lime _____ , composed of approximately 75% silicon dioxide , sodium oxide from sodium carbonate , calcium oxide , also called lime, and several minor additives.

Exam Probability: **Low**

28. *Answer choices:*

(see index for correct answer)

- a. EVOH
- b. Pullulan
- c. Tear tape
- d. Glass

Guidance: level 1

:: ::

In production, research, retail, and accounting, a _____ is the value of money that has been used up to produce something or deliver a service, and hence is not available for use anymore. In business, the _____ may be one of acquisition, in which case the amount of money expended to acquire it is counted as _____. In this case, money is the input that is gone in order to acquire the thing. This acquisition _____ may be the sum of the _____ of production as incurred by the original producer, and further _____s of transaction as incurred by the acquirer over and above the price paid to the producer. Usually, the price also includes a mark-up for profit over the _____ of production.

Exam Probability: **High**

29. *Answer choices:*

(see index for correct answer)

- a. Character
- b. hierarchical perspective
- c. corporate values
- d. Cost

Guidance: level 1

:: Production and manufacturing ::

_____ is a theory of management that analyzes and synthesizes workflows. Its main objective is improving economic efficiency, especially labor productivity. It was one of the earliest attempts to apply science to the engineering of processes and to management. _____ is sometimes known as Taylorism after its founder, Frederick Winslow Taylor.

Exam Probability: **Medium**

30. *Answer choices:*

(see index for correct answer)

- a. Master production schedule
- b. Production engineering
- c. Bill of materials
- d. Scientific management

Guidance: level 1

:: E-commerce ::

_____ is the activity of buying or selling of products on online services or over the Internet. Electronic commerce draws on technologies such as mobile commerce, electronic funds transfer, supply chain management, Internet marketing, online transaction processing, electronic data interchange , inventory management systems, and automated data collection systems.

Exam Probability: **High**

31. *Answer choices:*

(see index for correct answer)

- a. Friend-to-friend
- b. Mobile banking
- c. E-commerce
- d. ICOCA

Guidance: level 1

:: Business planning ::

_____ is a critical component to the successful delivery of any project, programme or activity. A stakeholder is any individual, group or organization that can affect, be affected by, or perceive itself to be affected by a programme.

Exam Probability: **Medium**

32. *Answer choices:*

(see index for correct answer)

- a. operational planning
- b. Business war games
- c. Joint decision trap
- d. Exit planning

Guidance: level 1

:: Promotion and marketing communications ::

The _____ of American Manufacturers, now ThomasNet, is an online platform for supplier discovery and product sourcing in the US and Canada. It was once known as the "big green books" and "Thomas Registry", and was a multi-volume directory of industrial product information covering 650,000 distributors, manufacturers and service companies within 67,000-plus industrial categories that is now published on ThomasNet.

Exam Probability: **High**

33. *Answer choices:*

(see index for correct answer)

- a. Promotional representative
- b. Media guide
- c. Cresta International Advertising Awards
- d. Thomas Register

Guidance: level 1

:: Project management ::

A _____ is a type of bar chart that illustrates a project schedule, named after its inventor, Henry Gantt, who designed such a chart around the years 1910–1915. Modern _____ s also show the dependency relationships between activities and current schedule status.

Exam Probability: **Medium**

34. *Answer choices:*

(see index for correct answer)

- a. Gantt chart
- b. Project engineering
- c. Project manufacturing
- d. Project workforce management

Guidance: level 1

:: Procurement ::

Purchasing is the formal process of buying goods and services. The _____ can vary from one organization to another, but there are some common key elements.

Exam Probability: **Medium**

35. *Answer choices:*

(see index for correct answer)

- a. Collateral Billing number
- b. Purchasing process
- c. Commodity management
- d. Knife catcher

Guidance: level 1

:: Project management ::

_____ is a work methodology emphasizing the parallelisation of tasks , which is sometimes called simultaneous engineering or integrated product development using an integrated product team approach. It refers to an approach used in product development in which functions of design engineering, manufacturing engineering, and other functions are integrated to reduce the time required to bring a new product to market.

Exam Probability: **High**

36. *Answer choices:*

(see index for correct answer)

- a. Costab
- b. Concurrent engineering
- c. Project sponsorship
- d. Risk management plan

Guidance: level 1

:: Information technology management ::

_____ concerns a cycle of organizational activity: the acquisition of information from one or more sources, the custodianship and the distribution of that information to those who need it, and its ultimate disposition through archiving or deletion.

Exam Probability: **High**

37. *Answer choices:*

(see index for correct answer)

- a. Information model
- b. Information Technology Infrastructure Library
- c. Virtual filing cabinet
- d. Information management

Guidance: level 1

:: Product management ::

_____ is the state of being which occurs when an object, service, or practice is no longer wanted even though it may still be in good working order; however, the international standard EN62402 _____ Management - Application Guide defines _____ as being the "transition from availability of products by the original manufacturer or supplier to unavailability". _____ frequently occurs because a replacement has become available that has, in sum, more advantages compared to the disadvantages incurred by maintaining or repairing the original. Obsolete also refers to something that is already disused or discarded, or antiquated. Typically, _____ is preceded by a gradual decline in popularity.

Exam Probability: **High**

38. *Answer choices:*

(see index for correct answer)

- a. Diffusion of innovations
- b. Consumer adoption of technological innovations
- c. business name
- d. Service life

Guidance: level 1

:: ::

_____ is a kind of action that occur as two or more objects have an effect upon one another. The idea of a two-way effect is essential in the concept of _____ , as opposed to a one-way causal effect. A closely related term is interconnectivity, which deals with the _____ s of _____ s within systems: combinations of many simple _____ s can lead to surprising emergent phenomena. _____ has different tailored meanings in various sciences. Changes can also involve _____ .

Exam Probability: **High**

39. *Answer choices:*

(see index for correct answer)

- a. similarity-attraction theory
- b. deep-level diversity
- c. imperative
- d. personal values

Guidance: level 1

:: Data interchange standards ::

_____ is the concept of businesses electronically communicating information that was traditionally communicated on paper, such as purchase orders and invoices. Technical standards for EDI exist to facilitate parties transacting such instruments without having to make special arrangements.

Exam Probability: **Low**

40. *Answer choices:*

(see index for correct answer)

- a. Domain Application Protocol
- b. Electronic data interchange
- c. Data Interchange Standards Association
- d. Interaction protocol

Guidance: level 1

:: Commerce ::

A _____ is an employee within a company, business or other organization who is responsible at some level for buying or approving the acquisition of goods and services needed by the company. Responsible for buying the best quality products, goods and services for their company at the most competitive prices, _____ s work in a wide range of sectors for many different organizations. The position responsibilities may be the same as that of a buyer or purchasing agent, or may include wider supervisory or managerial responsibilities. A _____ may oversee the acquisition of materials needed for production, general supplies for offices and facilities, equipment, or construction contracts. A _____ often supervises purchasing agents and buyers, but in small companies the _____ may also be the purchasing agent or buyer. The _____ position may also carry the title "Procurement Manager" or in the public sector, "Procurement Officer". He or she can come from both an Engineering or Economics background.

Exam Probability: **Low**

41. *Answer choices:*

(see index for correct answer)

- a. Purchasing manager
- b. E-receipt
- c. Trade credit
- d. Reseller

Guidance: level 1

:: Distribution, retailing, and wholesaling ::

_____ measures the performance of a system. Certain goals are defined and the _____ gives the percentage to which those goals should be achieved. Fill rate is different from _____ .

Exam Probability: **Low**

42. *Answer choices:*

(see index for correct answer)

- a. Foodservice distributor
- b. Hypermarket
- c. Concession
- d. Service level

Guidance: level 1

:: Information technology management ::

The term _____ is used to refer to periods when a system is unavailable. _____ or outage duration refers to a period of time that a system fails to provide or perform its primary function. Reliability, availability, recovery, and unavailability are related concepts. The unavailability is the proportion of a time-span that a system is unavailable or offline. This is usually a result of the system failing to function because of an unplanned event, or because of routine maintenance .

Exam Probability: **High**

43. *Answer choices:*

(see index for correct answer)

- a. Test effort
- b. Enterprise content management
- c. Early-arriving fact
- d. Information Technology Infrastructure Library

Guidance: level 1

:: Management accounting ::

_____ are costs that are not directly accountable to a cost object. _____ may be either fixed or variable. _____ include administration, personnel and security costs. These are those costs which are not directly related to production. Some _____ may be overhead. But some overhead costs can be directly attributed to a project and are direct costs.

Exam Probability: **Medium**

44. *Answer choices:*

(see index for correct answer)

- a. Management accounting
- b. Total benefits of ownership
- c. Indirect costs
- d. Pre-determined overhead rate

Guidance: level 1

:: ::

A _____ consists of an orchestrated and repeatable pattern of business activity enabled by the systematic organization of resources into processes that transform materials, provide services, or process information. It can be depicted as a sequence of operations, the work of a person or group, the work of an organization of staff, or one or more simple or complex mechanisms.

Exam Probability: **High**

45. *Answer choices:*

(see index for correct answer)

- a. Sarbanes-Oxley act of 2002
- b. Workflow
- c. deep-level diversity
- d. Character

Guidance: level 1

:: Help desk ::

Data center management is the collection of tasks performed by those responsible for managing ongoing operation of a data center This includes Business service management and planning for the future.

Exam Probability: **Medium**

46. *Answer choices:*

(see index for correct answer)

- a. SysAid Technologies
- b. Help desk
- c. Technical support
- d. Vitalyst

Guidance: level 1

:: Industrial equipment ::

_____s are heat exchangers typically used to provide heat to the bottom of industrial distillation columns. They boil the liquid from the bottom of a distillation column to generate vapors which are returned to the column to drive the distillation separation. The heat supplied to the column by the _____ at the bottom of the column is removed by the condenser at the top of the column.

Exam Probability: **Medium**

47. *Answer choices:*

(see index for correct answer)

- a. Thermal wheel
- b. Cellulose insulating material plant
- c. Production packer
- d. Reboiler

Guidance: level 1

:: Quality assurance ::

Organizations that issue credentials or certify third parties against official standards are themselves formally accredited by _____ bodies ; hence they are sometimes known as "accredited certification bodies". The _____ process ensures that their certification practices are acceptable, typically meaning that they are competent to test and certify third parties, behave ethically and employ suitable quality assurance.

Exam Probability: **High**

48. *Answer choices:*

(see index for correct answer)

- a. Accreditation
- b. The Compliance Team
- c. National Certification Corporation
- d. HP Quality Center

Guidance: level 1

:: Process management ::

_____ is a statistics package developed at the Pennsylvania State University by researchers Barbara F. Ryan, Thomas A. Ryan, Jr., and Brian L. Joiner in 1972. It began as a light version of OMNITAB 80, a statistical analysis program by NIST. Statistical analysis software such as _____ automates calculations and the creation of graphs, allowing the user to focus more on the analysis of data and the interpretation of results. It is compatible with other _____ , Inc. software.

Exam Probability: **High**

49. *Answer choices:*

(see index for correct answer)

- a. business process re-engineering
- b. Process flow diagram
- c. SREDIM
- d. Minitab

Guidance: level 1

:: Management ::

An _____ is a loosely coupled, self-organizing network of firms that combine their economic output to provide products and services offerings to the market. Firms in the _____ may operate independently, for example, through market mechanisms, or cooperatively through agreements and contracts. They provide value added service or product to the OEM.

Exam Probability: **Low**

50. *Answer choices:*

(see index for correct answer)

- a. Gemba
- b. Just in time

- c. Intelligent customer
- d. Extended enterprise

Guidance: level 1

:: Metals ::

A _____ is a material that, when freshly prepared, polished, or fractured, shows a lustrous appearance, and conducts electricity and heat relatively well. _____ s are typically malleable or ductile. A _____ may be a chemical element such as iron, or an alloy such as stainless steel.

Exam Probability: **High**

51. *Answer choices:*

(see index for correct answer)

- a. Metals of antiquity
- b. Half-metal
- c. Metal
- d. Thulium

Guidance: level 1

:: Process management ::

When used in the context of communication networks, such as Ethernet or packet radio, _____ or network _____ is the rate of successful message delivery over a communication channel. The data these messages belong to may be delivered over a physical or logical link, or it can pass through a certain network node. _____ is usually measured in bits per second, and sometimes in data packets per second or data packets per time slot.

Exam Probability: **High**

52. *Answer choices:*

(see index for correct answer)

- a. YAWL
- b. GROW model
- c. Business triage
- d. Business process discovery

Guidance: level 1

:: Insulators ::

A _____ is a piece of soft cloth large enough either to cover or to enfold a great portion of the user's body, usually when sleeping or otherwise at rest, thereby trapping radiant bodily heat that otherwise would be lost through convection, and so keeping the body warm.

Exam Probability: **High**

53. *Answer choices:*

(see index for correct answer)

- a. Pentafluoropropane
- b. Malter effect
- c. Sleeping bag
- d. Thermal pad

Guidance: level 1

:: Management ::

_____ is a process by which entities review the quality of all factors involved in production. ISO 9000 defines _____ as "A part of quality management focused on fulfilling quality requirements".

Exam Probability: **Medium**

54. *Answer choices:*

(see index for correct answer)

- a. Control limits
- b. Managerial economics
- c. Profitable growth
- d. Fall guy

Guidance: level 1

:: ::

An _____ is, most an organized examination or formal evaluation exercise. In engineering activities _____ involves the measurements, tests, and gauges applied to certain characteristics in regard to an object or activity. The results are usually compared to specified requirements and standards for determining whether the item or activity is in line with these targets, often with a Standard _____ Procedure in place to ensure consistent checking. _____ s are usually non-destructive.

Exam Probability: **High**

55. *Answer choices:*

(see index for correct answer)

- a. empathy
- b. imperative
- c. cultural
- d. Inspection

Guidance: level 1

:: Time management ::

_____ is the process of planning and exercising conscious control of time spent on specific activities, especially to increase effectiveness, efficiency, and productivity. It involves a juggling act of various demands upon a person relating to work, social life, family, hobbies, personal interests and commitments with the finiteness of time. Using time effectively gives the person "choice" on spending/managing activities at their own time and expediency.

Exam Probability: **High**

56. *Answer choices:*

(see index for correct answer)

- a. Time perception
- b. Getting Things Done
- c. HabitRPG
- d. Sufficient unto the day is the evil thereof

Guidance: level 1

:: Finance ::

_____ is a financial estimate intended to help buyers and owners determine the direct and indirect costs of a product or system. It is a management accounting concept that can be used in full cost accounting or even ecological economics where it includes social costs.

Exam Probability: **High**

57. Answer choices:

(see index for correct answer)

- a. CBDC NORTIP
- b. Tangible common equity
- c. Remote deposit
- d. Structured sale

Guidance: level 1

:: ::

_____ is the process of finding an estimate, or approximation, which is a value that is usable for some purpose even if input data may be incomplete, uncertain, or unstable. The value is nonetheless usable because it is derived from the best information available. Typically, _____ involves "using the value of a statistic derived from a sample to estimate the value of a corresponding population parameter". The sample provides information that can be projected, through various formal or informal processes, to determine a range most likely to describe the missing information. An estimate that turns out to be incorrect will be an overestimate if the estimate exceeded the actual result, and an underestimate if the estimate fell short of the actual result.

Exam Probability: **Medium**

58. Answer choices:

(see index for correct answer)

- a. co-culture

- b. imperative
- c. information systems assessment
- d. cultural

Guidance: level 1

:: Monopoly (economics) ::

_____ are "efficiencies formed by variety, not volume". For example, a gas station that sells gasoline can sell soda, milk, baked goods, etc through their customer service representatives and thus achieve gasoline companies _____ .

Exam Probability: **Low**

59. *Answer choices:*
(see index for correct answer)

- a. Dominance
- b. Complementary monopoly
- c. Economies of scope
- d. Supracompetitive pricing

Guidance: level 1

Commerce

Commerce relates to "the exchange of goods and services, especially on a large scale." It includes legal, economic, political, social, cultural and technological systems that operate in any country or internationally.

:: E-commerce ::

_____ is the activity of buying or selling of products on online services or over the Internet. Electronic commerce draws on technologies such as mobile commerce, electronic funds transfer, supply chain management, Internet marketing, online transaction processing, electronic data interchange , inventory management systems, and automated data collection systems.

Exam Probability: **Medium**

1. *Answer choices:*

(see index for correct answer)

- a. PayXpert
- b. Types of E-commerce
- c. Digital currency
- d. Confinity

Guidance: level 1

:: ::

_____ is the amount of time someone works beyond normal working hours. The term is also used for the pay received for this time. Normal hours may be determined in several ways.

Exam Probability: **Low**

2. *Answer choices:*

(see index for correct answer)

- a. Overtime
- b. open system
- c. personal values
- d. empathy

Guidance: level 1

:: Payments ::

A _____ or government incentive is a form of financial aid or support extended to an economic sector generally with the aim of promoting economic and social policy. Although commonly extended from government, the term _____ can relate to any type of support – for example from NGOs or as implicit subsidies. Subsidies come in various forms including: direct and indirect.

Exam Probability: **Low**

3. *Answer choices:*

(see index for correct answer)

- a. County payments
- b. Incentive payments
- c. Direct Payments
- d. Subsidy

Guidance: level 1

:: E-commerce ::

A _____ is a financial transaction involving a very small sum of money and usually one that occurs online. A number of _____ systems were proposed and developed in the mid-to-late 1990s, all of which were ultimately unsuccessful. A second generation of _____ systems emerged in the 2010s.

Exam Probability: **Low**

4. *Answer choices:*

(see index for correct answer)

- a. Plantify
- b. Micropayment
- c. SMS banking
- d. ChannelAdvisor

Guidance: level 1

:: Market structure and pricing ::

_____ has historically emerged in two separate types of discussions in economics, that of Adam Smith on the one hand, and that of Karl Marx on the other hand. Adam Smith in his writing on economics stressed the importance of laissez-faire principles outlining the operation of the market in the absence of dominant political mechanisms of control, while Karl Marx discussed the working of the market in the presence of a controlled economy sometimes referred to as a command economy in the literature. Both types of _____ have been in historical evidence throughout the twentieth century and twenty-first century.

Exam Probability: **Low**

5. *Answer choices:*

(see index for correct answer)

- a. Open-source economics
- b. Liberalization
- c. Open source
- d. Market structure

Guidance: level 1

:: E-commerce ::

_____ , cybersecurity or information technology security is the protection of computer systems from theft or damage to their hardware, software or electronic data, as well as from disruption or misdirection of the services they provide.

Exam Probability: **High**

6. *Answer choices:*

(see index for correct answer)

- a. Computer security
- b. PapiNet
- c. IBill

- d. Micropayment

Guidance: level 1

:: Monopoly (economics) ::

A _____ exists when a specific person or enterprise is the only supplier of a particular commodity. This contrasts with a monopsony which relates to a single entity's control of a market to purchase a good or service, and with oligopoly which consists of a few sellers dominating a market. Monopolies are thus characterized by a lack of economic competition to produce the good or service, a lack of viable substitute goods, and the possibility of a high _____ price well above the seller's marginal cost that leads to a high _____ profit. The verb monopolise or monopolize refers to the process by which a company gains the ability to raise prices or exclude competitors. In economics, a _____ is a single seller. In law, a _____ is a business entity that has significant market power, that is, the power to charge overly high prices. Although monopolies may be big businesses, size is not a characteristic of a _____ . A small business may still have the power to raise prices in a small industry .

Exam Probability: **Low**

7. *Answer choices:*

(see index for correct answer)

- a. Wartime Law on Industrial Property
- b. Copyright law of the European Union
- c. Chamberlinian monopolistic competition
- d. Monopoly

Guidance: level 1

:: Business terms ::

_____ning is an organization's process of defining its strategy, or direction, and making decisions on allocating its resources to pursue this strategy. It may also extend to control mechanisms for guiding the implementation of the strategy. _____ning became prominent in corporations during the 1960s and remains an important aspect of strategic management. It is executed by _____ners or strategists, who involve many parties and research sources in their analysis of the organization and its relationship to the environment in which it competes.

Exam Probability: **Low**

8. *Answer choices:*
(see index for correct answer)

- a. customer base
- b. Strategic plan
- c. year-to-date
- d. back office

Guidance: level 1

:: ::

_____ is the administration of an organization, whether it is a business, a not-for-profit organization, or government body. _____ includes the activities of setting the strategy of an organization and coordinating the efforts of its employees to accomplish its objectives through the application of available resources, such as financial, natural, technological, and human resources. The term "_____" may also refer to those people who manage an organization.

Exam Probability: **Medium**

9. *Answer choices:*

(see index for correct answer)

- a. hierarchical
- b. cultural
- c. personal values
- d. imperative

Guidance: level 1

:: Computer access control ::

_____ is the act of confirming the truth of an attribute of a single piece of data claimed true by an entity. In contrast with identification, which refers to the act of stating or otherwise indicating a claim purportedly attesting to a person or thing's identity, _____ is the process of actually confirming that identity. It might involve confirming the identity of a person by validating their identity documents, verifying the authenticity of a website with a digital certificate, determining the age of an artifact by carbon dating, or ensuring that a product is what its packaging and labeling claim to be. In other words, _____ often involves verifying the validity of at least one form of identification.

Exam Probability: **Low**

10. *Answer choices:*

(see index for correct answer)

- a. EAuthentication
- b. Integrated Windows Authentication
- c. Authentication
- d. LinOTP

Guidance: level 1

:: ::

A _____ is a person or firm who arranges transactions between a buyer and a seller for a commission when the deal is executed. A _____ who also acts as a seller or as a buyer becomes a principal party to the deal. Neither role should be confused with that of an agent—one who acts on behalf of a principal party in a deal.

Exam Probability: **Medium**

11. *Answer choices:*

(see index for correct answer)

- a. Sarbanes-Oxley act of 2002
- b. hierarchical
- c. Character
- d. Broker

Guidance: level 1

:: Supply chain management terms ::

In business and finance, _____ is a system of organizations, people, activities, information, and resources involved in moving a product or service from supplier to customer. _____ activities involve the transformation of natural resources, raw materials, and components into a finished product that is delivered to the end customer. In sophisticated _____ systems, used products may re-enter the _____ at any point where residual value is recyclable. _____ s link value chains.

Exam Probability: **Low**

12. *Answer choices:*

(see index for correct answer)

- a. Most valuable customers
- b. Supply chain
- c. Final assembly schedule
- d. Consumable

Guidance: level 1

:: Commodities ::

In economics, a _____ is an economic good or service that has full or substantial fungibility: that is, the market treats instances of the good as equivalent or nearly so with no regard to who produced them. Most commodities are raw materials, basic resources, agricultural, or mining products, such as iron ore, sugar, or grains like rice and wheat. Commodities can also be mass-produced unspecialized products such as chemicals and computer memory.

Exam Probability: **High**

13. *Answer choices:*

(see index for correct answer)

- a. Commodity pathway diversion
- b. Commoditization

- c. Commodity
- d. IRely

Guidance: level 1

:: Marketing ::

_____ comes from the Latin neg and otsia referring to businessmen who, unlike the patricians, had no leisure time in their industriousness; it held the meaning of business until the 17th century when it took on the diplomatic connotation as a dialogue between two or more people or parties intended to reach a beneficial outcome over one or more issues where a conflict exists with respect to at least one of these issues. Thus, _____ is a process of combining divergent positions into a joint agreement under a decision rule of unanimity.

Exam Probability: **Medium**

14. *Answer choices:*
(see index for correct answer)

- a. Business-to-employee
- b. Sales contest
- c. Negotiation
- d. Customer lifetime value

Guidance: level 1

:: Retailing ::

A _____ or trolley, also known by a variety of other names, is a cart supplied by a shop, especially supermarkets, for use by customers inside the shop for transport of merchandise to the checkout counter during shopping. In many cases customers can then also use the cart to transport their purchased goods to their vehicles, but some carts are designed to prevent them from leaving the shop.

Exam Probability: **High**

15. *Answer choices:*

(see index for correct answer)

- a. Second-hand shop
- b. Store-within-a-store
- c. Pop-up retail
- d. Slatwall

Guidance: level 1

:: Hospitality industry ::

_____ refers to the relationship between a guest and a host, wherein the host receives the guest with goodwill, including the reception and entertainment of guests, visitors, or strangers. Louis, chevalier de Jaucourt describes _____ in the Encyclopédie as the virtue of a great soul that cares for the whole universe through the ties of humanity.

Exam Probability: **Low**

16. *Answer choices:*

(see index for correct answer)

- a. Hospitality
- b. Travel insurance
- c. Restaurant ware
- d. Cover charge

Guidance: level 1

:: ::

An _____ is a contingent motivator. Traditional _____ s are extrinsic motivators which reward actions to yield a desired outcome. The effectiveness of traditional _____ s has changed as the needs of Western society have evolved. While the traditional _____ model is effective when there is a defined procedure and goal for a task, Western society started to require a higher volume of critical thinkers, so the traditional model became less effective. Institutions are now following a trend in implementing strategies that rely on intrinsic motivations rather than the extrinsic motivations that the traditional _____ s foster.

Exam Probability: **Low**

17. *Answer choices:*

(see index for correct answer)

- a. Incentive
- b. deep-level diversity
- c. Sarbanes-Oxley act of 2002
- d. levels of analysis

Guidance: level 1

:: ::

A _____ or _____ s is a type of footwear and not a specific type of shoe. Most _____ s mainly cover the foot and the ankle, while some also cover some part of the lower calf. Some _____ s extend up the leg, sometimes as far as the knee or even the hip. Most _____ s have a heel that is clearly distinguishable from the rest of the sole, even if the two are made of one piece. Traditionally made of leather or rubber, modern _____ s are made from a variety of materials. _____ s are worn both for their functionality protecting the foot and leg from water, extreme cold, mud or hazards or providing additional ankle support for strenuous activities with added traction requirements , or may have hobnails on their undersides to protect against wear and to get better grip; and for reasons of style and fashion.

Exam Probability: **Medium**

18. *Answer choices:*

(see index for correct answer)

- a. Sarbanes-Oxley act of 2002
- b. empathy

- c. imperative
- d. Character

Guidance: level 1

:: ::

A trade union is an association of workers forming a legal unit or legal personhood, usually called a "bargaining unit", which acts as bargaining agent and legal representative for a unit of employees in all matters of law or right arising from or in the administration of a collective agreement. Labour unions typically fund the formal organisation, head office, and legal team functions of the labour union through regular fees or union dues. The delegate staff of the labour union representation in the workforce are made up of workplace volunteers who are appointed by members in democratic elections.

Exam Probability: **Low**

19. *Answer choices:*

(see index for correct answer)

- a. empathy
- b. Character
- c. corporate values
- d. Labor union

Guidance: level 1

:: ::

The _____ or just chief executive, is the most senior corporate, executive, or administrative officer in charge of managing an organization especially an independent legal entity such as a company or nonprofit institution. CEOs lead a range of organizations, including public and private corporations, non-profit organizations and even some government organizations. The CEO of a corporation or company typically reports to the board of directors and is charged with maximizing the value of the entity, which may include maximizing the share price, market share, revenues or another element. In the non-profit and government sector, CEOs typically aim at achieving outcomes related to the organization's mission, such as reducing poverty, increasing literacy, etc.

Exam Probability: **Medium**

20. *Answer choices:*

(see index for correct answer)

- a. Chief executive officer
- b. interpersonal communication
- c. information systems assessment
- d. deep-level diversity

Guidance: level 1

:: Industrial Revolution ::

The _____, now also known as the First _____, was the transition to new manufacturing processes in Europe and the US, in the period from about 1760 to sometime between 1820 and 1840. This transition included going from hand production methods to machines, new chemical manufacturing and iron production processes, the increasing use of steam power and water power, the development of machine tools and the rise of the mechanized factory system. The _____ also led to an unprecedented rise in the rate of population growth.

Exam Probability: **High**

21. *Answer choices:*

(see index for correct answer)

- a. Pinsley Mill
- b. Cromford Mill
- c. Spinning jenny
- d. Lancashire Loom

Guidance: level 1

:: Confidence tricks ::

_____ is the fraudulent attempt to obtain sensitive information such as usernames, passwords and credit card details by disguising oneself as a trustworthy entity in an electronic communication. Typically carried out by email spoofing or instant messaging, it often directs users to enter personal information at a fake website which matches the look and feel of the legitimate site.

Exam Probability: **High**

22. *Answer choices:*

(see index for correct answer)

- a. Hot reading
- b. Ponzi scheme
- c. Thai zig zag scam
- d. Phishing

Guidance: level 1

:: Commerce ::

An _____ is a bank that offers card association branded payment cards directly to consumers. The name is derived from the practice of issuing payment to the acquiring bank on behalf of its customer.

Exam Probability: **Low**

23. *Answer choices:*

(see index for correct answer)

- a. Video rental shop
- b. Factory
- c. Issuing bank
- d. Acquiring bank

Guidance: level 1

:: International trade ::

A _____ is a document issued by a carrier to acknowledge receipt of cargo for shipment. Although the term historically related only to carriage by sea, a _____ may today be used for any type of carriage of goods.

Exam Probability: **High**

24. *Answer choices:*

(see index for correct answer)

- a. Bill of lading
- b. Combined Nomenclature
- c. Indian Ocean trade
- d. Competitiveness

Guidance: level 1

:: Management ::

A _____ is an idea of the future or desired result that a person or a group of people envisions, plans and commits to achieve. People endeavor to reach _____ s within a finite time by setting deadlines.

Exam Probability: **Medium**

25. *Answer choices:*

(see index for correct answer)

- a. Goal
- b. Earned value management
- c. Intelligent customer
- d. Design leadership

Guidance: level 1

:: Commercial item transport and distribution ::

A _____, forwarder, or forwarding agent, also known as a non-vessel operating common carrier , is a person or company that organizes shipments for individuals or corporations to get goods from the manufacturer or producer to a market, customer or final point of distribution. Forwarders contract with a carrier or often multiple carriers to move the goods. A forwarder does not move the goods but acts as an expert in the logistics network. These carriers can use a variety of shipping modes, including ships, airplanes, trucks, and railroads, and often do utilize multiple modes for a single shipment. For example, the _____ may arrange to have cargo moved from a plant to an airport by truck, flown to the destination city, then moved from the airport to a customer's building by another truck.

Exam Probability: **Low**

26. *Answer choices:*

(see index for correct answer)

- a. MC Freight Systems
- b. Supply chain management
- c. Port centric logistics
- d. Skid unit

Guidance: level 1

:: Banking ::

A _____ is a financial institution that accepts deposits from the public and creates credit. Lending activities can be performed either directly or indirectly through capital markets. Due to their importance in the financial stability of a country, _____ s are highly regulated in most countries. Most nations have institutionalized a system known as fractional reserve _____ ing under which _____ s hold liquid assets equal to only a portion of their current liabilities. In addition to other regulations intended to ensure liquidity, _____ s are generally subject to minimum capital requirements based on an international set of capital standards, known as the Basel Accords.

Exam Probability: **High**

27. *Answer choices:*

(see index for correct answer)

- a. Variance risk premium
- b. Bank run

- c. Anonymous Internet banking
- d. Narrow banking

Guidance: level 1

:: Evaluation ::

_____ is a way of preventing mistakes and defects in manufactured products and avoiding problems when delivering products or services to customers; which ISO 9000 defines as "part of quality management focused on providing confidence that quality requirements will be fulfilled". This defect prevention in _____ differs subtly from defect detection and rejection in quality control and has been referred to as a shift left since it focuses on quality earlier in the process .

Exam Probability: **Medium**

28. *Answer choices:*
(see index for correct answer)

- a. Impact assessment
- b. CESG Claims Tested Mark
- c. Formative assessment
- d. Continuous assessment

Guidance: level 1

_____ Holdings, Inc. is an American company operating a worldwide online payments system that supports online money transfers and serves as an electronic alternative to traditional paper methods like checks and money orders. The company operates as a payment processor for online vendors, auction sites, and many other commercial users, for which it charges a fee in exchange for benefits such as one-click transactions and password memory. _____'s payment system, also called _____, is considered a type of payment rail.

Exam Probability: **High**

29. *Answer choices:*

(see index for correct answer)

- a. Character
- b. imperative
- c. PayPal
- d. empathy

Guidance: level 1

Business Model Canvas is a strategic management and lean startup template for developing new or documenting existing business models. It is a visual chart with elements describing a firm's or product's value proposition, infrastructure, customers, and finances. It assists firms in aligning their activities by illustrating potential trade-offs.

Exam Probability: **Low**

30. *Answer choices:*

(see index for correct answer)

- a. deep-level diversity
- b. hierarchical
- c. surface-level diversity
- d. Cost structure

Guidance: level 1

_____ is a marketing communication that employs an openly sponsored, non-personal message to promote or sell a product, service or idea. Sponsors of _____ are typically businesses wishing to promote their products or services. _____ is differentiated from public relations in that an advertiser pays for and has control over the message. It differs from personal selling in that the message is non-personal, i.e., not directed to a particular individual. _____ is communicated through various mass media, including traditional media such as newspapers, magazines, television, radio, outdoor _____ or direct mail; and new media such as search results, blogs, social media, websites or text messages. The actual presentation of the message in a medium is referred to as an advertisement, or "ad" or advert for short.

Exam Probability: **High**

31. *Answer choices:*

(see index for correct answer)

- a. deep-level diversity
- b. Advertising
- c. surface-level diversity
- d. interpersonal communication

Guidance: level 1

:: E-commerce ::

_____ is the business-to-business or business-to-consumer or business-to-government purchase and sale of supplies, work, and services through the Internet as well as other information and networking systems, such as electronic data interchange and enterprise resource planning.

Exam Probability: **High**

32. *Answer choices:*

(see index for correct answer)

- a. E-commerce in Southeast Asia
- b. Quisk
- c. E-procurement
- d. TXT402

Guidance: level 1

:: Fraud ::

In law, _____ is intentional deception to secure unfair or unlawful gain, or to deprive a victim of a legal right. _____ can violate civil law, a criminal law, or it may cause no loss of money, property or legal right but still be an element of another civil or criminal wrong. The purpose of _____ may be monetary gain or other benefits, for example by obtaining a passport, travel document, or driver's license, or mortgage _____, where the perpetrator may attempt to qualify for a mortgage by way of false statements.

Exam Probability: **Low**

33. *Answer choices:*

(see index for correct answer)

- a. Fraud
- b. Long firm
- c. Plastic shaman
- d. 419 scams

Guidance: level 1

:: Stochastic processes ::

_____ in its modern meaning is a "new idea, creative thoughts, new imaginations in form of device or method". _____ is often also viewed as the application of better solutions that meet new requirements, unarticulated needs, or existing market needs. Such _____ takes place through the provision of more-effective products, processes, services, technologies, or business models that are made available to markets, governments and society. An _____ is something original and more effective and, as a consequence, new, that "breaks into" the market or society. _____ is related to, but not the same as, invention, as _____ is more apt to involve the practical implementation of an invention to make a meaningful impact in the market or society, and not all _____ s require an invention. _____ often manifests itself via the engineering process, when the problem being solved is of a technical or scientific nature. The opposite of _____ is exnovation.

Exam Probability: **High**

34. Answer choices:

(see index for correct answer)

- a. M/G/1 queue
- b. Zero-order process
- c. Hitting time
- d. Innovation

Guidance: level 1

:: ::

An _____ is the production of goods or related services within an economy. The major source of revenue of a group or company is the indicator of its relevant _____ . When a large group has multiple sources of revenue generation, it is considered to be working in different industries. Manufacturing _____ became a key sector of production and labour in European and North American countries during the Industrial Revolution, upsetting previous mercantile and feudal economies. This came through many successive rapid advances in technology, such as the production of steel and coal.

Exam Probability: **Low**

35. Answer choices:

(see index for correct answer)

- a. process perspective
- b. Industry

- c. levels of analysis
- d. similarity-attraction theory

Guidance: level 1

:: Industry ::

_____ , also known as flow production or continuous production, is the production of large amounts of standardized products, including and especially on assembly lines. Together with job production and batch production, it is one of the three main production methods.

Exam Probability: **Low**

36. *Answer choices:*
(see index for correct answer)

- a. Sunrise industry
- b. Cleaner
- c. Maintenance engineering
- d. Energy policy

Guidance: level 1

:: Commerce ::

A _____ is an employee within a company, business or other organization who is responsible at some level for buying or approving the acquisition of goods and services needed by the company. Responsible for buying the best quality products, goods and services for their company at the most competitive prices, _____ s work in a wide range of sectors for many different organizations. The position responsibilities may be the same as that of a buyer or purchasing agent, or may include wider supervisory or managerial responsibilities. A _____ may oversee the acquisition of materials needed for production, general supplies for offices and facilities, equipment, or construction contracts. A _____ often supervises purchasing agents and buyers, but in small companies the _____ may also be the purchasing agent or buyer. The _____ position may also carry the title "Procurement Manager" or in the public sector, "Procurement Officer". He or she can come from both an Engineering or Economics background.

Exam Probability: **High**

37. *Answer choices:*

(see index for correct answer)

- a. Purchasing manager
- b. Barter
- c. Agio
- d. Deal transaction

Guidance: level 1

:: Basic financial concepts ::

_____ is a sustained increase in the general price level of goods and services in an economy over a period of time. When the general price level rises, each unit of currency buys fewer goods and services; consequently, _____ reflects a reduction in the purchasing power per unit of money a loss of real value in the medium of exchange and unit of account within the economy. The measure of _____ is the _____ rate, the annualized percentage change in a general price index, usually the consumer price index, over time. The opposite of _____ is deflation.

Exam Probability: **Medium**

38. *Answer choices:*

(see index for correct answer)

- a. Inflation
- b. Base effect
- c. balloon payment
- d. Tax shield

Guidance: level 1

:: ::

_____ is the practice of deliberately managing the spread of information between an individual or an organization and the public. _____ may include an organization or individual gaining exposure to their audiences using topics of public interest and news items that do not require direct payment. This differentiates it from advertising as a form of marketing communications. _____ is the idea of creating coverage for clients for free, rather than marketing or advertising. But now, advertising is also a part of greater PR Activities. An example of good _____ would be generating an article featuring a client, rather than paying for the client to be advertised next to the article. The aim of _____ is to inform the public, prospective customers, investors, partners, employees, and other stakeholders and ultimately persuade them to maintain a positive or favorable view about the organization, its leadership, products, or political decisions. _____ professionals typically work for PR and marketing firms, businesses and companies, government, and public officials as PIOs and nongovernmental organizations, and nonprofit organizations. Jobs central to _____ include account coordinator, account executive, account supervisor, and media relations manager.

Exam Probability: **High**

39. *Answer choices:*

(see index for correct answer)

- a. levels of analysis
- b. Public relations
- c. Sarbanes-Oxley act of 2002
- d. cultural

Guidance: level 1

:: ::

_____ is the extraction of valuable minerals or other geological materials from the earth, usually from an ore body, lode, vein, seam, reef or placer deposit. These deposits form a mineralized package that is of economic interest to the miner.

Exam Probability: **High**

40. *Answer choices:*

(see index for correct answer)

- a. Mining
- b. empathy
- c. process perspective
- d. interpersonal communication

Guidance: level 1

:: ::

_____ , in general use, is a devotion and faithfulness to a nation, cause, philosophy, country, group, or person. Philosophers disagree on what can be an object of _____ , as some argue that _____ is strictly interpersonal and only another human being can be the object of _____ . The definition of _____ in law and political science is the fidelity of an individual to a nation, either one's nation of birth, or one's declared home nation by oath .

Exam Probability: **Low**

41. *Answer choices:*

(see index for correct answer)

- a. open system
- b. functional perspective
- c. cultural
- d. Character

Guidance: level 1

:: ::

A _____ consists of one people who live in the same dwelling and share meals. It may also consist of a single family or another group of people. A dwelling is considered to contain multiple _____ s if meals or living spaces are not shared. The _____ is the basic unit of analysis in many social, microeconomic and government models, and is important to economics and inheritance.

Exam Probability: **Low**

42. *Answer choices:*

(see index for correct answer)

- a. functional perspective
- b. hierarchical

- c. Household
- d. co-culture

Guidance: level 1

:: Minimum wage ::

A _____ is the lowest remuneration that employers can legally pay their workers—the price floor below which workers may not sell their labor. Most countries had introduced _____ legislation by the end of the 20th century.

Exam Probability: **High**

43. *Answer choices:*

(see index for correct answer)

- a. National Anti-Sweating League
- b. Minimum wage
- c. Working poor
- d. Minimum wage in Taiwan

Guidance: level 1

:: Materials ::

A _____ , also known as a feedstock, unprocessed material, or primary commodity, is a basic material that is used to produce goods, finished products, energy, or intermediate materials which are feedstock for future finished products. As feedstock, the term connotes these materials are bottleneck assets and are highly important with regard to producing other products. An example of this is crude oil, which is a _____ and a feedstock used in the production of industrial chemicals, fuels, plastics, and pharmaceutical goods; lumber is a _____ used to produce a variety of products including all types of furniture. The term " _____ " denotes materials in minimally processed or unprocessed in states; e.g., raw latex, crude oil, cotton, coal, raw biomass, iron ore, air, logs, or water i.e. "...any product of agriculture, forestry, fishing and any other mineral that is in its natural form or which has undergone the transformation required to prepare it for internationally marketing in substantial volumes."

Exam Probability: **Medium**

44. *Answer choices:*

(see index for correct answer)

- a. Raw material
- b. Tensometer
- c. Nanophase
- d. Slag

Guidance: level 1

:: Warrants issued in Hong Kong Stock Exchange ::

_____ is a chemical element with symbol Ag and atomic number 47. A soft, white, lustrous transition metal, it exhibits the highest electrical conductivity, thermal conductivity, and reflectivity of any metal. The metal is found in the Earth's crust in the pure, free elemental form , as an alloy with gold and other metals, and in minerals such as argentite and chlorargyrite. Most _____ is produced as a byproduct of copper, gold, lead, and zinc refining.

Exam Probability: **High**

45. *Answer choices:*

(see index for correct answer)

- a. China Shenhua Energy Company
- b. Hong Kong Stock Exchange
- c. China Railway Engineering Corporation
- d. Silver

Guidance: level 1

:: Project management ::

_____ is the right to exercise power, which can be formalized by a state and exercised by way of judges, appointed executives of government, or the ecclesiastical or priestly appointed representatives of a God or other deities.

Exam Probability: **High**

46. Answer choices:

(see index for correct answer)

- a. Authority
- b. Project manufacturing
- c. Point of total assumption
- d. American Society of Professional Estimators

Guidance: level 1

:: ::

A _____ is a structured form of play, usually undertaken for enjoyment and sometimes used as an educational tool. _____ s are distinct from work, which is usually carried out for remuneration, and from art, which is more often an expression of aesthetic or ideological elements. However, the distinction is not clear-cut, and many _____ s are also considered to be work or art.

Exam Probability: **Low**

47. Answer choices:

(see index for correct answer)

- a. surface-level diversity
- b. levels of analysis
- c. Game
- d. Sarbanes-Oxley act of 2002

Guidance: level 1

:: Logistics ::

_____ is generally the detailed organization and implementation of a complex operation. In a general business sense, _____ is the management of the flow of things between the point of origin and the point of consumption in order to meet requirements of customers or corporations. The resources managed in _____ may include tangible goods such as materials, equipment, and supplies, as well as food and other consumable items. The _____ of physical items usually involves the integration of information flow, materials handling, production, packaging, inventory, transportation, warehousing, and often security.

Exam Probability: **Low**

48. *Answer choices:*
(see index for correct answer)

- a. Logistics
- b. DASH7
- c. Liquid logistics
- d. Trailer tracking

Guidance: level 1

:: Workplace ::

_____ is asystematic determination of a subject's merit, worth and significance, using criteria governed by a set of standards. It can assist an organization, program, design, project or any other intervention or initiative to assess any aim, realisable concept/proposal, or any alternative, to help in decision-making; or to ascertain the degree of achievement or value in regard to the aim and objectives and results of any such action that has been completed. The primary purpose of _____, in addition to gaining insight into prior or existing initiatives, is to enable reflection and assist in the identification of future change.

Exam Probability: **Medium**

49. *Answer choices:*

(see index for correct answer)

- a. Evaluation
- b. Workplace conflict
- c. Control freak
- d. Queen bee syndrome

Guidance: level 1

:: Auctioneering ::

A _____ is one of several similar kinds of auctions. Most commonly, it means an auction in which the auctioneer begins with a high asking price, and lowers it until some participant accepts the price, or it reaches a predetermined reserve price. This has also been called a clock auction or open-outcry descending-price auction. This type of auction is good for auctioning goods quickly, since a sale never requires more than one bid. Strategically, it's similar to a first-price sealed-bid auction.

Exam Probability: **Low**

50. *Answer choices:*
(see index for correct answer)

- a. Reppert School of Auctioneering
- b. Chinese auction
- c. Dutch auction
- d. Auction catalog

Guidance: level 1

:: E-commerce ::

_____ is a type of performance-based marketing in which a business rewards one or more affiliates for each visitor or customer brought by the affiliate's own marketing efforts.

Exam Probability: **Low**

51. *Answer choices:*

(see index for correct answer)

- a. Affiliate marketing
- b. Electronic billing
- c. Social commerce
- d. Boston Computer Exchange

Guidance: level 1

:: Summary statistics ::

_____ is the number of occurrences of a repeating event per unit of time. It is also referred to as temporal _____ , which emphasizes the contrast to spatial _____ and angular _____ . The period is the duration of time of one cycle in a repeating event, so the period is the reciprocal of the _____ . For example: if a newborn baby's heart beats at a _____ of 120 times a minute, its period—the time interval between beats—is half a second . _____ is an important parameter used in science and engineering to specify the rate of oscillatory and vibratory phenomena, such as mechanical vibrations, audio signals , radio waves, and light.

Exam Probability: **Medium**

52. *Answer choices:*

(see index for correct answer)

- a. Generalized entropy index
- b. Five-number summary

- c. Frequency
- d. Lorenz asymmetry coefficient

Guidance: level 1

:: Supply chain management ::

_____ is a variable pricing strategy, based on understanding, anticipating and influencing consumer behavior in order to maximize revenue or profits from a fixed, time-limited resource. As a specific, inventory-focused branch of revenue management, _____ involves strategic control of inventory to sell the right product to the right customer at the right time for the right price. This process can result in price discrimination, in which customers consuming identical goods or services are charged different prices. _____ is a large revenue generator for several major industries; Robert Crandall, former Chairman and CEO of American Airlines, gave _____ its name and has called it "the single most important technical development in transportation management since we entered deregulation."

Exam Probability: **Medium**

53. *Answer choices:*

(see index for correct answer)

- a. Supply chain security
- b. Service management
- c. Calculating demand forecast accuracy
- d. Yield management

Guidance: level 1

:: ::

A _____ or GM is an executive who has overall responsibility for managing both the revenue and cost elements of a company's income statement, known as profit & loss responsibility. A _____ usually oversees most or all of the firm's marketing and sales functions as well as the day-to-day operations of the business. Frequently, the _____ is responsible for effective planning, delegating, coordinating, staffing, organizing, and decision making to attain desirable profit making results for an organization.

Exam Probability: **Medium**

54. *Answer choices:*

(see index for correct answer)

- a. personal values
- b. Sarbanes-Oxley act of 2002
- c. General manager
- d. information systems assessment

Guidance: level 1

:: Decision theory ::

Within economics the concept of _____ is used to model worth or value, but its usage has evolved significantly over time. The term was introduced initially as a measure of pleasure or satisfaction within the theory of utilitarianism by moral philosophers such as Jeremy Bentham and John Stuart Mill. But the term has been adapted and reapplied within neoclassical economics, which dominates modern economic theory, as a _____ function that represents a consumer's preference ordering over a choice set. As such, it is devoid of its original interpretation as a measurement of the pleasure or satisfaction obtained by the consumer from that choice.

Exam Probability: **Medium**

55. *Answer choices:*

(see index for correct answer)

- a. Distinction bias
- b. Utility
- c. Rational planning model
- d. Decision-matrix method

Guidance: level 1

:: Asset ::

In financial accounting, an _____ is any resource owned by the business. Anything tangible or intangible that can be owned or controlled to produce value and that is held by a company to produce positive economic value is an _____. Simply stated, _____ s represent value of ownership that can be converted into cash. The balance sheet of a firm records the monetary value of the _____ s owned by that firm. It covers money and other valuables belonging to an individual or to a business.

Exam Probability: **Medium**

56. *Answer choices:*

(see index for correct answer)

- a. Current asset
- b. Fixed asset

Guidance: level 1

:: ::

Competition arises whenever at least two parties strive for a goal which cannot be shared: where one`s gain is the other`s loss.

Exam Probability: **Low**

57. *Answer choices:*

(see index for correct answer)

- a. Competitor
- b. Sarbanes-Oxley act of 2002
- c. deep-level diversity
- d. Character

Guidance: level 1

:: Theories ::

A _____ union is a type of multinational political union where negotiated power is delegated to an authority by governments of member states.

Exam Probability: **High**

58. *Answer choices:*
(see index for correct answer)

- a. Supranational
- b. incrementalism

Guidance: level 1

:: Securities (finance) ::

A _____ is a container that is traditionally constructed from stiff fibers, and can be made from a range of materials, including wood splints, runners, and cane. While most _____ s are made from plant materials, other materials such as horsehair, baleen, or metal wire can be used. _____ s are generally woven by hand. Some _____ s are fitted with a lid, while others are left open on top.

Exam Probability: **High**

59. *Answer choices:*

(see index for correct answer)

- a. Principal at risk notes
- b. Indirect holding system
- c. Bought out deal
- d. Basket

Guidance: level 1

Business ethics

Business ethics (also known as corporate ethics) is a form of applied ethics or professional ethics, that examines ethical principles and moral or ethical problems that can arise in a business environment. It applies to all aspects of business conduct and is relevant to the conduct of individuals and entire organizations. These ethics originate from individuals, organizational statements or from the legal system. These norms, values, ethical, and unethical practices are what is used to guide business. They help those businesses maintain a better connection with their stakeholders.

:: Coal ::

_____ is a combustible black or brownish-black sedimentary rock, formed as rock strata called _____ seams. _____ is mostly carbon with variable amounts of other elements; chiefly hydrogen, sulfur, oxygen, and nitrogen. _____ is formed if dead plant matter decays into peat and over millions of years the heat and pressure of deep burial converts the peat into _____. Vast deposits of _____ originates in former wetlands—called _____ forests—that covered much of the Earth's tropical land areas during the late Carboniferous and Permian times.

Exam Probability: **High**

1. *Answer choices:*

(see index for correct answer)

- a. Maceral
- b. Vitrinite
- c. Coal hole
- d. Coal

Guidance: level 1

:: Carbon finance ::

The _____ is an international treaty which extends the 1992 United Nations Framework Convention on Climate Change that commits state parties to reduce greenhouse gas emissions, based on the scientific consensus that global warming is occurring and it is extremely likely that human-made CO2 emissions have predominantly caused it. The _____ was adopted in Kyoto, Japan on 11 December 1997 and entered into force on 16 February 2005. There are currently 192 parties to the Protocol.

Exam Probability: **Low**

2. *Answer choices:*

(see index for correct answer)

- a. EcoAid
- b. Kyoto Protocol
- c. Carbon finance
- d. The London Accord

Guidance: level 1

:: Management ::

The term _____ refers to measures designed to increase the degree of autonomy and self-determination in people and in communities in order to enable them to represent their interests in a responsible and self-determined way, acting on their own authority. It is the process of becoming stronger and more confident, especially in controlling one's life and claiming one's rights.
_____ as action refers both to the process of self-_____ and to professional support of people, which enables them to overcome their sense of powerlessness and lack of influence, and to recognize and use their resources.
To do work with power.

Exam Probability: **Medium**

3. *Answer choices:*

(see index for correct answer)

- a. Empowerment
- b. Focused improvement
- c. Business model
- d. Wireless informatics

Guidance: level 1

:: Natural gas ::

_____ is a naturally occurring hydrocarbon gas mixture consisting primarily of methane, but commonly including varying amounts of other higher alkanes, and sometimes a small percentage of carbon dioxide, nitrogen, hydrogen sulfide, or helium. It is formed when layers of decomposing plant and animal matter are exposed to intense heat and pressure under the surface of the Earth over millions of years. The energy that the plants originally obtained from the sun is stored in the form of chemical bonds in the gas.

Exam Probability: **High**

4. *Answer choices:*

(see index for correct answer)

- a. Natural gas
- b. Natural-gas condensate
- c. Clathrate hydrate
- d. Reid vapor pressure

Guidance: level 1

:: Competition regulators ::

The _____ is an independent agency of the United States government, established in 1914 by the _____ Act. Its principal mission is the promotion of consumer protection and the elimination and prevention of anticompetitive business practices, such as coercive monopoly. It is headquartered in the _____ Building in Washington, D.C.

Exam Probability: **High**

5. *Answer choices:*

(see index for correct answer)

- a. Competition Appeal Tribunal
- b. Competition Bureau
- c. Federal Trade Commission
- d. Superintendency of Industry and Commerce

Guidance: level 1

:: Business ::

_____ , or built-in obsolescence, in industrial design and economics is a policy of planning or designing a product with an artificially limited useful life, so that it becomes obsolete after a certain period of time. The rationale behind this strategy is to generate long-term sales volume by reducing the time between repeat purchases .

Exam Probability: **Low**

6. *Answer choices:*

(see index for correct answer)

- a. Planned obsolescence
- b. Sales

- c. Religion and business
- d. Attribution

Guidance: level 1

:: ::

_____ is a non-governmental environmental organization with offices in over 39 countries and an international coordinating body in Amsterdam, the Netherlands. _____ was founded in 1971 by Irving Stowe, and Dorothy Stowe, Canadian and US ex-pat environmental activists. _____ states its goal is to "ensure the ability of the Earth to nurture life in all its diversity" and focuses its campaigning on worldwide issues such as climate change, deforestation, overfishing, commercial whaling, genetic engineering, and anti-nuclear issues. It uses direct action, lobbying, research, and ecotage to achieve its goals. The global organization does not accept funding from governments, corporations, or political parties, relying on three million individual supporters and foundation grants. _____ has a general consultative status with the United Nations Economic and Social Council and is a founding member of the INGO Accountability Charter, an international non-governmental organization that intends to foster accountability and transparency of non-governmental organizations.

Exam Probability: **Low**

7. *Answer choices:*

(see index for correct answer)

- a. process perspective
- b. cultural

- c. Greenpeace
- d. corporate values

Guidance: level 1

:: ::

A _____ is an astronomical body orbiting a star or stellar remnant that is massive enough to be rounded by its own gravity, is not massive enough to cause thermonuclear fusion, and has cleared its neighbouring region of _____ esimals.

Exam Probability: **High**

8. *Answer choices:*

(see index for correct answer)

- a. process perspective
- b. hierarchical
- c. levels of analysis
- d. Sarbanes-Oxley act of 2002

Guidance: level 1

:: Confidence tricks ::

A _____ is a business model that recruits members via a promise of payments or services for enrolling others into the scheme, rather than supplying investments or sale of products. As recruiting multiplies, recruiting becomes quickly impossible, and most members are unable to profit; as such, _____ s are unsustainable and often illegal.

Exam Probability: **High**

9. *Answer choices:*

(see index for correct answer)

- a. Cackle-bladder
- b. Salting
- c. Hongcheng Magic Liquid
- d. Pyramid scheme

Guidance: level 1

:: ::

_____ generally refers to a focus on the needs or desires of one's self. A number of philosophical, psychological, and economic theories examine the role of _____ in motivating human action.

Exam Probability: **Low**

10. *Answer choices:*

(see index for correct answer)

- a. co-culture
- b. hierarchical perspective
- c. levels of analysis
- d. Self-interest

Guidance: level 1

:: Price fixing convictions ::

_____ AG is a German multinational conglomerate company headquartered in Berlin and Munich and the largest industrial manufacturing company in Europe with branch offices abroad.

Exam Probability: **Medium**

11. *Answer choices:*

(see index for correct answer)

- a. Christmas tree production in Denmark
- b. ThyssenKrupp
- c. Hoffmann-La Roche
- d. Siemens

Guidance: level 1

:: ::

A _____ is a set of rules, often written, with regards to clothing. _____ s are created out of social perceptions and norms, and vary based on purpose, circumstances and occasions. Different societies and cultures are likely to have different _____ s.

Exam Probability: **Low**

12. *Answer choices:*

(see index for correct answer)

- a. deep-level diversity
- b. Dress code
- c. similarity-attraction theory
- d. surface-level diversity

Guidance: level 1

:: Agricultural labor ::

The _____ of America, or more commonly just _____ , is a labor union for farmworkers in the United States. It originated from the merger of two workers' rights organizations, the Agricultural Workers Organizing Committee led by organizer Larry Itliong, and the National Farm Workers Association led by César Chávez and Dolores Huerta. They became allied and transformed from workers' rights organizations into a union as a result of a series of strikes in 1965, when the mostly Filipino farmworkers of the AWOC in Delano, California initiated a grape strike, and the NFWA went on strike in support. As a result of the commonality in goals and methods, the NFWA and the AWOC formed the _____ Organizing Committee on August 22, 1966. This organization was accepted into the AFL-CIO in 1972 and changed its name to the _____ Union.

Exam Probability: **High**

13. *Answer choices:*

(see index for correct answer)

- a. United Farm Workers
- b. Bailleur
- c. Ethical purchasing groups
- d. Agricultural Wheel

Guidance: level 1

:: Ethical banking ::

A _____ or community development finance institution - abbreviated in both cases to CDFI - is a financial institution that provides credit and financial services to underserved markets and populations, primarily in the USA but also in the UK. A CDFI may be a community development bank, a community development credit union , a community development loan fund , a community development venture capital fund , a microenterprise development loan fund, or a community development corporation.

Exam Probability: **High**

14. *Answer choices:*

(see index for correct answer)

- a. Shared Interest
- b. Institute for Social Banking
- c. Citizens Bank of Canada
- d. Community development financial institution

Guidance: level 1

_____ is "property consisting of land and the buildings on it, along with its natural resources such as crops, minerals or water; immovable property of this nature; an interest vested in this an item of real property, buildings or housing in general. Also: the business of _____ ; the profession of buying, selling, or renting land, buildings, or housing." It is a legal term used in jurisdictions whose legal system is derived from English common law, such as India, England, Wales, Northern Ireland, United States, Canada, Pakistan, Australia, and New Zealand.

Exam Probability: **Low**

15. *Answer choices:*

(see index for correct answer)

- a. Character
- b. hierarchical perspective
- c. Real estate
- d. functional perspective

Guidance: level 1

:: Toxicology ::

_____ or lead-based paint is paint containing lead. As pigment, lead chromate, Lead oxide,, and lead carbonate are the most common forms. Lead is added to paint to accelerate drying, increase durability, maintain a fresh appearance, and resist moisture that causes corrosion. It is one of the main health and environmental hazards associated with paint. In some countries, lead continues to be added to paint intended for domestic use, whereas countries such as the U.S. and the UK have regulations prohibiting this, although _____ may still be found in older properties painted prior to the introduction of such regulations. Although lead has been banned from household paints in the United States since 1978, paint used in road markings may still contain it. Alternatives such as water-based, lead-free traffic paint are readily available, and many states and federal agencies have changed their purchasing contracts to buy these instead.

Exam Probability: **Low**

16. *Answer choices:*

(see index for correct answer)

- a. CIOMS/RUCAM scale
- b. Lead paint
- c. Toxicology
- d. Toxicology testing

Guidance: level 1

:: Corporate governance ::

_____ refers to the practice of members of a corporate board of directors serving on the boards of multiple corporations. A person that sits on multiple boards is known as a multiple director. Two firms have a direct interlock if a director or executive of one firm is also a director of the other, and an indirect interlock if a director of each sits on the board of a third firm. This practice, although widespread and lawful, raises questions about the quality and independence of board decisions.

Exam Probability: **Medium**

17. *Answer choices:*

(see index for correct answer)

- a. Interlocking directorate
- b. Yasser Akkaoui
- c. Corporate security
- d. InfoSTEP

Guidance: level 1

:: Financial regulatory authorities of the United States ::

The _____ is an agency of the United States government responsible for consumer protection in the financial sector. CFPB's jurisdiction includes banks, credit unions, securities firms, payday lenders, mortgage-servicing operations, foreclosure relief services, debt collectors and other financial companies operating in the United States.

Exam Probability: **Low**

18. *Answer choices:*

(see index for correct answer)

- a. Securities Investor Protection Corporation
- b. Operation Choke Point
- c. National Credit Union Administration
- d. Consumer Financial Protection Bureau

Guidance: level 1

:: ::

In ecology, a _____ is the type of natural environment in which a particular species of organism lives. It is characterized by both physical and biological features. A species' _____ is those places where it can find food, shelter, protection and mates for reproduction.

Exam Probability: **Low**

19. *Answer choices:*

(see index for correct answer)

- a. cultural
- b. surface-level diversity
- c. Character

- d. Sarbanes-Oxley act of 2002

Guidance: level 1

:: Anti-Revisionism ::

_____, officially the German Democratic Republic, was a country that existed from 1949 to 1990, when the eastern portion of Germany was part of the Eastern Bloc during the Cold War. It described itself as a socialist "workers' and peasants' state", and the territory was administered and occupied by Soviet forces at the end of World War II — the Soviet Occupation Zone of the Potsdam Agreement, bounded on the east by the Oder–Neisse line. The Soviet zone surrounded West Berlin but did not include it; as a result, West Berlin remained outside the jurisdiction of the GDR.

Exam Probability: **Medium**

20. *Answer choices:*
(see index for correct answer)

- a. New Communist Movement
- b. Party of Labour of Albania
- c. Ho Chi Minh Thought
- d. Chilean Communist Party

Guidance: level 1

:: ::

The American Recovery and Reinvestment Act of 2009, nicknamed the _____, was a stimulus package enacted by the 111th U.S. Congress and signed into law by President Barack Obama in February 2009. Developed in response to the Great Recession, the ARRA's primary objective was to save existing jobs and create new ones as soon as possible. Other objectives were to provide temporary relief programs for those most affected by the recession and invest in infrastructure, education, health, and renewable energy.

Exam Probability: **Low**

21. *Answer choices:*

(see index for correct answer)

- a. empathy
- b. Recovery Act
- c. co-culture
- d. process perspective

Guidance: level 1

:: Social philosophy ::

The _____ describes the unintended social benefits of an individual's self-interested actions. Adam Smith first introduced the concept in The Theory of Moral Sentiments, written in 1759, invoking it in reference to income distribution. In this work, however, the idea of the market is not discussed, and the word "capitalism" is never used.

Exam Probability: **High**

22. *Answer choices:*

(see index for correct answer)

- a. Freedom to contract
- b. vacancy chain
- c. Societal attitudes towards abortion
- d. Veil of Ignorance

Guidance: level 1

:: ::

The _____, the Calvinist work ethic or the Puritan work ethic is a work ethic concept in theology, sociology, economics and history that emphasizes that hard work, discipline and frugality are a result of a person's subscription to the values espoused by the Protestant faith, particularly Calvinism. The phrase was initially coined in 1904–1905 by Max Weber in his book The Protestant Ethic and the Spirit of Capitalism.

Exam Probability: **Low**

23. *Answer choices:*

(see index for correct answer)

- a. surface-level diversity
- b. hierarchical perspective
- c. functional perspective
- d. Protestant work ethic

Guidance: level 1

:: ::

The _____ of 1906 was the first of a series of significant consumer protection laws which was enacted by Congress in the 20th century and led to the creation of the Food and Drug Administration. Its main purpose was to ban foreign and interstate traffic in adulterated or mislabeled food and drug products, and it directed the U.S. Bureau of Chemistry to inspect products and refer offenders to prosecutors. It required that active ingredients be placed on the label of a drug's packaging and that drugs could not fall below purity levels established by the United States Pharmacopeia or the National Formulary. The Jungle by Upton Sinclair with its graphic and revolting descriptions of unsanitary conditions and unscrupulous practices rampant in the meatpacking industry, was an inspirational piece that kept the public's attention on the important issue of unhygienic meat processing plants that later led to food inspection legislation. Sinclair quipped, "I aimed at the public's heart and by accident I hit it in the stomach," as outraged readers demanded and got the pure food law.

Exam Probability: **Medium**

24. Answer choices:

(see index for correct answer)

- a. deep-level diversity
- b. process perspective
- c. levels of analysis
- d. Pure Food and Drug Act

Guidance: level 1

:: Ethically disputed business practices ::

_____ is the trading of a public company's stock or other securities by individuals with access to nonpublic information about the company. In various countries, some kinds of trading based on insider information is illegal. This is because it is seen as unfair to other investors who do not have access to the information, as the investor with insider information could potentially make larger profits than a typical investor could make. The rules governing _____ are complex and vary significantly from country to country. The extent of enforcement also varies from one country to another. The definition of insider in one jurisdiction can be broad, and may cover not only insiders themselves but also any persons related to them, such as brokers, associates and even family members. A person who becomes aware of non-public information and trades on that basis may be guilty of a crime.

Exam Probability: **High**

25. *Answer choices:*

(see index for correct answer)

- a. Suicide bidding
- b. Conflict of interest
- c. Banishment room
- d. Gaming the system

Guidance: level 1

:: Office work ::

_____ is the process and behavior in human interactions involving power and authority. It is also a tool to assess the operational capacity and to balance diverse views of interested parties. It is also known as office politics and organizational politics. It is the use of power and social networking within an organization to achieve changes that benefit the organization or individuals within it. Influence by individuals may serve personal interests without regard to their effect on the organization itself. Some of the personal advantages may include access to tangible assets, or intangible benefits such as status or pseudo-authority that influences the behavior of others. On the other hand, organizational politics can increase efficiency, form interpersonal relationships, expedite change, and profit the organization and its members simultaneously. Both individuals and groups may engage in office politics which can be highly destructive, as people focus on personal gains at the expense of the organization. "Self-serving political actions can negatively influence our social groupings, cooperation, information sharing, and many other organizational functions." Thus, it is vital to pay attention to organizational politics and create the right political landscape. "Politics is the lubricant that oils your organization's internal gears."
Office politics has also been described as "simply how power gets worked out on a practical, day-to-day basis."

Exam Probability: **Low**

26. *Answer choices:*

(see index for correct answer)

- a. Peter Principle
- b. Career woman
- c. Salaryman
- d. Electronic office

Guidance: level 1

:: Electronic feedback ::

_____ occurs when outputs of a system are routed back as inputs as part of a chain of cause-and-effect that forms a circuit or loop. The system can then be said to feed back into itself. The notion of cause-and-effect has to be handled carefully when applied to _____ systems.

Exam Probability: **Low**

27. *Answer choices:*

(see index for correct answer)

- a. Positive feedback
- b. Feedback

Guidance: level 1

:: United States federal defense and national security legislation ::

The USA _____ is an Act of the U.S. Congress that was signed into law by President George W. Bush on October 26, 2001. The title of the Act is a contrived three letter initialism preceding a seven letter acronym, which in combination stand for Uniting and Strengthening America by Providing Appropriate Tools Required to Intercept and Obstruct Terrorism Act of 2001. The acronym was created by a 23 year old Congressional staffer, Chris Kyle.

Exam Probability: **Low**

28. *Answer choices:*

(see index for correct answer)

- a. USA PATRIOT Act
- b. Export Administration Act

Guidance: level 1

:: Commercial crimes ::

_____ is an agreement between participants on the same side in a market to buy or sell a product, service, or commodity only at a fixed price, or maintain the market conditions such that the price is maintained at a given level by controlling supply and demand.

Exam Probability: **Low**

29. Answer choices:

(see index for correct answer)

- a. pilferage
- b. Gold laundering
- c. Price fixing
- d. Shanzhai

Guidance: level 1

:: Fraud ::

In law, _____ is intentional deception to secure unfair or unlawful gain, or to deprive a victim of a legal right. _____ can violate civil law, a criminal law, or it may cause no loss of money, property or legal right but still be an element of another civil or criminal wrong. The purpose of _____ may be monetary gain or other benefits, for example by obtaining a passport, travel document, or driver's license, or mortgage _____, where the perpetrator may attempt to qualify for a mortgage by way of false statements.

Exam Probability: **High**

30. Answer choices:

(see index for correct answer)

- a. Gone in 60 Seconds
- b. Welfare queen

- c. misleading advertising
- d. Fraud

Guidance: level 1

:: United States federal trade legislation ::

The _____ of 1914 established the Federal Trade Commission. The Act, signed into law by Woodrow Wilson in 1914, outlaws unfair methods of competition and outlaws unfair acts or practices that affect commerce.

Exam Probability: **High**

31. *Answer choices:*

(see index for correct answer)

- a. Warehousing Act
- b. Tariff of 1832
- c. Gould Amendment
- d. Section 22

Guidance: level 1

:: ::

In regulatory jurisdictions that provide for it, _____ is a group of laws and organizations designed to ensure the rights of consumers as well as fair trade, competition and accurate information in the marketplace. The laws are designed to prevent the businesses that engage in fraud or specified unfair practices from gaining an advantage over competitors. They may also provides additional protection for those most vulnerable in society. _____ laws are a form of government regulation that aim to protect the rights of consumers. For example, a government may require businesses to disclose detailed information about products—particularly in areas where safety or public health is an issue, such as food.

Exam Probability: **High**

32. *Answer choices:*

(see index for correct answer)

- a. information systems assessment
- b. hierarchical
- c. Consumer Protection
- d. corporate values

Guidance: level 1

:: Industry ::

_____ is the manner in which a given entity has decided to address issues of energy development including energy production, distribution and consumption. The attributes of _____ may include legislation, international treaties, incentives to investment, guidelines for energy conservation, taxation and other public policy techniques. Energy is a core component of modern economies. A functioning economy requires not only labor and capital but also energy, for manufacturing processes, transportation, communication, agriculture, and more.

Exam Probability: **High**

33. *Answer choices:*

(see index for correct answer)

- a. Low carbon leakage
- b. Sisyphism
- c. Consciousness Industry
- d. Standard Industrial Classification

Guidance: level 1

:: ::

The _____ was a severe worldwide economic depression that took place mostly during the 1930s, beginning in the United States. The timing of the _____ varied across nations; in most countries it started in 1929 and lasted until the late-1930s. It was the longest, deepest, and most widespread depression of the 20th century. In the 21st century, the _____ is commonly used as an example of how intensely the world's economy can decline.

Exam Probability: **Medium**

34. *Answer choices:*

(see index for correct answer)

- a. process perspective
- b. functional perspective
- c. Great Depression
- d. personal values

Guidance: level 1

:: Euthenics ::

_____ is an ethical framework and suggests that an entity, be it an organization or individual, has an obligation to act for the benefit of society at large. _____ is a duty every individual has to perform so as to maintain a balance between the economy and the ecosystems. A trade-off may exist between economic development, in the material sense, and the welfare of the society and environment, though this has been challenged by many reports over the past decade. _____ means sustaining the equilibrium between the two. It pertains not only to business organizations but also to everyone whose any action impacts the environment. This responsibility can be passive, by avoiding engaging in socially harmful acts, or active, by performing activities that directly advance social goals. _____ must be intergenerational since the actions of one generation have consequences on those following.

Exam Probability: **Low**

35. Answer choices:

(see index for correct answer)

- a. Social responsibility
- b. Family and consumer science
- c. Home economics
- d. Minnie Cumnock Blodgett

Guidance: level 1

:: ::

The _____ of 1977 is a United States federal law known primarily for two of its main provisions: one that addresses accounting transparency requirements under the Securities Exchange Act of 1934 and another concerning bribery of foreign officials. The Act was amended in 1988 and in 1998, and has been subject to continued congressional concerns, namely whether its enforcement discourages U.S. companies from investing abroad.

Exam Probability: **Low**

36. Answer choices:

(see index for correct answer)

- a. process perspective
- b. Foreign Corrupt Practices Act
- c. information systems assessment
- d. hierarchical perspective

Guidance: level 1

:: ::

_____ is the practice of deliberately managing the spread of information between an individual or an organization and the public. _____ may include an organization or individual gaining exposure to their audiences using topics of public interest and news items that do not require direct payment. This differentiates it from advertising as a form of marketing communications. _____ is the idea of creating coverage for clients for free, rather than marketing or advertising. But now, advertising is also a part of greater PR Activities.An example of good _____ would be generating an article featuring a client, rather than paying for the client to be advertised next to the article. The aim of _____ is to inform the public, prospective customers, investors, partners, employees, and other stakeholders and ultimately persuade them to maintain a positive or favorable view about the organization, its leadership, products, or political decisions. _____ professionals typically work for PR and marketing firms, businesses and companies, government, and public officials as PIOs and nongovernmental organizations, and nonprofit organizations. Jobs central to _____ include account coordinator, account executive, account supervisor, and media relations manager.

Exam Probability: **Low**

37. *Answer choices:*

(see index for correct answer)

- a. Character
- b. Public relations
- c. empathy

- d. interpersonal communication

Guidance: level 1

:: Business ethics ::

_____ is a type of harassment technique that relates to a sexual nature and the unwelcome or inappropriate promise of rewards in exchange for sexual favors. _____ includes a range of actions from mild transgressions to sexual abuse or assault. Harassment can occur in many different social settings such as the workplace, the home, school, churches, etc. Harassers or victims may be of any gender.

Exam Probability: **Medium**

38. *Answer choices:*

(see index for correct answer)

- a. Conspiracy of Fools
- b. Sweatshop
- c. Corporate Knights
- d. Sexual harassment

Guidance: level 1

:: ::

The _____, founded in 1912, is a private, nonprofit organization whose self-described mission is to focus on advancing marketplace trust, consisting of 106 independently incorporated local BBB organizations in the United States and Canada, coordinated under the Council of _____ s in Arlington, Virginia.

Exam Probability: **Low**

39. *Answer choices:*

(see index for correct answer)

- a. co-culture
- b. hierarchical perspective
- c. levels of analysis
- d. Better Business Bureau

Guidance: level 1

:: Leadership ::

_____ is a theory of leadership where a leader works with teams to identify needed change, creating a vision to guide the change through inspiration, and executing the change in tandem with committed members of a group; it is an integral part of the Full Range Leadership Model. _____ serves to enhance the motivation, morale, and job performance of followers through a variety of mechanisms; these include connecting the follower's sense of identity and self to a project and to the collective identity of the organization; being a role model for followers in order to inspire them and to raise their interest in the project; challenging followers to take greater ownership for their work, and understanding the strengths and weaknesses of followers, allowing the leader to align followers with tasks that enhance their performance.

Exam Probability: **High**

40. *Answer choices:*

(see index for correct answer)

- a. Tribal Leadership
- b. Consideration and Initiating Structure
- c. Transactional leadership
- d. Transformational leadership

Guidance: level 1

:: Power (social and political) ::

:::::::: is a form of reverence gained by a leader who has strong interpersonal relationship skills. _____, as an aspect of personal power, becomes particularly important as organizational leadership becomes increasingly about collaboration and influence, rather than command and control.

Exam Probability: **Low**

41. *Answer choices:*

(see index for correct answer)

- a. need for power
- b. Expert power
- c. Referent power

Guidance: level 1

:: ::

_____ is the collection of mechanisms, processes and relations by which corporations are controlled and operated. Governance structures and principles identify the distribution of rights and responsibilities among different participants in the corporation and include the rules and procedures for making decisions in corporate affairs. _____ is necessary because of the possibility of conflicts of interests between stakeholders, primarily between shareholders and upper management or among shareholders.

Exam Probability: **Low**

42. *Answer choices:*

(see index for correct answer)

- a. similarity-attraction theory
- b. functional perspective
- c. Corporate governance
- d. surface-level diversity

Guidance: level 1

:: Confidence tricks ::

A _____ is a form of fraud that lures investors and pays profits to earlier investors with funds from more recent investors. The scheme leads victims to believe that profits are coming from product sales or other means, and they remain unaware that other investors are the source of funds. A _____ can maintain the illusion of a sustainable business as long as new investors contribute new funds, and as long as most of the investors do not demand full repayment and still believe in the non-existent assets they are purported to own.

Exam Probability: **High**

43. *Answer choices:*

(see index for correct answer)

- a. Bride scam
- b. Patent safe

- c. Ponzi scheme
- d. Miracle cars scam

Guidance: level 1

:: Workplace ::

In business management, _____ is a management style whereby a manager closely observes and/or controls the work of his/her subordinates or employees.

Exam Probability: **Medium**

44. *Answer choices:*

(see index for correct answer)

- a. Occupational stress
- b. Micromanagement
- c. Workplace violence
- d. Workplace deviance

Guidance: level 1

:: White-collar criminals ::

_____ refers to financially motivated, nonviolent crime committed by businesses and government professionals. It was first defined by the sociologist Edwin Sutherland in 1939 as "a crime committed by a person of respectability and high social status in the course of their occupation". Typical _____ s could include wage theft, fraud, bribery, Ponzi schemes, insider trading, labor racketeering, embezzlement, cybercrime, copyright infringement, money laundering, identity theft, and forgery. Lawyers can specialize in _____ .

Exam Probability: **Medium**

45. *Answer choices:*

(see index for correct answer)

- a. Du Jun
- b. Tongsun Park

Guidance: level 1

:: Organizational structure ::

An _____ defines how activities such as task allocation, coordination, and supervision are directed toward the achievement of organizational aims.

Exam Probability: **Medium**

46. *Answer choices:*

(see index for correct answer)

- a. Unorganisation
- b. Automated Bureaucracy
- c. The Starfish and the Spider
- d. Organizational structure

Guidance: level 1

:: Private equity ::

In finance, a high-yield bond is a bond that is rated below investment grade. These bonds have a higher risk of default or other adverse credit events, but typically pay higher yields than better quality bonds in order to make them attractive to investors.

Exam Probability: **Medium**

47. *Answer choices:*
(see index for correct answer)

- a. Private money investing
- b. Divisional buyout
- c. Junk bond
- d. History of private equity and venture capital

Guidance: level 1

The _____ of 1973 serves as the enacting legislation to carry out the provisions outlined in The Convention on International Trade in Endangered Species of Wild Fauna and Flora. Designed to protect critically imperiled species from extinction as a "consequence of economic growth and development untempered by adequate concern and conservation", the ESA was signed into law by President Richard Nixon on December 28, 1973. The law requires federal agencies to consult with the Fish and Wildlife Service &/or the NOAA Fisheries Service to ensure their actions are not likely to jeopardize the continued existence of any listed species or result in the destruction or adverse modification of designated critical habitat of such species. The U.S. Supreme Court found that "the plain intent of Congress in enacting" the ESA "was to halt and reverse the trend toward species extinction, whatever the cost." The Act is administered by two federal agencies, the United States Fish and Wildlife Service and the National Marine Fisheries Service.

Exam Probability: **Low**

48. *Answer choices:*

(see index for correct answer)

- a. hierarchical perspective
- b. Endangered Species Act
- c. deep-level diversity
- d. empathy

Guidance: level 1

:: Corporate crime ::

_____ LLP, based in Chicago, was an American holding company. Formerly one of the "Big Five" accounting firms, the firm had provided auditing, tax, and consulting services to large corporations. By 2001, it had become one of the world's largest multinational companies.

Exam Probability: **High**

49. *Answer choices:*

(see index for correct answer)

- a. NatWest Three
- b. Arthur Andersen
- c. Allied Deals Inc.
- d. Equity Funding

Guidance: level 1

:: ::

The _____ is an 1848 political pamphlet by the German philosophers Karl Marx and Friedrich Engels. Commissioned by the Communist League and originally published in London just as the Revolutions of 1848 began to erupt, the Manifesto was later recognised as one of the world's most influential political documents. It presents an analytical approach to the class struggle and the conflicts of capitalism and the capitalist mode of production, rather than a prediction of communism's potential future forms.

Exam Probability: **Low**

50. *Answer choices:*

(see index for correct answer)

- a. hierarchical perspective
- b. deep-level diversity
- c. Sarbanes-Oxley act of 2002
- d. Communist Manifesto

Guidance: level 1

:: Renewable energy ::

_____ is the conversion of energy from sunlight into electricity, either directly using photovoltaics , indirectly using concentrated _____ , or a combination. Concentrated _____ systems use lenses or mirrors and tracking systems to focus a large area of sunlight into a small beam. Photovoltaic cells convert light into an electric current using the photovoltaic effect.

Exam Probability: **Medium**

51. *Answer choices:*

(see index for correct answer)

- a. Biomass
- b. Deep water source cooling

- c. Carbon Recycling International
- d. Grid balancing

Guidance: level 1

:: Minimum wage ::

A _____ is the lowest remuneration that employers can legally pay their workers—the price floor below which workers may not sell their labor. Most countries had introduced _____ legislation by the end of the 20th century.

Exam Probability: **Low**

52. *Answer choices:*

(see index for correct answer)

- a. National Anti-Sweating League
- b. Minimum wage
- c. Working poor
- d. Minimum wage in Taiwan

Guidance: level 1

:: ::

_____ is a cognitive process that elicits emotion and rational associations based on an individual's moral philosophy or value system. _____ stands in contrast to elicited emotion or thought due to associations based on immediate sensory perceptions and reflexive responses, as in sympathetic central nervous system responses. In common terms, _____ is often described as leading to feelings of remorse when a person commits an act that conflicts with their moral values. An individual's moral values and their dissonance with familial, social, cultural and historical interpretations of moral philosophy are considered in the examination of cultural relativity in both the practice and study of psychology. The extent to which _____ informs moral judgment before an action and whether such moral judgments are or should be based on reason has occasioned debate through much of modern history between theories of modern western philosophy in juxtaposition to the theories of romanticism and other reactionary movements after the end of the Middle Ages.

Exam Probability: **Medium**

53. *Answer choices:*
(see index for correct answer)

- a. hierarchical perspective
- b. surface-level diversity
- c. interpersonal communication
- d. Conscience

Guidance: level 1

:: Pyramid and Ponzi schemes ::

_____ was an Italian swindler and con artist in the U.S. and Canada. His aliases include Charles Ponci, Carlo, and Charles P. Bianchi. Born and raised in Italy, he became known in the early 1920s as a swindler in North America for his money-making scheme. He promised clients a 50% profit within 45 days or 100% profit within 90 days, by buying discounted postal reply coupons in other countries and redeeming them at face value in the United States as a form of arbitrage. In reality, Ponzi was paying earlier investors using the investments of later investors. While this type of fraudulent investment scheme was not originally invented by Ponzi, it became so identified with him that it now is referred to as a "Ponzi scheme". His scheme ran for over a year before it collapsed, costing his "investors" $20 million.

Exam Probability: **Medium**

54. *Answer choices:*

(see index for correct answer)

- a. Stanley Chais
- b. Charles Ponzi
- c. Scott W. Rothstein
- d. Matrix scheme

Guidance: level 1

:: Occupational safety and health ::

_____ is a chemical element with symbol Pb and atomic number 82. It is a heavy metal that is denser than most common materials. _____ is soft and malleable, and also has a relatively low melting point. When freshly cut, _____ is silvery with a hint of blue; it tarnishes to a dull gray color when exposed to air. _____ has the highest atomic number of any stable element and three of its isotopes are endpoints of major nuclear decay chains of heavier elements.

Exam Probability: **Low**

55. *Answer choices:*

(see index for correct answer)

- a. CLP Regulation
- b. Thermal work limit
- c. Contact dermatitis
- d. Lead

Guidance: level 1

:: Financial markets ::

The _____ is a United States federal government organization, established by Title I of the Dodd–Frank Wall Street Reform and Consumer Protection Act, which was signed into law by President Barack Obama on July 21, 2010. The Office of Financial Research is intended to provide support to the council.

Exam Probability: **High**

56. *Answer choices:*

(see index for correct answer)

- a. Risk arbitrage
- b. Financial Stability Oversight Council
- c. Floor broker
- d. Subscription

Guidance: level 1

:: ::

A _____ is the ability to carry out a task with determined results often within a given amount of time, energy, or both. _____ s can often be divided into domain-general and domain-specific _____ s. For example, in the domain of work, some general _____ s would include time management, teamwork and leadership, self-motivation and others, whereas domain-specific _____ s would be used only for a certain job. _____ usually requires certain environmental stimuli and situations to assess the level of _____ being shown and used.

Exam Probability: **Low**

57. *Answer choices:*

(see index for correct answer)

- a. functional perspective
- b. personal values
- c. deep-level diversity
- d. corporate values

Guidance: level 1

:: ::

_____ is an eight-block-long street running roughly northwest to southeast from Broadway to South Street, at the East River, in the Financial District of Lower Manhattan in New York City. Over time, the term has become a metonym for the financial markets of the United States as a whole, the American financial services industry , or New York–based financial interests.

Exam Probability: **Low**

58. *Answer choices:*

(see index for correct answer)

- a. Sarbanes-Oxley act of 2002
- b. empathy
- c. process perspective
- d. information systems assessment

Guidance: level 1

:: Cultural appropriation ::

_____ is a social and economic order that encourages the acquisition of goods and services in ever-increasing amounts. With the industrial revolution, but particularly in the 20th century, mass production led to an economic crisis: there was overproduction—the supply of goods would grow beyond consumer demand, and so manufacturers turned to planned obsolescence and advertising to manipulate consumer spending. In 1899, a book on _____ published by Thorstein Veblen, called The Theory of the Leisure Class, examined the widespread values and economic institutions emerging along with the widespread "leisure time" in the beginning of the 20th century. In it Veblen "views the activities and spending habits of this leisure class in terms of conspicuous and vicarious consumption and waste. Both are related to the display of status and not to functionality or usefulness."

Exam Probability: **Medium**

59. *Answer choices:*
(see index for correct answer)

- a. Blackface
- b. Consumerism
- c. Coon Chicken Inn
- d. Representation of African Americans in media

Guidance: level 1

Accounting

Accounting or accountancy is the measurement, processing, and communication of financial information about economic entities such as businesses and corporations. The modern field was established by the Italian mathematician Luca Pacioli in 1494. Accounting, which has been called the "language of business", measures the results of an organization's economic activities and conveys this information to a variety of users, including investors, creditors, management, and regulators.

:: Accounting ::

_____ are key sources of information and evidence used to prepare, verify and/or audit the financial statements. They also include documentation to prove asset ownership for creation of liabilities and proof of monetary and non monetary transactions.

Exam Probability: **Low**

1. *Answer choices:*

(see index for correct answer)

- a. Morison International
- b. Accounting records
- c. INPACT International
- d. Bookkeeping

Guidance: level 1

:: Investment ::

In economics, _____ is spending which increases the availability of fixed capital goods or means of production and goods inventories. It is the total spending on newly produced physical capital and on inventories —that is, gross investment—minus replacement investment, which simply replaces depreciated capital goods. It is productive capital formation plus net additions to the stock of housing and the stock of inventories.

Exam Probability: **Low**

2. *Answer choices:*

(see index for correct answer)

- a. Self-invested personal pension
- b. Juniperus Capital
- c. Special settlement
- d. Net investment

Guidance: level 1

:: Generally Accepted Accounting Principles ::

> An _____ or profit and loss account is one of the financial statements of a company and shows the company's revenues and expenses during a particular period.

Exam Probability: **High**

3. *Answer choices:*

(see index for correct answer)

- a. Fin 48
- b. Income statement
- c. Profit
- d. Deprival value

Guidance: level 1

:: Stock market ::

_____ is a form of stock which may have any combination of features not possessed by common stock including properties of both an equity and a debt instrument, and is generally considered a hybrid instrument. _____ s are senior to common stock, but subordinate to bonds in terms of claim and may have priority over common stock in the payment of dividends and upon liquidation. Terms of the _____ are described in the issuing company's articles of association or articles of incorporation.

Exam Probability: **High**

4. *Answer choices:*

(see index for correct answer)

- a. Central securities depository
- b. Stock market data systems
- c. Instinet
- d. Accelerated Return Note

Guidance: level 1

:: Accounting in the United States ::

The _____ is the internal audit profession's most widely recognized advocate, educator, and provider of standards, guidance, and certifications. Established in 1941, the IIA today serves more than 200,000 members from more than 170 countries and territories. IIA's global headquarters are in Lake Mary, Fla., United States.

Exam Probability: **High**

5. *Answer choices:*

(see index for correct answer)

- a. Certified Public Accountant
- b. Accounting Today
- c. Positive assurance
- d. Institute of Internal Auditors

Guidance: level 1

:: Insurance terms ::

A _____ in the broadest sense is a natural person or other legal entity who receives money or other benefits from a benefactor. For example, the _____ of a life insurance policy is the person who receives the payment of the amount of insurance after the death of the insured.

Exam Probability: **High**

6. *Answer choices:*

(see index for correct answer)

- a. Beneficiary
- b. Community rating
- c. Cash value
- d. Gross premiums written

Guidance: level 1

:: Accounting terminology ::

In accounting/accountancy, _____ are journal entries usually made at the end of an accounting period to allocate income and expenditure to the period in which they actually occurred. The revenue recognition principle is the basis of making _____ that pertain to unearned and accrued revenues under accrual-basis accounting. They are sometimes called Balance Day adjustments because they are made on balance day.

Exam Probability: **Medium**

7. *Answer choices:*

(see index for correct answer)

- a. double-entry bookkeeping
- b. Fund accounting
- c. Accounts payable
- d. Adjusting entries

Guidance: level 1

:: Financial ratios ::

A _____ or accounting ratio is a relative magnitude of two selected numerical values taken from an enterprise's financial statements. Often used in accounting, there are many standard ratios used to try to evaluate the overall financial condition of a corporation or other organization. _____s may be used by managers within a firm, by current and potential shareholders of a firm, and by a firm's creditors. Financial analysts use _____s to compare the strengths and weaknesses in various companies. If shares in a company are traded in a financial market, the market price of the shares is used in certain _____s.

Exam Probability: **High**

8. *Answer choices:*

(see index for correct answer)

- a. Return on capital
- b. Debt-to-capital ratio
- c. Operating ratio
- d. Financial ratio

Guidance: level 1

:: Financial economics ::

A _____ is defined to include property of any kind held by an assessee, whether connected with their business or profession or not connected with their business or profession. It includes all kinds of property, movable or immovable, tangible or intangible, fixed or circulating. Thus, land and building, plant and machinery, motorcar, furniture, jewellery, route permits, goodwill, tenancy rights, patents, trademarks, shares, debentures, securities, units, mutual funds, zero-coupon bonds etc. are _____ s.

Exam Probability: **High**

9. *Answer choices:*

(see index for correct answer)

- a. Collateralized fund obligation
- b. No-trade theorem
- c. Consumer leverage ratio
- d. Forward rate

Guidance: level 1

:: Stock market ::

A _____ , equity market or share market is the aggregation of buyers and sellers of stocks , which represent ownership claims on businesses; these may include securities listed on a public stock exchange, as well as stock that is only traded privately. Examples of the latter include shares of private companies which are sold to investors through equity crowdfunding platforms. Stock exchanges list shares of common equity as well as other security types, e.g. corporate bonds and convertible bonds.

Exam Probability: **Medium**

10. *Answer choices:*

(see index for correct answer)

- a. Foolish Four
- b. Slippage
- c. Share price
- d. Stock Market

Guidance: level 1

:: Tax reform ::

_____ is the process of changing the way taxes are collected or managed by the government and is usually undertaken to improve tax administration or to provide economic or social benefits. _____ can include reducing the level of taxation of all people by the government, making the tax system more progressive or less progressive, or simplifying the tax system and making the system more understandable or more accountable.

Exam Probability: **High**

11. *Answer choices:*

(see index for correct answer)

- a. Rational economic exchange
- b. Goods and Services Tax

- c. Joseph A. Pechman
- d. 2006 Puerto Rico budget crisis

Guidance: level 1

:: Financial statements ::

A Statement of changes in equity and similarly the statement of changes in owner's equity for a sole trader, statement of changes in partners' equity for a partnership, statement of changes in Shareholders' equity for a Company or statement of changes in Taxpayers' equity for Government financial statements is one of the four basic financial statements.

Exam Probability: **Low**

12. *Answer choices:*

(see index for correct answer)

- a. Consolidated financial statement
- b. Quarterly finance report
- c. Statement of retained earnings
- d. Government financial statements

Guidance: level 1

:: Accounting ::

_____ are designed to facilitate the process of journalizing and posting transactions. They are used for the most frequent transactions in a business. For example, in merchandising businesses, companies acquire merchandise from vendors, and then in turn sell the merchandise to individuals or other businesses. Sales and purchases are the most common transactions for the merchandising businesses. A business such as a retail store will record the following transactions many times a day for sales on account and cash sales.

Exam Probability: **High**

13. *Answer choices:*

(see index for correct answer)

- a. Efficiency Based Absorption Costing
- b. Special journals
- c. Della mercatura e del mercante perfetto
- d. European training programs

Guidance: level 1

:: Business models ::

A _____ is a company that owns enough voting stock in another firm to control management and operation by influencing or electing its board of directors. The company is deemed a subsidiary of the _____ .

Exam Probability: **Medium**

14. Answer choices:

(see index for correct answer)

- a. Co-operative Wholesale Society
- b. Organizational architecture
- c. Parent company
- d. Very small business

Guidance: level 1

:: Financial accounting ::

In macroeconomics and international finance, the _____ is one of two primary components of the balance of payments, the other being the current account. Whereas the current account reflects a nation's net income, the _____ reflects net change in ownership of national assets.

Exam Probability: **High**

15. Answer choices:

(see index for correct answer)

- a. Book value
- b. Advance payment
- c. Commuted cash value
- d. Capital account

Guidance: level 1

:: Commercial crimes ::

_____ is the act of withholding assets for the purpose of conversion of such assets, by one or more persons to whom the assets were entrusted, either to be held or to be used for specific purposes. _____ is a type of financial fraud. For example, a lawyer might embezzle funds from the trust accounts of their clients; a financial advisor might embezzle the funds of investors; and a husband or a wife might embezzle funds from a bank account jointly held with the spouse.

Exam Probability: **Medium**

16. *Answer choices:*

(see index for correct answer)

- a. Shill
- b. Counterfeit
- c. FATF blacklist
- d. Embezzlement

Guidance: level 1

:: Accounting in the United States ::

Established in 1988, the _____ is a professional organization of fraud examiners. Its activities include producing fraud information, tools and training. The ACFE grants the professional designation of Certified Fraud Examiner. The ACFE is the world's largest anti-fraud organization and is a provider of anti-fraud training and education, with more than 85,000 members.

Exam Probability: **Medium**

17. *Answer choices:*

(see index for correct answer)

- a. Accounting Today
- b. Accounting Principles Board
- c. Association of Certified Fraud Examiners
- d. Certified Government Financial Manager

Guidance: level 1

:: ::

_____ is a costing method that identifies activities in an organization and assigns the cost of each activity to all products and services according to the actual consumption by each. This model assigns more indirect costs into direct costs compared to conventional costing.

Exam Probability: **Low**

18. *Answer choices:*

(see index for correct answer)

- a. surface-level diversity
- b. Sarbanes-Oxley act of 2002
- c. deep-level diversity
- d. Activity-based costing

Guidance: level 1

:: Retail financial services ::

A _____ is a prepaid stored-value money card, usually issued by a retailer or bank, to be used as an alternative to cash for purchases within a particular store or related businesses. _____ s are also given out by employers or organizations as rewards or gifts. They may also be distributed by retailers and marketers as part of a promotion strategy, to entice the recipient to come in or return to the store, and at times such cards are called cash cards. _____ s are generally redeemable only for purchases at the relevant retail premises and cannot be cashed out, and in some situations may be subject to an expiry date or fees. American Express, MasterCard, and Visa offer generic _____ s which need not be redeemed at particular stores, and which are widely used for cashback marketing strategies. A feature of these cards is that they are generally anonymous and are disposed of when the stored value on a card is exhausted.

Exam Probability: **Low**

19. *Answer choices:*

(see index for correct answer)

- a. Gift card
- b. Financial management advisor
- c. Certificate of Deposit Account Registry Service
- d. History of pawnbroking

Guidance: level 1

:: Types of business entity ::

A sole _____ , also known as the sole trader, individual entrepreneurship or _____ , is a type of enterprise that is owned and run by one person and in which there is no legal distinction between the owner and the business entity. A sole trader does not necessarily work 'alone'—it is possible for the sole trader to employ other people.

Exam Probability: **Low**

20. *Answer choices:*

(see index for correct answer)

- a. Aktiengesellschaft
- b. Virtual limited liability company
- c. Proprietorship
- d. European Private Company

Guidance: level 1

:: ::

_____ is a process whereby a person assumes the parenting of another, usually a child, from that person's biological or legal parent or parents. Legal _____ s permanently transfers all rights and responsibilities, along with filiation, from the biological parent or parents.

Exam Probability: **High**

21. *Answer choices:*

(see index for correct answer)

- a. Adoption
- b. empathy
- c. information systems assessment
- d. open system

Guidance: level 1

:: Valuation (finance) ::

The _____ is one of three major groups of methodologies, called valuation approaches, used by appraisers. It is particularly common in commercial real estate appraisal and in business appraisal. The fundamental math is similar to the methods used for financial valuation, securities analysis, or bond pricing. However, there are some significant and important modifications when used in real estate or business valuation.

Exam Probability: **Medium**

22. *Answer choices:*

(see index for correct answer)

- a. Expertization
- b. The Appraisal Foundation
- c. Chepakovich valuation model
- d. Diminution in value

Guidance: level 1

:: Management accounting ::

In business, a _____ is a division that gains revenue from product sales or service provided. The manager in _____ is accountable for revenue only.

Exam Probability: **High**

23. *Answer choices:*

(see index for correct answer)

- a. RCA open-source application
- b. Contribution margin
- c. Average per-bit delivery cost
- d. Management control system

Guidance: level 1

:: Tax credits ::

A _____ is a tax incentive which allows certain taxpayers to subtract the amount of the credit they have accrued from the total they owe the state. It may also be a credit granted in recognition of taxes already paid or, as in the United Kingdom, a form of state support.

Exam Probability: **Medium**

24. *Answer choices:*

(see index for correct answer)

- a. Railroad Track Maintenance Tax Credit
- b. Child tax credit
- c. Disability tax credit
- d. Earned income tax credit

Guidance: level 1

:: ::

_____ is the process of making predictions of the future based on past and present data and most commonly by analysis of trends. A commonplace example might be estimation of some variable of interest at some specified future date. Prediction is a similar, but more general term. Both might refer to formal statistical methods employing time series, cross-sectional or longitudinal data, or alternatively to less formal judgmental methods. Usage can differ between areas of application: for example, in hydrology the terms "forecast" and "_____" are sometimes reserved for estimates of values at certain specific future times, while the term "prediction" is used for more general estimates, such as the number of times floods will occur over a long period.

Exam Probability: **High**

25. *Answer choices:*

(see index for correct answer)

- a. functional perspective
- b. interpersonal communication
- c. cultural
- d. Forecasting

Guidance: level 1

:: Accounting source documents ::

_____ is a letter sent by a customer to a supplier to inform the supplier that their invoice has been paid. If the customer is paying by cheque, the _____ often accompanies the cheque. The advice may consist of a literal letter or of a voucher attached to the side or top of the cheque.

Exam Probability: **High**

26. *Answer choices:*

(see index for correct answer)

- a. Bank statement
- b. Superbill
- c. Parcel audit
- d. Remittance advice

Guidance: level 1

:: Financial accounting ::

In accounting, _____ is the value of an asset according to its balance sheet account balance. For assets, the value is based on the original cost of the asset less any depreciation, amortization or impairment costs made against the asset. Traditionally, a company's _____ is its total assets minus intangible assets and liabilities. However, in practice, depending on the source of the calculation, _____ may variably include goodwill, intangible assets, or both. The value inherent in its workforce, part of the intellectual capital of a company, is always ignored. When intangible assets and goodwill are explicitly excluded, the metric is often specified to be "tangible _____".

Exam Probability: **Medium**

27. *Answer choices:*

(see index for correct answer)

- a. Fixed asset register
- b. Authorised capital
- c. Carry
- d. Asset recovery

Guidance: level 1

:: Generally Accepted Accounting Principles ::

Expenditure is an outflow of money to another person or group to pay for an item or service, or for a category of costs. For a tenant, rent is an _____ . For students or parents, tuition is an _____ . Buying food, clothing, furniture or an automobile is often referred to as an _____ . An _____ is a cost that is "paid" or "remitted", usually in exchange for something of value. Something that seems to cost a great deal is "expensive". Something that seems to cost little is "inexpensive". "_____ s of the table" are _____ s of dining, refreshments, a feast, etc.

Exam Probability: **Medium**

28. *Answer choices:*

(see index for correct answer)

- a. Expense
- b. Earnings before interest, taxes and depreciation
- c. AICPA Statements of Position
- d. Fin 48

Guidance: level 1

:: Financial accounting ::

_____ refers to any one of several methods by which a company, for 'financial accounting' or tax purposes, depreciates a fixed asset in such a way that the amount of depreciation taken each year is higher during the earlier years of an asset's life. For financial accounting purposes, _____ is expected to be much more productive during its early years, so that depreciation expense will more accurately represent how much of an asset's usefulness is being used up each year. For tax purposes, _____ provides a way of deferring corporate income taxes by reducing taxable income in current years, in exchange for increased taxable income in future years. This is a valuable tax incentive that encourages businesses to purchase new assets.

Exam Probability: **Low**

29. *Answer choices:*
(see index for correct answer)

- a. Exit rate
- b. Intangibles
- c. Financial Condition Report
- d. Deferred Acquisition Costs

Guidance: level 1

:: Accounting in the United States ::

_____ refers to a Memorandum of Understanding signed in September 2002 between the Financial Accounting Standards Board, the US standard setter, and the International Accounting Standards Board. The agreement is so called as it was reached in Norwalk.

Exam Probability: **Medium**

30. *Answer choices:*

(see index for correct answer)

- a. Association of Certified Fraud Examiners
- b. Financial Accounting Foundation
- c. Norwalk Agreement
- d. Federal Accounting Standards Advisory Board

Guidance: level 1

:: Accounting systems ::

In bookkeeping, a _____ statement is a process that explains the difference on a specified date between the bank balance shown in an organization's bank statement, as supplied by the bank and the corresponding amount shown in the organization's own accounting records.

Exam Probability: **High**

31. *Answer choices:*

(see index for correct answer)

- a. control account
- b. Debits and credits
- c. Substance over form
- d. Cookie jar accounting

Guidance: level 1

:: Insolvency ::

_____ is the process in accounting by which a company is brought to an end in the United Kingdom, Republic of Ireland and United States. The assets and property of the company are redistributed. _____ is also sometimes referred to as winding-up or dissolution, although dissolution technically refers to the last stage of _____. The process of _____ also arises when customs, an authority or agency in a country responsible for collecting and safeguarding customs duties, determines the final computation or ascertainment of the duties or drawback accruing on an entry.

Exam Probability: **Low**

32. *Answer choices:*

(see index for correct answer)

- a. Bankruptcy
- b. Preferential creditor
- c. Insolvency

- d. Official Committee of Equity Security Holders

Guidance: level 1

:: Banking ::

A _____ is a financial account maintained by a bank for a customer. A _____ can be a deposit account, a credit card account, a current account, or any other type of account offered by a financial institution, and represents the funds that a customer has entrusted to the financial institution and from which the customer can make withdrawals. Alternatively, accounts may be loan accounts in which case the customer owes money to the financial institution.

Exam Probability: **High**

33. *Answer choices:*

(see index for correct answer)

- a. Bank account
- b. Peer-to-peer lending
- c. Lender of last resort
- d. U-turn

Guidance: level 1

:: Corporate crime ::

_____ LLP, based in Chicago, was an American holding company. Formerly one of the "Big Five" accounting firms, the firm had provided auditing, tax, and consulting services to large corporations. By 2001, it had become one of the world's largest multinational companies.

Exam Probability: **Low**

34. *Answer choices:*

(see index for correct answer)

- a. Arthur Andersen
- b. Tip and Trade
- c. Arthur Andersen LLP v. United States
- d. Corporate Manslaughter and Corporate Homicide Act 2007

Guidance: level 1

:: Auditing ::

A _____, also called "Internal _____", is a term of financial audit, internal audit and Enterprise Risk Management. It means the overall attitude, awareness and actions of directors and management regarding the internal control system and its importance to the entity. They express it in management style, corporate culture, values, philosophy and operating style, the organisational structure, and human resources policies and procedures.

Exam Probability: **Medium**

35. Answer choices:

(see index for correct answer)

- a. International Register of Certificated Auditors
- b. Control environment
- c. Clinical audit
- d. Environmental audit

Guidance: level 1

:: Management accounting ::

A _____ is an organizational unit headed by a manager, who is responsible for its activities and results. In responsibility accounting, revenues and cost information are collected and reported on by _____ s.

Exam Probability: **Low**

36. Answer choices:

(see index for correct answer)

- a. Owner earnings
- b. Extended cost
- c. Resource consumption accounting
- d. Inventory valuation

Guidance: level 1

:: Financial accounting ::

_____ in accounting is the process of treating investments in associate companies. Equity accounting is usually applied where an investor entity holds 20–50% of the voting stock of the associate company. The investor records such investments as an asset on its balance sheet. The investor`s proportional share of the associate company`s net income increases the investment , and proportional payments of dividends decrease it. In the investor's income statement, the proportional share of the investor's net income or net loss is reported as a single-line item.

Exam Probability: **Medium**

37. *Answer choices:*

(see index for correct answer)

- a. Equity method
- b. Convenience translation
- c. Mark-to-market accounting
- d. Financial Condition Report

Guidance: level 1

:: Inventory ::

_____ is the maximum amount of goods, or inventory, that a company can possibly sell during this fiscal year. It has the formula.

Exam Probability: **Low**

38. *Answer choices:*

(see index for correct answer)

- a. LIFO
- b. Reorder point
- c. Cost of goods available for sale
- d. Stock mix

Guidance: level 1

:: Accounting in the United States ::

The _____ was formed by the American Institute of Certified Public Accountants in 1972, and developed the Objective of Financial Statements. The committee's goal was to create financial statements that helped external users make decisions about the economics of companies. In 1978, the Financial Accounting Standards Board, whose purpose is to develop generally accepted accounting principles, adopted the key objectives established by the _____

Exam Probability: **Low**

39. Answer choices:

(see index for correct answer)

- a. Certified Government Financial Manager
- b. Norwalk Agreement
- c. Trueblood Committee
- d. Comprehensive Performance Assessment

Guidance: level 1

_____ is the act of compensating someone for an out-of-pocket expense by giving them an amount of money equal to what was spent.

Exam Probability: **Low**

40. Answer choices:

(see index for correct answer)

- a. similarity-attraction theory
- b. Reimbursement
- c. Sarbanes-Oxley act of 2002
- d. co-culture

Guidance: level 1

:: Financial statements ::

In financial accounting, a _____ or statement of financial position or statement of financial condition is a summary of the financial balances of an individual or organization, whether it be a sole proprietorship, a business partnership, a corporation, private limited company or other organization such as Government or not-for-profit entity. Assets, liabilities and ownership equity are listed as of a specific date, such as the end of its financial year. A _____ is often described as a "snapshot of a company's financial condition". Of the four basic financial statements, the _____ is the only statement which applies to a single point in time of a business' calendar year.

Exam Probability: **Medium**

41. *Answer choices:*

(see index for correct answer)

- a. Financial report
- b. Balance sheet
- c. Statement on Auditing Standards No. 70: Service Organizations
- d. Quarterly finance report

Guidance: level 1

:: Inventory ::

It requires a detailed physical count, so that the company knows exactly how many of each goods brought on specific dates remained at year end inventory. When this information is found, the amount of goods are multiplied by their purchase cost at their purchase date, to get a number for the ending inventory cost.

Exam Probability: **Low**

42. *Answer choices:*

(see index for correct answer)

- a. Specific identification
- b. Stock mix
- c. Stock-taking
- d. Order picking

Guidance: level 1

:: ::

_____ science is the application of science to criminal and civil laws, mainly—on the criminal side—during criminal investigation, as governed by the legal standards of admissible evidence and criminal procedure.

Exam Probability: **Low**

43. *Answer choices:*

(see index for correct answer)

- a. empathy
- b. Sarbanes-Oxley act of 2002
- c. cultural
- d. Forensic

Guidance: level 1

:: Ethically disputed business practices ::

_____, in accounting, is the act of intentionally influencing the process of financial reporting to obtain some private gain. _____ involves the alteration of financial reports to mislead stakeholders about the organization's underlying performance, or to "influence contractual outcomes that depend on reported accounting numbers."

Exam Probability: **High**

44. *Answer choices:*

(see index for correct answer)

- a. Cream skimming
- b. Earnings management
- c. at-will
- d. Anti-competitive practices

Guidance: level 1

:: Pharmaceutical industry ::

A _____ is a document in which data collected for a clinical trial is first recorded. This data is usually later entered in the case report form. The International Conference on Harmonisation of Technical Requirements for Registration of Pharmaceuticals for Human Use guidelines define _____s as "original documents, data, and records." _____s contain source data, which is defined as "all information in original records and certified copies of original records of clinical findings, observations, or other activities in a clinical trial necessary for the reconstruction and evaluation of the trial."

Exam Probability: **High**

45. *Answer choices:*

(see index for correct answer)

- a. Safety monitoring
- b. Good clinical practice
- c. Pharmaceutical sales representative
- d. Pharmaceutical Marketing and Management

Guidance: level 1

:: Fundamental analysis ::

_____ is the monetary value of earnings per outstanding share of common stock for a company.

Exam Probability: **Low**

46. *Answer choices:*

(see index for correct answer)

- a. Continuing value
- b. Goldman Sachs asset management factor model
- c. Earnings per share
- d. Growth stock

Guidance: level 1

:: Generally Accepted Accounting Principles ::

The _____ principle is a cornerstone of accrual accounting together with the matching principle. They both determine the accounting period in which revenues and expenses are recognized. According to the principle, revenues are recognized when they are realized or realizable, and are earned, no matter when cash is received. In cash accounting – in contrast – revenues are recognized when cash is received no matter when goods or services are sold.

Exam Probability: **High**

47. *Answer choices:*

(see index for correct answer)

- a. Profit
- b. Cash method of accounting
- c. Operating income before depreciation and amortization
- d. Revenue recognition

Guidance: level 1

:: Asset ::

In accounting, a _____ is any asset which can reasonably be expected to be sold, consumed, or exhausted through the normal operations of a business within the current fiscal year or operating cycle. Typical _____ s include cash, cash equivalents, short-term investments, accounts receivable, stock inventory, supplies, and the portion of prepaid liabilities which will be paid within a year. In simple words, assets which are held for a short period are known as _____ s. Such assets are expected to be realised in cash or consumed during the normal operating cycle of the business.

Exam Probability: **Low**

48. *Answer choices:*

(see index for correct answer)

- a. Current asset
- b. Asset

Guidance: level 1

:: Accounting systems ::

In accounting, the _____ is an account in the general ledger for which a corresponding subsidiary ledger has been created. The subsidiary ledger allows for tracking transactions within the _____ in more detail. Individual transactions are posted both to the _____ and the corresponding subsidiary ledger, and the totals for both are compared when preparing a trial balance to ensure accuracy.

Exam Probability: **Low**

49. *Answer choices:*

(see index for correct answer)

- a. Momentum accounting and triple-entry bookkeeping
- b. Off-balance sheet
- c. Entity concept
- d. Single-entry bookkeeping system

Guidance: level 1

:: Income taxes ::

An _____ is a tax imposed on individuals or entities that varies with respective income or profits. _____ generally is computed as the product of a tax rate times taxable income. Taxation rates may vary by type or characteristics of the taxpayer.

Exam Probability: **High**

50. *Answer choices:*

(see index for correct answer)

- a. Income tax
- b. Negative income tax
- c. American Society of Tax Problem Solvers
- d. Rouanet Law

Guidance: level 1

:: Management accounting ::

"_____ s are the structural determinants of the cost of an activity, reflecting any linkages or interrelationships that affect it". Therefore we could assume that the _____ s determine the cost behavior within the activities, reflecting the links that these have with other activities and relationships that affect them.

Exam Probability: **Medium**

51. *Answer choices:*

(see index for correct answer)

- a. Certified Management Accountants of Canada
- b. Hedge accounting
- c. Management accounting
- d. Cost driver

Guidance: level 1

:: ::

A _____ is the period used by governments for accounting and budget purposes, which varies between countries. It is also used for financial reporting by business and other organizations. Laws in many jurisdictions require company financial reports to be prepared and published on an annual basis, but generally do not require the reporting period to align with the calendar year. Taxation laws generally require accounting records to be maintained and taxes calculated on an annual basis, which usually corresponds to the _____ used for government purposes. The calculation of tax on an annual basis is especially relevant for direct taxation, such as income tax. Many annual government fees—such as Council rates, licence fees, etc.—are also levied on a _____ basis, while others are charged on an anniversary basis.

Exam Probability: **Low**

52. *Answer choices:*

(see index for correct answer)

- a. personal values
- b. hierarchical
- c. open system
- d. empathy

Guidance: level 1

:: Management accounting ::

A _____ is a cost that differs between alternatives being considered. In order for a cost to be a _____ it must be.

Exam Probability: **Medium**

53. *Answer choices:*
(see index for correct answer)

- a. Average per-bit delivery cost
- b. Relevant cost
- c. Net present value
- d. Double counting

Guidance: level 1

:: Investment ::

In finance, the benefit from an _____ is called a return. The return may consist of a gain realised from the sale of property or an _____, unrealised capital appreciation, or _____ income such as dividends, interest, rental income etc., or a combination of capital gain and income. The return may also include currency gains or losses due to changes in foreign currency exchange rates.

Exam Probability: **Medium**

54. *Answer choices:*

(see index for correct answer)

- a. APMEX
- b. American Bullion
- c. Tactical asset allocation
- d. Investment

Guidance: level 1

:: Legal terms ::

_____ or _____ interest, in law, is anything that functions contrary to a party's interest. This word should not be confused with averse.

Exam Probability: **High**

55. *Answer choices:*

(see index for correct answer)

- a. As is
- b. In-chambers opinion
- c. Adverse
- d. Actual notice

Guidance: level 1

:: E-commerce ::

A _____ is a plastic payment card that can be used instead of cash when making purchases. It is similar to a credit card, but unlike a credit card, the money is immediately transferred directly from the cardholder's bank account when performing a transaction.

Exam Probability: **Low**

56. *Answer choices:*

(see index for correct answer)

- a. Superdistribution
- b. Auction software
- c. Debit card
- d. APazari Desktop

Guidance: level 1

:: Manufacturing ::

_____ costs are all manufacturing costs that are related to the cost object but cannot be traced to that cost object in an economically feasible way.

Exam Probability: **High**

57. *Answer choices:*

(see index for correct answer)

- a. Industrial Valley
- b. Manufacturing overhead
- c. Build to order
- d. Gunsmith

Guidance: level 1

:: Accounting in the United States ::

The _____ is a private-sector, nonprofit corporation created by the Sarbanes–Oxley Act of 2002 to oversee the audits of public companies and other issuers in order to protect the interests of investors and further the public interest in the preparation of informative, accurate and independent audit reports. The PCAOB also oversees the audits of broker-dealers, including compliance reports filed pursuant to federal securities laws, to promote investor protection. All PCAOB rules and standards must be approved by the U.S. Securities and Exchange Commission .

Exam Probability: **Low**

58. *Answer choices:*

(see index for correct answer)

- a. Positive assurance
- b. Association of Government Accountants
- c. Public Company Accounting Oversight Board
- d. Other comprehensive income

Guidance: level 1

:: Inventory ::

In business and accounting/accountancy, _____ or continuous inventory describes systems of inventory where information on inventory quantity and availability is updated on a continuous basis as a function of doing business. Generally this is accomplished by connecting the inventory system with order entry and in retail the point of sale system. In this case, book inventory would be exactly the same as, or almost the same, as the real inventory.

Exam Probability: **High**

59. *Answer choices:*

(see index for correct answer)

- a. Average cost method
- b. Perpetual inventory
- c. Order picking
- d. Specific identification

Guidance: level 1

INDEX: Correct Answers

Foundations of Business

1. d: Restructuring

2. a: Negotiation

3. b: Brainstorming

4. b: Capitalism

5. a: Business model

6. : Stock exchange

7. b: Information technology

8. b: Partnership

9. : Payment

10. d: Dimension

11. a: Reputation

12. b: Law

13. b: Gross domestic product

14. a: Business

15. b: Customs

16. : Sharing

17. d: Career

18. a: Common stock

19. : Corporation

20. c: Accounting

21. : Demand

22. c: Benchmarking

23. d: Arthur Andersen

24. c: Fixed cost

25. d: Utility

26. : Advertising

27. a: Arbitration

28. : Evaluation

29. a: Outsourcing

30. d: Bias

31. a: Internal control

32. b: Trade

33. a: Currency

34. b: Case study

35. b: Purchasing

36. a: Health

37. d: Total quality management

38. : Empowerment

39. b: Market value

40. b: Authority

41. c: Risk

42. b: Question

43. : Return on investment

44. c: Specification

45. : Best practice

46. c: Business process

47. d: Globalization

48. a: Labor relations

49. : Stock

50. : Buyer

51. d: Organizational structure

52. b: Industry

53. b: Sexual harassment

54. : Selling

55. a: Creativity

56. a: Net income

57. b: Economies of scale

58. d: Opportunity cost

59. b: Strategic alliance

Management

1. d: Supply chain management

2. : Supply chain

3. : Mass customization

4. a: Negotiation

5. b: Enabling

6. d: Organizational commitment

7. c: Reinforcement

8. c: Decentralization

9. c: Office

10. d: Performance management

11. : Compromise

12. b: World Trade Organization

13. a: Leadership style

14. b: North American Free Trade Agreement

15. d: Bias

16. : Enron

17. : Code

18. c: Intellectual property

19. a: Board of directors

20. c: Labor force

21. a: Theory X

22. a: Revenue

23. b: Utility

24. : Human capital

25. b: Employment

26. d: Total cost

27. : Hotel

28. c: Frequency

29. a: Variable cost

30. d: Corporate governance

31. d: Size

32. : Project management

33. a: Strategic management

34. b: Organizational performance

35. b: Motivation

36. : Property

37. a: Fixed cost

38. : Officer

39. : Entrepreneurship

40. c: Tariff

41. d: Standard deviation

42. c: Logistics

43. b: Control chart

44. b: Market research

45. a: Problem

46. b: Affirmative action

47. d: Inspection

48. a: Recruitment

49. b: Leadership development

50. : Project team

51. : Self-assessment

52. b: Linear programming

53. b: Entrepreneur

54. d: Specification

55. d: European Union

56. b: Social loafing

57. : Halo effect

58. : Goal setting

59. c: Bounded rationality

Business law

1. d: Limited partnership

2. : Securities Act

3. a: Personal property

4. d: Money laundering

5. : Pregnancy discrimination

6. a: Misrepresentation

7. a: Condition precedent

8. b: Firm

9. b: Contract law

10. c: Liquidated damages

11. b: Contract Clause

12. c: Advertising

13. c: Tangible

14. : Indictment

15. c: Statute of limitations

16. : Investment

17. a: Statute of frauds

18. a: Appellate Court

19. b: Parol evidence

20. : Anticipatory repudiation

21. c: Injunction

22. c: Certiorari

23. c: Opening statement

24. d: Marketing

25. b: Security agreement

26. : Ratification

27. c: Committee

28. c: Punitive

29. a: Shares

30. b: Independent contractor

31. c: Trial

32. a: Substantive law

33. c: Labor relations

34. c: Beneficiary

35. b: Corporate governance

36. b: Authority

37. a: Relevant market

38. c: Proximate cause

39. d: Restraint of trade

40. : Buyer

41. b: Incentive

42. c: Wage

43. a: Impossibility

44. : Federal Arbitration Act

45. d: Service mark

46. d: Ford

47. : Due diligence

48. a: Lanham Act

49. c: Insolvency

50. : Undue influence

51. b: Bad faith

52. b: Uniform Commercial Code

53. : Arbitration clause

54. c: Subsidiary

55. d: Negotiable instrument

56. b: Real property

57. a: Writ

58. d: Competitor

59. c: Plaintiff

Finance

1. d: Par value

2. : Cost accounting

3. a: Indenture

4. c: Capital stock

5. : Financial management

6. b: Loan

7. : Risk assessment

8. b: Standard deviation

9. a: Taxation

10. d: Mortgage

11. c: Fixed cost

12. : Property

13. c: Income

14. a: Tax rate

15. d: Capital market

16. c: Finance

17. b: Aging

18. d: Financial risk

19. c: Monetary policy

20. a: Pension fund

21. b: Subsidiary ledger

22. b: Fiscal year

23. a: Bond market

24. d: Financial Accounting Standards Board

25. : Municipal bond

26. a: Commercial paper

27. b: S corporation

28. b: Initial public offering

29. b: Call option

30. d: Matching principle

31. c: Shares

32. a: Net profit

33. d: Cost of goods sold

34. d: Capital asset

35. c: Petty cash

36. b: Budget

37. : Total cost

38. b: Money market

39. : Liquidity

40. b: Debtor

41. : Competition

42. d: Citigroup

43. : Certified Public Accountant

44. : Capital budgeting

45. a: General ledger

46. a: Public Company Accounting Oversight Board

47. a: Annual report

48. b: Hedge

49. b: Average Cost

50. : Bank account

51. b: Interest rate

52. b: Cash management

53. c: Yield to maturity

54. a: Interest

55. c: Trial balance

56. d: Bank

57. d: Exchange rate

58. b: Risk premium

59. c: Goldman Sachs

Human resource management

1. : Retirement

2. a: Halo effect

3. c: Career management

4. : Delayering

5. c: Needs analysis

6. d: Questionnaire

7. d: Expatriate

8. c: Pay grade

9. c: Union shop

10. d: Organizational justice

11. a: Action learning

12. d: Intellectual capital

13. a: Exit interview

14. : Unfair labor practice

15. d: Self-actualization

16. b: Golden parachute

17. a: Employment

18. : Employee stock

19. : Interview

20. c: Cafeteria plan

21. d: American Federation of Government Employees

22. : Drug test

23. c: Leadership development

24. a: Impression management

25. a: Social media

26. a: Balanced scorecard

27. b: Mining

28. : Internal consistency

29. b: Functional job analysis

30. c: Executive compensation

31. d: Resignation

32. c: Nearshoring

33. a: Collaboration

34. c: Merit pay

35. : Substance abuse

36. c: Vesting

37. b: Socialization

38. c: Just cause

39. c: Mobile recruiting

40. d: Telecommuting

41. d: Job enlargement

42. a: Analysis

43. c: Conformity

44. : Public administration

45. a: Reasonable person

46. a: Global workforce

47. : Whistleblower

48. : Cross-training

49. a: Cross-functional team

50. b: Workforce management

51. c: Love contract

52. d: Goal setting

53. a: Bundy v. Jackson

54. a: Seniority

55. : E-HRM

56. : Closed shop

57. d: Competitive advantage

58. a: Census

59. : Employee assistance program

Information systems

1. c: Input device

2. d: Information silo

3. a: Blogger

4. b: Mozy

5. d: Switch

6. d: Questionnaire

7. c: Sustainable

8. : System

9. b: PayPal

10. d: Sensitivity analysis

11. b: Monopoly

12. : Wiki

13. c: Government-to-citizen

14. b: Consumer-to-business

15. d: Picasa

16. b: Privacy policy

17. b: Information systems

18. c: Authentication

19. : Freemium

20. b: Business process management

21. c: Text mining

22. d: Data warehouse

23. a: Spyware

24. a: Asset

25. a: Kinect

26. : Payment card

27. : Information technology

28. c: Google

29. c: Geocoding

30. c: Transport Layer Security

31. : Debit card

32. : Interactivity

33. c: Social commerce

34. b: Enterprise application

35. a: Open source

36. d: Interoperability

37. a: Fault tolerance

38. d: Information management

39. d: Disaster recovery plan

40. a: Cookie

41. : Semantic Web

42. d: Diagram

43. d: Computer security

44. c: Top-level domain

45. : Downtime

46. d: Content management system

47. b: Data integrity

48. a: Query by Example

49. b: M-Pesa

50. c: Privacy

51. a: Intrusion detection system

52. c: Magnetic tape

53. b: Backup

54. c: Carnivore

55. d: Content management

56. : E-commerce

57. b: Total cost of ownership

58. : Business-to-business

59. d: Consumerization

Marketing

1. d: Market segments

2. b: Data warehouse

3. b: Question

4. a: Trial

5. b: Expense

6. b: Globalization

7. c: Market development

8. a: Insurance

9. : Customer experience

10. d: American Express

11. : Customer

12. : Aid

13. b: Blog

14. c: Adoption

15. a: Purchasing

16. d: Star

17. : Variable cost

18. a: Mass marketing

19. : North American Free Trade Agreement

20. : Consumer Protection

21. : Economy

22. a: Respondent

23. : Mass customization

24. d: Logistics

25. c: Productivity

26. b: Disintermediation

27. : Organizational structure

28. b: Total Quality Management

29. a: Secondary data

30. : Green marketing

31. c: Inventory

32. b: Warehouse

33. a: Direct selling

34. a: Pricing

35. a: Brand loyalty

36. : Distribution channel

37. d: Marketing plan

38. d: Strategic alliance

39. c: Services marketing

40. b: Technology

41. a: Negotiation

42. a: Competitive advantage

43. b: Shares

44. d: Communication

45. : Brand management

46. : Empowerment

47. c: Perception

48. : Creative brief

49. c: Sherman Antitrust Act

50. b: Franchising

51. d: Research and development

52. : Logo

53. a: Brand equity

54. a: Global marketing

55. b: Planning

56. b: Nonprofit

57. a: Information system

58. a: Brand extension

59. : Health

Manufacturing

1. : DMAIC

2. b: Process capability

3. : Supply chain

4. c: Waste

5. b: Kanban

6. d: Capacity planning

7. b: Schedule

8. : Quality by Design

9. d: Project team

10. : Goal

11. c: Project management

12. b: Joint Commission

13. b: Control limits

14. : Expediting

15. a: Reflux

16. b: Total cost

17. b: Purchase order

18. d: Histogram

19. a: Retail

20. c: Durability

21. d: Statistical process control

22. b: Furnace

23. b: Third-party logistics

24. : Sales

25. a: Flowchart

26. a: Malcolm Baldrige National Quality Award

27. : Rolling

28. d: Glass

29. d: Cost

30. d: Scientific management

31. c: E-commerce

32. : Stakeholder management

33. d: Thomas Register

34. a: Gantt chart

35. b: Purchasing process

36. b: Concurrent engineering

37. d: Information management

38. : Obsolescence

39. : Interaction

40. b: Electronic data interchange

41. a: Purchasing manager

42. d: Service level

43. : Downtime

44. c: Indirect costs

45. b: Workflow

46. c: Technical support

47. d: Reboiler

48. a: Accreditation

49. d: Minitab

50. d: Extended enterprise

51. c: Metal

52. : Throughput

53. : Blanket

54. : Quality control

55. d: Inspection

56. : Time management

57. : Total cost of ownership

58. : Estimation

59. c: Economies of scope

Commerce

1. : E-commerce

2. a: Overtime

3. d: Subsidy

4. b: Micropayment

5. d: Market structure

6. a: Computer security

7. d: Monopoly

8. b: Strategic plan

9. : Management

10. c: Authentication

11. d: Broker

12. b: Supply chain

13. c: Commodity

14. c: Negotiation

15. : Shopping cart

16. a: Hospitality

17. a: Incentive

18. : Boot

19. d: Labor union

20. a: Chief executive officer

21. : Industrial Revolution

22. d: Phishing

23. c: Issuing bank

24. a: Bill of lading

25. a: Goal

26. : Freight forwarder

27. : Bank

28. : Quality assurance

29. c: PayPal

30. d: Cost structure

31. b: Advertising

32. c: E-procurement

33. a: Fraud

34. d: Innovation

35. b: Industry

36. : Mass production

37. a: Purchasing manager

38. a: Inflation

39. b: Public relations

40. a: Mining

41. : Loyalty

42. c: Household

43. b: Minimum wage

44. a: Raw material

45. d: Silver

46. a: Authority

47. c: Game

48. a: Logistics

49. a: Evaluation

50. c: Dutch auction

51. a: Affiliate marketing

52. c: Frequency

53. d: Yield management

54. c: General manager

55. b: Utility

56. c: Asset

57. a: Competitor

58. a: Supranational

59. d: Basket

Business ethics

1. d: Coal

2. b: Kyoto Protocol

3. a: Empowerment

4. a: Natural gas

5. c: Federal Trade Commission

6. a: Planned obsolescence

7. c: Greenpeace

8. : Planet

9. d: Pyramid scheme

10. d: Self-interest

11. d: Siemens

12. b: Dress code

13. a: United Farm Workers

14. d: Community development financial institution

15. c: Real estate

16. b: Lead paint

17. a: Interlocking directorate

18. d: Consumer Financial Protection Bureau

19. : Habitat

20. : East Germany

21. b: Recovery Act

22. : Invisible hand

23. d: Protestant work ethic

24. d: Pure Food and Drug Act

25. : Insider trading

26. : Workplace politics

27. b: Feedback

28. c: Patriot Act

29. c: Price fixing

30. d: Fraud

31. : Federal Trade Commission Act

32. c: Consumer Protection

33. : Energy policy

34. c: Great Depression

35. a: Social responsibility

36. b: Foreign Corrupt Practices Act

37. b: Public relations

38. d: Sexual harassment

39. d: Better Business Bureau

40. d: Transformational leadership

41. c: Referent power

42. c: Corporate governance

43. c: Ponzi scheme

44. b: Micromanagement

45. c: White-collar crime

46. d: Organizational structure

47. c: Junk bond

48. b: Endangered Species Act

49. b: Arthur Andersen

50. d: Communist Manifesto

51. : Solar power

52. b: Minimum wage

53. d: Conscience

54. b: Charles Ponzi

55. d: Lead

56. b: Financial Stability Oversight Council

57. : Skill

58. : Wall Street

59. b: Consumerism

Accounting

1. b: Accounting records

2. d: Net investment

3. b: Income statement

4. : Preferred stock

5. d: Institute of Internal Auditors

6. a: Beneficiary

7. d: Adjusting entries

8. d: Financial ratio

9. : Capital asset

10. d: Stock Market

11. : Tax reform

12. c: Statement of retained earnings

13. b: Special journals

14. c: Parent company

15. d: Capital account

16. d: Embezzlement

17. c: Association of Certified Fraud Examiners

18. d: Activity-based costing

19. a: Gift card

20. c: Proprietorship

21. a: Adoption

22. : Income approach

23. : Revenue center

24. : Tax credit

25. d: Forecasting

26. d: Remittance advice

27. : Book value

28. a: Expense

29. : Accelerated depreciation

30. c: Norwalk Agreement

31. : Bank reconciliation

32. : Liquidation

33. a: Bank account

34. a: Arthur Andersen

35. b: Control environment

36. : Responsibility center

37. a: Equity method

38. c: Cost of goods available for sale

39. c: Trueblood Committee

40. b: Reimbursement

41. b: Balance sheet

42. a: Specific identification

43. d: Forensic

44. b: Earnings management

45. : Source document

46. c: Earnings per share

47. d: Revenue recognition

48. a: Current asset

49. : Controlling account

50. a: Income tax

51. d: Cost driver

52. : Fiscal year

53. b: Relevant cost

54. d: Investment

55. c: Adverse

56. c: Debit card

57. b: Manufacturing overhead

58. c: Public Company Accounting Oversight Board

59. b: Perpetual inventory

CPSIA information can be obtained
at www.ICGtesting.com
Printed in the USA
LVHW011543301019
635718LV00004B/388/P